THE HEART UNVEILED

"These early plays are a revelation of the
continuing development of the greatest
theatrical imagination since Shakespeare ...
[They] represent one of the largest
repository of types available from a single
theatrical mind: the Don Juan in reverse,
the sex-starved widow ... the meddler,
the boor, the hypocrite ... the pretentious
mother, the dumb bride, the vain bank
director, the misogynistic clerk, the
talkative wife—to name but a few
of Chekhov's remarkable collection.
With them Chekhov made a fascinating
exposé of the human heart. . . . His
themes are the eternal ones: the dangers
of snobbery, ignorance, cruelty,
marriage, bondage, and the lures and
snares of the eternal feminine. After
Shakespeare and Molière, what other man
of the theater has shown us so much
of ourselves?"

From the Introduction.

ALEX SZOGYI, Professor of French at Hunter
College, is author of *An Analysis of Chekhov's Plays*
and translator of Chekhov's *The Sea Gull* and
Gorky's *The Lower Depths*. He has directed and
acted in several of the plays in this collection.
A Guggenheim grant awarded to Professor Szogyi
enabled him to finish this volume.

A BANTAM CLASSIC

TEN EARLY PLAYS

by

CHEKHOV

TRANSLATED AND
WITH AN INTRODUCTION BY
ALEX SZOGYI
—Hunter College

BANTAM BOOKS
NEW YORK / TORONTO / LONDON

ACKNOWLEDGMENTS

I wish to thank the John Simon Guggenheim Foundation for its generous help to me during the time I did these translations.

I dedicate these translations to the memory of Mme. Marguerite Peyre. To Henri Peyre, Ruth Berman, Karen Clements, Walter Kerr, Robert Penn Warren, and Philip Thompson, my deepest thanks for their help and encouragement.

TEN EARLY PLAYS BY CHEKHOV
A Bantam Classic / published September 1965

Library of Congress Catalog Card Number: 65-22484

Bantam Books are published by Bantam Books, Inc., a subsidiary of Grosset & Dunlap, Inc. Its trade-mark, consisting of the words "Bantam Books" and the portrayal of a bantam, is registered in the United States Patent office and in other countries. Marca Registrada. Bantam Books, Inc., 271 Madison Avenue, New York, N. Y. 10016.

PRINTED IN THE UNITED STATES OF AMERICA

CONTENTS

of bourgeois manners and mores, perhaps the most accurate portrayal of bourgeois foibles after Molière and before Perelman.

The Bear, or *The Boor,* as it is alternately translated from the Russian *myedvyed,* was Chekhov's most successful play during his lifetime. It remains his most often performed short play. It has about it an effortless quality which makes us believe Chekhov's assertion that subjects for his "vaudevilles" simply gushed out of him like oil from a Baku well. The play was adapted from a French vaudeville, *Les Jirons de Cadillac* by Pierre Berton, which Chekhov knew in a Russian adaptation, *Conquerors Are Above Criticism.* Chekhov wrote his own adaptation (originally the situation concerned a lady and a sailor) for the actor, Solovtsov, who played the sailor. *The Bear* became so lucrative that he called it his milchcow. (It brought him more money than any of his short stories.) It is a classic tale that would not seem out of place in the works of Boccaccio or even Chaucer. It reveals an irresistible comic logic and a line of logical action. A widow mourns her husband's death overmuch, and this despite the fact that he was unfaithful to her during his lifetime. She is visited by a boorish landowner trying to collect one of her husband's debts. He ends up dueling her and they fall madly in love. The movement of the play is extravagantly exuberant. Its cleverest psychological detail is its most humorous one: the widow, Popova, provides well for Toby, her husband's favorite horse. In his memory, she asks that his favorite horse be fed an extra bag of oats. At the end of the play, as she is kissing her new lover, she takes time out from her embrace to order a servant not to give Toby any oats at all that day. The relentless pace and humor of the play centers on its total adherence to logic. The bear, Smirnov, keeps insisting he needs his money to pay his creditors—that he cannot wait. The heroine, Popova, keeps insisting, in her own right, that she will have no money until her steward returns and that she is in no mood to talk finances. Each maintains his own position. They come to blows inevitably and the intensity of the explosion leads to sexual expression rather than violence. Popova's struggle with fidelity to the memory of her own faithless spouse is so earnest and her lapse into infidelity so sudden that one cannot help laughing at the triumphant revenge of human nature. A work of art is rarely both profound and obvious at the same time. Shakespeare was both profound and obvious in *Hamlet*. Works such as *King Lear* and *The Sea Gull* are not more profound, but they are much less obvious. At the heart of *The Bear* is a fidelity to human nature; given two such peppery personalities with such stubborn propensities, their meeting will result either in murder—or romance. The cream of the jest is that the widow is just a bit more boorish than her visitor. Thus, the title is slightly ambiguous.

The Proposal is the most highly stylized of Chekhov's early plays. It is a Molièresque play of types: the hypochondriacal suitor, the stubborn daughter, the oily father eager to marry off his daughter. It is bourgeois satire to the marrow. The daughter, Natalya Stepanovna, insists the neighboring land is hers no matter how much her prospective suitor, Lomov, insists it is not. The neat twist of the plot, the kernel of irony, is her violent despair when she realizes that Lomov came to propose to her and that she has perhaps lost him as a result of her boorish insistence on having her own way. The argument continues just as violently when he returns: this time the subject shifts to the relative merits of their respective dogs. The confusion remains total even at the end, as the despairing father, Chubukov, proposes champagne to celebrate the approaching nuptials. The characters in Chekhov's farces are led to a moment of truth. The nervous suitor and the snobbish bride in *The Proposal,* the boor and the hypocritical widow in *The Bear*—are led to reveal themselves as they actually are. The audience recognizes them before they reveal themselves. The initial illusion or misunderstanding is dissipated and we see the reality: the comedy of sudden realization. Natalya Stepanovna will fight for her convictions to the distraction of all the males around her and she will continue arguing to her dying day, as will her sickly suitor, but they will have to pause momentarily to accomplish the rituals which make life's continuation possible. They will embrace and continue arguing happily ever after. This play was also an instantaneous success (1888) and was enjoyed even by the tsar. Its success perhaps results from its basic kernel of truthful humor: the girl wants to get married; the boy does, too. Their snobbery and stubbornness almost prevent them from getting together. The meaning of the play is obvious throughout but never commented upon: it is thoroughly "dramatized," as so few plays ever are. The meaning of Chekhov's plays is implicit in the nature of the characters he chose to portray.

In 1889, Chekhov wrote a one-act comedy entitled *Tatyana Repina* for his friend and publisher Suvorin. It was a parody of a play of Suvorin's which was sent to Chekhov by the author as a gesture of friendship. The play was Chekhov's reply. It is a satire on the marriage ceremony, with full quotes from the Bible. Suvorin ordered two copies to be printed, one for himself and one for Chekhov. Chekhov wished to forget about the prank and, in characteristic modesty, struck his name from his copy.

The Reluctant Tragedian (also known as *The Tragedian in Spite of Himself*) taps the same vein as *On The Harmfulness of Tobacco*. It is a long list of woes poured out by a poor henpecked husband, Tolkachov, to his friend Murashkin. Tolkachov is the put-upon husband, constantly running errands for his wife and their neighbors. Hearing him out, Murashkin finally asks him whether he knows a certain woman of the region. Tolkachov admits he does. Then Murashkin asks for the same kind of favor. Tolkachov loses control and goes berserk. The role, written for the actor Varlamov, was adapted from a short story which was, in Chekhov's opinion, an old moth-eaten tale. The tale itself is spicier: the censor dictated omission of a lewdly funny detail—the wife vents her accumulated sensual feelings on her husband at night. It seems that the play was almost as successful as *The Bear* and *The Proposal*. The moral, implicit within the play, is quite plain: Don't advertise your troubles or you may tempt fate. Its naive simplicity has something of the tone of a medieval farce. He who laughs last . . .

The Wedding is one of the funniest of all Chekhov's plays. It is his most bourgeois play. The scene is a wedding for which a general is traditionally imported, and presumably hired, to *épater les bourgeois*. The general of this occasion turns out to be a second-class officer in the navy, retired, and an inveterate babbler who cannot stop boasting about his naval days. There is a series of amusing types portrayed: the widow, Zmeyukina, who won't sing but insists on being fanned; the predatory bridegroom, the dumb bride, the miserly mother, the ignorant father; the crazy Greek confectioner; and the daughter's former suitor, Yat, a presumptuous would-be intellectual snob. The play is a snapshot of human vanity and bourgeois values. Slowly and irrevocably, the wedding is turned into meaningless ritual and nightmare. The humor bubbles along relentlessly, as each of the characters cannot help behaving characteristically. The joyous mood turns macabre as the "general" refuses to keep quiet. The play is adapted from two of Chekhov's short stories, "A Marriage of Convenience" and "A Wedding with a General," and a short humorous sketch, "The Marriage Season." Chekhov intended it as a satire on the common practice of hiring generals to grace shopkeepers' weddings. Chekhov lived below an apartment rented out for weddings and he and his brothers improvised wedding parties, imitating the ridiculous aspects of the ritual. The play lives up to one of Chekhov's tenets for the one-act play: the development of a complete confusion. The play's technique exposes rigidity of action—the refusal of the "general" to stop talking about his naval days conforms to Bergson's definition of the comic as a reversal from human to automatically rigid behavior. The farce depends on the rhythm of the acceleration of the rigidity. Farce, in general, is perhaps just that: an acceleration of ordinary reality. *The Wedding* relentlessly maintains a straight face, an apparent fidelity to reality even when it is completely out of hand.

The Anniversary (also known as *The Jubilee* and *The Celebration*) is the last of Chekhov's one-act plays (written in December 1891, and revised in 1902) and quite possibly the best. Based on a short story, "A Helpless Creature," it contains the same elements of bourgeois humor as *The Proposal* and *The Wedding*. It concentrates on bourgeois pomp and circumstance as it presents the celebration of the fifteenth anniversary of a bank; and, as his name is Shipuchin, the bank president Shipuchin has prepared his own acceptance speech and purchased his own silver urn to be presented to himself in commemoration of the great moment. He is thwarted from carrying out his plans by his frivolous wife and Merchutkina, the unwelcome guest who nearly drives Schipuchin mad with an unreasonable request of money for her worthless husband. Add only one other ingredient, a woman hater, the assistant scribe Hirin, a model of misogynistic behavior, and a wild farce ensues, closer to the brothers Marx than any other part of Chekhov's work. As usual, the villains are the ladies—their endless chatter and overweening demands are the ruination of peace and quiet in their ambience. Chekhov's bourgeois farces are universally comprehensible because they exaggerate only the rhythm of the action, never the character. In ordinary life people are every bit as rigid as these comic characters. But life does not always give us the opportunity to see them foiled as ingeniously. Though *The Anniversary* is at once a commentary on masculine vanity and feminine temerity, it was also geared as an exposé of the private banks in Russia. Chekhov's most skillful farce is a fitting conclusion to his collection of one-act plays. One other play, *The Night Before the Trial*, remained unfinished; an earlier comedy, *Diamond Cuts Diamond*, has not been found. There were other vaudeville pieces, too, with tantalizing names like "When the Hen Clucks" and "The Clean-shaven Secretary with a Pistol," and posterity may be fortunate enough to locate them.

The two other plays included in this collection are Chekhov's two full-length plays prior to *The Sea Gull: Ivanov* and *The Wood Demon.* Perhaps the most eloquently disillusioned hero since Hamlet, Ivanov is often considered the symbol of late nineteenth-century Russian decadence. Actually, *Ivanov* is a highly complex drama which has moments of melodrama and ironic comedy. The play contains many fine scenes. The moments given to the Jewish wife, Sarah, are unequaled in all of Chekhov's work for poignancy and searing drama. The second act is a masterful satire of bourgeois *mœurs*, as exemplified by the Lyebedev household. Zinaida Savishna is the most consummate miser since Molière's Harpagon. The last act is a turnabout on a wedding scene in which everything goes wrong. The quartet of tearful wedding guests in Act IV blends pathos and bathos as skilfully as anywhere else in Chekhov's work. Most of *Ivanov* is straight bourgeois satire. Its characters are caricatures of bourgeois types: Marfutka Babakina, the vain widow; Borkin, the scoundrel's scoundrel; Lyebedev, the henpecked husband; Kosich, the inveterate card player for whom life is one grand slam after another; and Avdotya Nazarovna, the mean old matchmaker-midwife. Lvov, the honest doctor, is one of Chekhov's few relentlessly cruel portraits. Ivanov himself is a victim of his own melancholia, a man old before his time and hounded to suicide by his uncomprehending compatriots. *Ivanov* is Chekhov's most Ibsenian play. Ivanov is as scrupulously honest as Camus' Meursault, the stranger in society. He is the spiritual descendant of Platonov, with the same fascination for self-destructive acts. All told, *Ivanov* is Chekhov's first mature work and deserves to be performed as often as his later plays.

The Wood Demon is a neglected play. To date, there has not been a single New York performance of the play (although it was done in Springfield, Massachusetts, summer of 1963, by the Ivy Players). Chekhov revised *The Wood Demon* and made it *Uncle Vanya*, which contains many but not all of the characters of the earlier play. The two plays work their materials out in almost diametrically opposed directions. The Elena of *The Wood Demon* is a much more interesting woman than the shallow beauty of *Uncle Vanya*. She is given an opportunity to leave her husband, the pedant Serebryakov, and return to him at the climax of the last act. The "Waffles" of *The Wood Demon* is much more useful to the plot and his speeches are better characterized. *Uncle Vanya*'s great moment, the attempted shooting at the end of the third act, became Chekhov's brilliant solution to his quest for an action at once humorous and pathetic. Vanya's counterpart in *The Wood Demon*, George, commits suicide. This suicide produces the major difference in the plot structure of the two plays. The fourth act of *The Wood Demon* is a joyous midsummer night's dream revelry with a Shakespearean lightness of touch. Its happy ending touches none of the melancholy depths of *Uncle Vanya*'s dénouement but its solution is just as equitable. *The Wood Demon* contains some of the most amusing of all Chekhovian characters: Fyodor Orlovski, the madcap lover and soldier of fortune, is the spiritual descendant of the wild horsethief Osip of *Platonov*, and the eternal meddler Borkin of *Ivanov*. Fyodor's joie de vivre is one of the major elements of *The Wood Demon*. Chekhov omitted him from *Uncle Vanya*, though he gave part of his character to Doctor Astrov. Zheltoukhin, the vain young gentleman, and his housekeeper-sister Julia, are also unique to *The Wood Demon*. Chekov's friend Prince Urusov once wrote him a letter (January 27, 1899) telling him how much better *The Wood Demon* was than his later play. He felt that Chekhov had spoiled *The Wood Demon* by rewriting it, that the earlier play was more novel and daring—perhaps he was right. The plays ought to be staged together and separately for they give us two insights into Chekhovian drama. The earlier play is more moral, influenced by Tolstoy, a work which concerns itself with the destruction of society by malevolent attitudes. The later play is more resigned, much more pessimistic and psychologically oriented rather than morally indignant. They represent the Chekhov of 1889 and 1897 and give us a better insight into Chekhov's development as a playwright than any essay that might contrast the two works.

The Wood Demon will doubtlessly be enjoyed innocently by those who have never seen or read the later masterwork.

Although Chekhov finally evolved a highly distilled, sensitive, subtle time-defying technique, his later plays still retain the comic characterization and the farcical plotting of the early one-act and full-length plays. These early plays are a revelation of the continuing development of the greatest theatrical imagination since Shakespeare. For actors and directors, these plays represent one of the largest repository of types available from a single theatrical mind: the Don Juan in reverse, the sex-starved widow, the henpecked husband, the elderly drunken actor, the miserly dowager, the inveterate card player, the meddler, the boor, the hypocrite, the hypochondriac, the femme fatale, the lover of the forests, the pampered professor, the extravagant lover, the perennial student of life, the member of the wedding, the avaricious bridegroom, the pretentious mother, the dumb bride, the vain bank director, the misogynistic clerk, the talkative wife —to name but a few of Chekhov's remarkable collection. With them Chekhov made a fascinating exposé of the human heart.

Chekhov's early plays belong with his later plays: before the public, as a gentle and very funny reminder of what man becomes in society. His themes are the eternal ones: the dangers of snobbery, ignorance, cruelty, marriage, bondage, and the lures and snares of the eternal feminine. After Shakespeare and Molière, what other man of the theater has shown us so much of ourselves?

IVANOV

❧

A Drama in Four Acts

CHARACTERS

Nikolai Alexeyevich Ivanov, *permanent member of the county council*

Anna Petrovna, *his wife, nee Sarah Abramson*

Matvyey Semyonovich, Count Shabyelski, *his uncle on his mother's side*

Pavel Kirilich Lyebedev, *chairman of the county council*

Zinaida Savishna, *his wife*

Sasha, *Lyebedev's daughter, aged twenty*

Yevgeny Konstantinovich Lvov, *young district doctor*

Marfa Yegorovna Babakina, *young widow, landowner, daughter of a rich merchant*

Dmitri Nikitich Kosich, *tax official*

Mikhail Mikhailovich Borkin, *distant relation of Ivanov and manager of his estate*

Avdotya Nazarovna, *old woman of uncertain occupation*

Yegoruska, *foarder at Lyebedevs'*

First, Second, Third, and Fourth Guests

Pyotr, *Ivanov's servant*

Gavrila, *Lyebedev's servant*

Visitors of Both Sexes, Servants

The action takes place in one of the provinces of central Russia.

Act I

Garden of IVANOV *estate. To the left, façade of the house with terrace. One window open. In front of the terrace, a wide semicircular space, from which, center and right, paths lead into the garden. On the right side of the garden, garden furniture and tables. On one of the last, a lamp burns. It is getting on toward evening. As the curtain rises, a piano and cello duet is heard from indoors.*

(IVANOV *is seated at a table reading a book.* BORKIN, *wearing large boots, carrying a gun, comes into sight from the back of the garden; he is a bit tight. Seeing* IVANOV, *he tiptoes up to him; coming alongside him, he aims the gun at his face.*)

IVANOV (*seeing* BORKIN, *starts, jumps up*). Misha, my God. . . . You frightened me. . . . I'm upset enough as it is; you and your stupid jokes. . . . (*Sits down.*) You frightened me and you're so happy about it. . . .

BORKIN (*laughs loudly*). There, there! . . . I'm sorry, I'm sorry. (*Sits down beside him.*) I won't do it again, really I won't. . . . (*Takes off his peaked cap.*) It's hot. You won't believe me, my friend, but I've covered some fifteen miles in the last three hours. . . . I'm worn out. . . . Feel . . . how my heart's beating.

IVANOV (*continues reading*). All right, later on. . . .

BORKIN. No, feel it now. (*Takes* IVANOV's *hand and holds it to his chest.*) Do you hear? *Po-pom, po-pom, po-pom.* That means I've got heart trouble. Any minute, it could mean sudden death. Listen, would you be sorry if I died?

IVANOV. I'm reading. . . . Later on . . .

15

BORKIN. No, seriously, would you be sorry if I were to die suddenly? Nikolai Alexeyevich, would you be sorry if I died?

IVANOV. Don't bother me!

BORKIN. My dear fellow, tell me: would you be sorry?

IVANOV. I'm sorry that you smell of vodka. Misha, that's disgusting.

BORKIN (laughs). Do I really smell? That's surprising . . . not that there's anything really surprising about it. I came across one of the inspectors at Plesniky, and the truth is we downed about eight drinks together. As a matter of fact, drinking is very harmful. Listen, is it harmful, really? Eh? Is it harmful?

IVANOV. This is getting to be unbearable. . . . Misha, I want you to understand this is a mockery. . . .

BORKIN. Well, well. . . . I'm sorry, I'm sorry! Possess your soul in patience, keep calm. . . . (Gets up and goes off.) What astonishing people; you can't even talk to them. (Returns.) Oh, yes! I almost forgot. . . . I think you'd better give me eighty-two rubles! . . .

IVANOV. Why eighty-two rubles?

BORKIN. The workmen have to be paid tomorrow.

IVANOV. I don't have it.

BORKIN. Thank you very much! (Imitates him.) I don't have it. . . . You know the workmen have to be paid, don't you?

IVANOV. No, I don't. And I don't have it today. Wait till the first of the month, when I expect my salary.

BORKIN. What's the use of talking with people like you . . . the workmen won't come for their money on the first of the month; they'll be there tomorrow morning! . . .

IVANOV. Well, what can I do about it now? Well then, irritate me, nag away. . . . Where did you develop this irritating habit of pestering me just at the very moment I'm reading, writing, or . . .

BORKIN. I ask you: must the workmen be paid or not? Oh, what's the use of talking to you! . . . (*Waves his hands.*) Nice proprietor you are, damn you, you landowner. . . . You and your scientific farming. . . . Thousands of acres of land —and no money in your pockets. It's like having a wine cellar and no corkscrew. . . . See if I don't sell the horses tomorrow! Yes, I will! I sold the oats before they were ready for harvesting, and tomorrow I'll just sell the rye. (*Paces the stage.*) You think I'll stand on ceremony? Yes? Well, I won't, not with you. That's not the way I do things. . . .

(*Offstage,* SHABYELSKI *and* ANNA PETROVNA.)

VOICE OF SHABYELSKI (*through the window*). Playing with you is impossible. . . . You have no more ear for music than a stunned pike and your touch is outrageous.

ANNA PETROVNA (*appears at the open window*). Who was that talking here just now? Was it you, Misha? Why are you pacing up and down like that?

BORKIN. What is there to do, other than pace up and down, when you have to deal with your *cher* Nicolas— over there?

ANNA PETROVNA. Listen, Misha, please bring some hay to the croquet lawn.

BORKIN (*waving his hand*). Leave me alone, please. . . .

ANNA PETROVNA. Tsk, tsk, what a tone of voice . . . it doesn't suit you. If you want women to like you, you must never be angry or high and mighty with them. . . . (*To her husband.*) Nikolai, let's go do some somersaults in the hay! . . .

IVANOV. Aniuta, it's bad for you to stand by the open window. Go in, please. . . . (*Shouts.*) Uncle, will you shut the window!

(*The window is shut.*)

BORKIN. And don't forget that two days from now you'll have to pay Lyebedev the interest.

IVANOV. I know. I'll be at Lyebedev's today and I'll ask him to wait. . . . (*Looks at his watch.*)

BORKIN. When are you going?

IVANOV. Right away.

BORKIN (*quick on the uptake*). Wait, wait! Let me see, isn't today Shurochka's birthday . . . tsk, tsk, tsk, tsk . . . and I almost forgot. . . . What a memory, eh? (*Jumps about.*) I'm off. . . . I'll go for a swim, and chew some mint, and take a few drops of spirits of ammonia, and then I'll be ready to start all over again. . . . My dear friend, Nikolai Alexeyevich, my old mother, you sweetheart, if you weren't always so nervous and depressed, constantly moaning about yourself, we could accomplish some great things together! I'd do anything for you . . . would you like me to marry Marfusha Babakina for you? Half the dowry would be yours . . . no, not half; take it all, all!

IVANOV. If I were you, I wouldn't talk such nonsense.

BORKIN. No, I'm serious! Would you like me to marry Marfusha? We'll divide the dowry. . . . But why am I talking to you like this? Could you understand? (*Imitates him.*) "If I were you, I wouldn't talk such nonsense." You're a good, intelligent man but you don't have enough nerve, do you understand, chutzpah! If you could only take a swing at something. You're a nervous wreck, a weakling. If you were a normal man, then in the space of a year you'd make a million. Take me, for instance, if I had two thousand three hundred rubles right now, I'd have twenty thousand in two weeks. Don't you believe me? Do you think that's nonsense? No, it's not nonsense. . . . You give me the twenty-three hundred rubles and in one week I'll give you twenty thousand. On the other side of the river, Osianov is selling a strip of land, right across from us, for twenty-three hundred rubles. If we bought that strip, then both sides of the land would be ours. And if both sides were ours, then, you understand, we'd have the right to dam the river. You see? We'll build a mill, and as soon as we announce our in-

tention to build a dam, then everybody living down the
river will raise an uproar, and we'll say: "*Kommen Sie
hierher*—if you don't want the dam, you must pay up." You
understand? The Zarev factory will give us five thousand,
Korolkov three thousand, the monastery five thousand. . . .

IVANOV. It's all very tricky, Misha. . . . If you don't want
to quarrel with me, then keep it to yourself.

BORKIN (*sitting down at the table*). Of course! . . . I knew
it! You won't do anything yourself and you're tying my
hands. . . .

SHABYELSKI (*coming out of the house, with* LVOV). Doctors are the same as lawyers; the only difference is that
lawyers only rob you, but doctors rob and kill you, too . . .
present company excepted (*Sits down on a small divan.*)
Charlatans, swindlers. . . . It might be that in some paradise
you would come across an exception to the general rule, but
. . . in the course of my life, I've spent some twenty thousand on doctors and I haven't come across one of them
who wasn't an out-and-out swindler.

BORKIN (*to* IVANOV). Yes, you do nothing yourself but
you tie my hands. That's why we have no money. . . .

SHABYELSKI. As I was saying, present company excepted.
. . . It may be there are some exceptions, but all the same
. . . (*Yawns.*)

IVANOV (*closing his book*). Well, Doctor, what do you say?

LVOV (*looking down at the window*). What I said in the
morning: she must leave for the Crimea immediately. (*Paces
up and down.*)

SHABYELSKI (*bursts out laughing*). To the Crimea! . . .
Why aren't we two doctors, Misha? It's so simple. . . . If any
old Mademoiselle Angot or Ophelia starts coughing or sneez-
ing from sheer boredom, take a piece of paper and write out
a prescription based on scientific principles: to begin with, a
young doctor, then a trip to the Crimea, and in the Crimea,
a Tartar guide. . . .

IVANOV (*to the* COUNT). Oh, stop it, you old nag. (*To* LVOV.) To go to the Crimea, you need the wherewithal. Suppose it were possible to find it—what if she positively refuses to go . . .

LVOV. Yes, she refuses. (*Pause.*)

BORKIN. Listen, Doctor, is Anna Petrovna really so seriously ill that it's necessary for her to go to the Crimea?

LVOV (*looks at the window*). Yes, she has consumption. . . .

BORKIN. Pss! . . . that's not so good. . . . For a long time now I've seen from the look on her face that she won't last long.

LVOV. Sh! . . . Not so loud . . . you can be heard in the house. . . . (*Pause.*)

BORKIN (*sighing*). Such is our life. . . . A man's life is like a flower; it grows luxuriously in the field: along comes a billygoat and eats it up—and then no more flower. . . .

SHABYELSKI. It's all nonsense, nonsense, nonsense. . . . (*Yawns.*) Stuff and nonsense. (*Pause.*)

BORKIN. Gentlemen, I have once again been trying to teach Nikolai Alexeyevich the value of money. I've given him the clue to a wonderful business, but, as usual, my seed fell on barren ground. You can't make him understand. . . . Just look at him: melancholy, dreary, gloomy, spleen, blues . . .

SHABYELSKI (*rises and stretches*). You're such a genius, such a smart head; you teach everybody how to live, but if you only taught me anything once. . . . Well, smart head, teach me how to live.

BORKIN (*gets up*). I'm going for a swim. . . . Good-by, everybody! (*To the* COUNT.) There are at least twenty ways. . . . If I were in your situation, I'd make twenty thousand in a week. (*Goes off.*)

SHABYELSKI (*goes after him*). In what way? Well, show me, smart head.

BORKIN. There's nothing to show. It's very simple. . . . (*Returns.*) Nikolai Alexeyevich, give me a ruble! (IVANOV *quietly gives him the money.*) Merci! (*To the* COUNT.) You've still got a few trumps in your hand.

SHABYELSKI (*following him*). Well, what are they?

BORKIN. If I were in your shoes, in a week I'd have twenty thousand, if not more. (*Goes out with the* COUNT.)

IVANOV (*after a pause*). Useless, superfluous talk, being forced to answer all those stupid questions—all this, Doctor, has made me sick and tired. I've become so irritable, hot-tempered, rude, and petty that I don't recognize myself. Every day I have a headache, I can't sleep, my ears are ringing. . . . I have positively nowhere I can go . . . simply nowhere. . . .

LVOV. Nikolai Alexeyevich, I must have a serious talk with you.

IVANOV. Go ahead.

LVOV. It's about Anna Petrovna. (*Sits down.*) She hasn't agreed to go to the Crimea, but she would go with you.

IVANOV (*after a moment's thought*). For both of us to go, we'd have to have the means. I couldn't get such a long holiday. I've already taken one this year. . . .

LVOV. It's possible you're right. Let's think beyond that. The best medicine for tuberculosis—is absolute peace and quiet, but your wife never has a moment's peace. She's continually troubled by your attitude to her. Forgive me, I'm upset about it and I must speak frankly. Your conduct is killing her. (*Pause.*) Nikolai Alexeyevich, let me think better of you!

IVANOV. All that is true, true. . . . I suppose I'm to blame, but my mind is so confused; I'm constrained by a kind of indolence. I don't have the strength to understand myself. I don't understand other people any better than I do myself. (*Glances at the window.*) They can hear us; let's go for a walk. (*They rise.*) My dear friend, I'd like to tell you the whole thing from the beginning, but it's a long story and a complicated one; it would last till morning. (*They walk.*) Aniuta is a remarkable, an extraordinary woman. . . . For my sake, she changed her religion, denied her mother and father, gave up her wealth, and if I asked for a hundred other sacrifices, she would have made them without blinking an eye. Well, there's nothing remarkable about me and I've sacrificed nothing. But it's a long story. . . . The crux of the matter, my dear doctor, is . . . the gist of it is, I was passionately in love with her when I married, and I swore I'd love her forever, but . . . five years have passed; she still loves me, but I . . . (*Helpless gesture with hands.*) Here you are telling me that she'll die soon, and I feel neither love nor pity, but a sort of emptiness and weariness. From someone else's viewpoint, I must really seem terrible; I myself don't understand what's happening to me. . . . (*They walk down the lane.*)

(SHABYELSKI *enters, then* ANNA PETROVNA.)

SHABYELSKI (*enters, laughing loudly*). In all honesty, he's not a swindler, he's a thinking man, a virtuoso! They should put up a monument to his memory. He's a nice combination of present-day rottenness, no matter how you look at it: lawyer, doctor, businessman, banker. (*Sits down on lowest step of terrace.*) It seems he's never finished any of his studies anywhere, it's astonishing . . . and what a genius of a scoundrel he might have been if he could also have assimilated some culture and the humanities! "You could make twenty thousand in a week!" he tells me. "You still have an ace of trump in your hand—your title—Count." (*Laughs loudly.*) "For you, there isn't a girl who wouldn't give up her dowry with love in her heart."

(ANNA PETROVNA *opens the window and looks down.*)

"Would you like," he asked, "for me to matchmake for you with Marfoosha?" *Qui est-ce que c'est* Marfusha? Oh, it's that Balabalkina, Babakalkina . . . that one that looks like a laundress.

ANNA PETROVNA. Is that you, Count?

SHABYELSKI. What's that?

(ANNA PETROVNA *laughs.*)

(*With a Jewish accent.*) For vot are you laffink?

ANNA PETROVNA. I was thinking of something you said. Do you remember what you said at dinner? A repentant thief, a horse . . . how did it go?

SHABYELSKI. A baptized Jew, a repentant thief, a sick horse: they're all the same.

ANNA PETROVNA (*laughs*). You can't even make a simple joke without malice. You're a malicious man. Joking aside, Count, you are very malicious. Living with you is tedious and terrible. You're always grumbling and complaining; according to you, everybody is a scoundrel and a villain. Tell me, Count, frankly: have you ever said a good word about anybody?

SHABYELSKI. What kind of cross-examination is this?

ANNA PETROVNA. We've been living under the same roof now for five years, and I've never once heard you speak of other people calmly, without gall or bitter laughter. What harm have they done you? Do you really think you're better than everybody else?

SHABYELSKI. I don't think that at all. I'm just as much of a scoundrel and a swine in a skullcap as everybody else, *Mauvais ton,* an old shoe. I'm always denigrating myself. Who am I? What am I? I was rich, free and a little happy, but now . . . I'm a parasite, a sponge, a useless fool. I show my indignation, my disdain, and they answer me with laughter; I laugh and they nod their heads sadly and say: "The old man is balmy." . . . But most often they don't hear me at all or take any notice of me. . . .

ANNA PETROVNA (*softly*). It's screeching again. . . .

SHABYELSKI. What's screeching?

ANNA PETROVNA. The owl. It screeches every night.

SHABYELSKI. Let it screech. Things can't get any worse than they are. (*Stretches himself.*) Oh, my dearest Sarah, if I won a hundred or two hundred thousand or so, I'd show you. I'd make you sit up and take notice! You'd never see me again. I'd have gotten away from this hole, from your damned charity and my feet wouldn't come this way again till the last judgment was upon me. . . .

ANNA PETROVNA. And what would you have done if you'd won the money?

SHABYELSKI (*after a moment's thought*). First of all, I'd go to Moscow and listen to the gypsies' songs. . . . Then, after that, I'd go to Paris. I'd rent an apartment and go to the Russian chu... regula.ly. . . .

ANNA PETROVNA. What else?

SHABYELSKI. Every day I'd sit by my wife's grave and think. I'd have sat by her grave till I died. My wife is buried in Paris. . . . (*Pause.*)

ANNA PETROVNA. Terribly depressing. . . . Shall we play another duet, what do you say?

SHABYELSKI. Fine, get the music ready.

IVANOV (*comes down the lane, with* LVOV). My friend, you only finished your studies last year. You're still young and hale and hearty. And I am thirty-five years old. I'm entitled to give you advice. Don't marry a Jewess or a neurotic or a bluestocking but choose for yourself some ordinary, dull girl who doesn't sparkle or talk superfluously. In general, build your whole life on the commonplace. The duller and more monotonous the backdrop of your life, the better. My friend, don't try to battle with the multitude singlehanded. Don't go battling windmills. Don't knock your head against the wall. . . . May God keep you from all kinds of scientific farming, newfangled schools for peasants, and passionate speechmaking. . . . Shut yourself up in your little shell and do your little deeds, live what God has in store for you. . . . That's better, more honest, and healthier. As for the life

I've led—how tiresome it's been! Oh, how tiresome! Only mistakes, injustice, absurdity. (*Sees the* COUNT, *irritated.*) Always you, Uncle, with your nose poking everywhere, you never give me a chance to talk to anybody!

SHABYELSKI (*in a tearful voice*). Where can I go? I have no refuge. (*Jumps up and goes into the house.*)

IVANOV (*shouts after him*). Well, I'm sorry! I'm sorry! (*To* Lvov.) Why did I hurt his feelings? I'm positively unnerved. I must do something about myself. . . .

LVOV (*perturbed*). Nikolai Alexeyevich, I've listened to you and . . . excuse me, I'd like to speak frankly, without beating about the bush. In your voice, in every intonation, not to mention the words you speak, there is so much heartless egotism, so much cold cruelty. A person is dying near you, because she is near you; her days are numbered, and you . . . you can allow yourself not to love and you can go about giving advice, analyzing your feelings. . . . I can't express it well to you; I don't have the gift of eloquence, but . . . I have a deep dislike for you.

IVANOV. Perhaps, perhaps . . . you see it from the outside . . . it's quite possible you do see through me, and that I'm very much at fault. . . . (*Listens.*) It sounds as if the horses are ready. I have to change my clothes. (*Walks toward the house, then stops.*) You don't like me, Doctor, and you don't conceal it. Your sincerity does you credit. . . . (*Goes into the house.*)

LVOV (*alone*). Damn it! I missed my chance again; I didn't say anything to him that I should have. . . . I can't talk to him coldbloodedly! Every time I open my mouth and say one word, something right here (*Points to his chest.*) begins to suffocate and turn over inside me; my tongue gets stuck in my mouth. I hate this Tartuffe, this . . . high and mighty impostor. . . . There he is, going out. . . . His unhappy wife's only pleasure is to be near him; he's the breath of life for her, she begs him to spend only one evening with her, and he . . . he can't . . . you see, for him, home is too stifling and too close. If he spent only one evening at home, he'd have to shoot himself in the head from sheer boredom. Poor fellow . . . he needs more elbow-room to start some new low tricks. . . . Oh, I know why you go every evening to visit those Lyebedevs! I know!

(*Enter* IVANOV, *wearing hat and coat,* SHABYELSKI, *and* ANNA PETROVNA.)

SHABYELSKI (*coming out of the house with* IVANOV *and* ANNA PETROVNA). Really, Nikolai, this is inhuman . . . you go out every evening by yourself, and we're left alone. We have to go to bed at eight o'clock from sheer boredom. It's disgraceful! It's no way to live! And why should you be able to go out, and not us? Why?

ANNA PETROVNA. Count, leave him alone! Let him go, let him. . . .

IVANOV (*to his wife*). And where would you go, with your illness? You're ill and you're not allowed outside after sunset. Ask the doctor here. You're not a child, Aniuta, be reasonable. . . . (*To the* COUNT.) And why do you want to go there?

SHABYELSKI. I'd go visit the devil in hell or jump right into a crocodile's jaws, just so I wouldn't have to stay here. I'm bored here. I'm dying of boredom. I bother everybody. You leave me at home so that she won't be here alone and upset, but I upset her and nag her to death!

ANNA PETROVNA. Leave him alone, Count, leave him alone! Let him go, if it means so much to him.

IVANOV. Anya, why do you take that tone? You know I'm not going there for enjoyment! I have to talk to them about the promissory note.

ANNA PETROVNA. I don't understand why you try to justify yourself so much. Go on! Who's holding you back?

IVANOV. My God, let's not eat each other up! Is all this necessary!

SHABYELSKI (*in a tearful voice*). Nicolas, my dear, I ask you, take me along with you! To get a look at all those rascals and scoundrels there might be entertaining. You know I haven't been anywhere since Easter!

IVANOV (*irritated*). All right, let's go! How annoying you all are.

SHABYELSKI. Yes? Well, *merci, merci*. . . . (*Gaily takes his arm and leads him off to the side.*) May I wear your straw hat?

IVANOV. Yes, you may, only hurry, please!

(*The* COUNT *runs into the house.*)

How annoying you are! My God, what am I saying? Anya, I've been talking to you in an impossible tone. I've never been this way before. Well, bye-bye, Anya, I'll be back by one o'clock.

ANNA PETROVNA. Kolya, my darling, stay at home!

IVANOV (*troubled*). My darling, my own, poor unhappy girl, I beg of you, don't prevent me from going out in the evenings. It's cruel and unjust on my part, but let me do this injustice! The house is unbearable to me. As soon as the sun goes down, I'm overcome with a feeling of yearning! Don't ask me why. I don't know why. I swear I don't know. It's depressing here, but when I go to the Lyebedevs', it's even worse; and when I come back here, I'm still depressed and so it goes the whole night long. . . . It makes me despair! . . .

ANNA PETROVNA. Kolya . . . stay home! We'll talk, as we used to. . . . We'll have supper together, and we'll read. . . . The grumbler and I have practiced many duets for you. . . . (*Putting her arms around him.*) Stay! . . . (*Pause.*) I don't understand you. This has been going on for a whole year. Why have you changed?

IVANOV. I don't know, I don't know. . . .

ANNA PETROVNA. Why don't you want me to go out with you, together, in the evenings?

IVANOV. If you really want to know, then I should tell you. It's cruel to say it, but it's better . . . when the melancholy yearning begins, I . . . I begin not to love you. I run from you at those times. You see, I have to get away from home.

ANNA PETROVNA. Melancholy yearning. I understand, I understand. . . . You know what, Kolya? Try to sing and laugh and get angry, the way you used to. . . . Stay, and we'll have a laugh, and drink brandy; your melancholy will fly away in a minute. Do you want me to sing? Or shall we go and sit in your study, in the dark, as we used to, and you'll tell me all about your melancholy yearning. . . . You have such tormented eyes! I'll look into them and cry, and we'll both feel easier. . . . (Laughs and cries.) So, what is it, Kolya? The flowers return in the spring, but the happiness—no? Yes? All right, go, go. . . .

IVANOV. Pray for me to God, Anya! (He goes, stops, and thinks.) No, I can't! (Goes out.)

ANNA PETROVNA. Go! . . . (Sits down at the table.)

LVOV (pacing back and forth on the stage). Anna Petrovna, make it a rule: as soon as the clock strikes six o'clock, you should go inside and not come out until the next morning. The evening dampness is bad for you.

ANNA PETROVNA. I understand.

LVOV. What do you mean, "I understand"! I'm speaking seriously.

ANNA PETROVNA. And I don't want to be serious. (Coughs.)

LVOV. You see—you're coughing already. . . .

SHABYELSKI (coming out of the house with hat and overcoat). And where's Nikolai? Are the horses ready? (Goes quickly to kiss ANNA PETROVNA's hand.) Good evening, my lovely one! (Grimaces. Yiddish accent.) Gevalt! Shcuse, pliz! (Goes out quickly.)

LVOV. What a clown! (Pause; the sound of a harmonica being played far away.)

ANNA PETROVNA. How depressing! The coachman and the cooks are doing a little dancing, and I . . . I'm like an abandoned one; Yevgeny Konstantinovich, why are you walking around so much? Come here and sit down! . . .

Lvov. I can't sit. (*Pause*.)

ANNA PETROVNA. In the kitchen they're playing "The Starling." (*Sings*.) "Starling, starling, where have you been? On the hillside drinking vodka." (*Pause*.) Doctor, do you have a father and a mother?

Lvov. My father is dead, but my mother is alive.

ANNA PETROVNA. Don't you miss your mother?

Lvov. I don't have time to miss anybody.

ANNA PETROVNA (*laughs*). The flowers return every spring, but the happiness—no. Who told me that? God give me a better memory. . . . I think it most likely Nikolai. (*Listening*.) The owl's screeching again!

Lvov. Well, let it screech.

ANNA PETROVNA. I'm beginning to think that fate has cheated me, Doctor. Lots of people who are no better than I am live happily and don't pay anything for their happiness. I've paid for everything, positively for everything! And how dearly! Why must I pay such a terrible interest? My dear friend, you've always been so considerate with me, so delicate, so afraid to tell me the truth, but do you think I don't know what my illness is? I know only too well. However, it's boring to talk about that. . . . (*In a Yiddish accent*.) Shcuse, pliz! Do you know how to tell funny stories?

Lvov. No, I don't.

ANNA PETROVNA. Nikolai does. And I'm starting to get a little surprised about how unfair people are: why don't they respond to love with love and why do they pay back truth with lies? Tell me: how much longer are my mother and father going to keep on hating me? They live fifty miles away from here and yet day and night, even in my sleep, I can feel their hatred. And how can I understand Nikolai's melancholy? He says that it's only in the evenings he doesn't love me, when the depressed feeling comes on him. That I understand and I believe it's true, but it's possible he might stop loving me altogether! Of course, that's not possible, but—suppose he has? No, no, I mustn't have thoughts like that. (*Sings.*) "Starling, starling, where have you been? . . ." (*Winces.*) What frightening thoughts I have! . . . You don't have a family, Doctor, and there's a lot you don't understand. . . .

Lvov. You're surprised . . . (*Sits down beside her.*) No, I . . . I'm surprised, surprised at you! Well, explain it to me, make me understand, how is it that you, an intelligent, upright woman, almost like a saint, allowed yourself to be so outrageously deceived and dragged into this owl's nest? Why are you here? What do you have in common with that cold, heartless . . . but let's leave your husband out of this . . . what do you have in common with these shallow, commonplace surroundings? Oh, my God! That eternal grumbler; that raving maniac of a count; and that scoundrel of scoundrels, Misha, with his vile expressions! . . . Explain it to me, why are you here? How did you get here?

Anna Petrovna (*laughs*). That's how he used to talk. . . . Just like that. . . . But he's got bigger eyes than you have, and when he would begin to talk so heatedly, about anything, they burned like coals. . . . Keep on talking, talk! . . .

Lvov (*gets up and waves his hands*). Why should I keep on talking? Go inside. . . .

Anna Petrovna. You say that Nikolai is like this, that and the other. . . . But do you really know him? Can you really get to know a man in half a year? He's a remarkable man, Doctor, and I'm sorry you didn't know him two or three years ago. He has his yearning now, he keeps quiet, doesn't do anything, but in the past— What a charming man! I fell in love with him at first sight. (*Laughs.*) I took one look, and the mousetrap went bang! He said: Let's go . . . and I cut everything off for him, as you know, like snipping rotten leaves with scissors, and I went. . . . (*Pauses.*) And now it's changed. . . . Now he goes to the Lyebedevs' to distract himself with other women, and I . . . sit in the garden and listen to the owl screeching. . . .

(*Outside the* WATCHMAN *taps to frighten away thieves.*)

Doctor, don't you have any brothers?

LVOV. No, I don't. (ANNA PETROVNA *sobs.*) Well, what now? What's the matter?

ANNA PETROVNA (*gets up*). I can't stand it any more, Doctor. I'm going there. . . .

LVOV. Going where?

ANNA PETROVNA. There, where he is. . . . I'm going. . . . Please harness the horses. (*Runs into the house.*)

LVOV. No, I positively refuse to treat anybody under such conditions! It's not that they haven't paid me anything, but they turn me inside out. No, I refuse! I've had enough! I refuse! (*Goes into the house.*)

CURTAIN

Act II

The living room of the LYEBEDEVS' *house—leads straight into the garden; doors to the right and left; old, expensive furniture. Chandeliers, a candelabra, and paintings, all under slipcovers.*

(ZINAIDA SAVISHNA *sits on the sofa. On either side of her there are elderly ladies in armchairs; young people occupy straight-backed chairs. In the back, near the entrance to the garden, the guests are playing cards; among the players,* KOSICH, AVDOTYA NAZAROVNA, *and* YEGORUSHKA. GAVRILA *stands by the door at the right; the* MAID *passes around plates of refreshments. Guests circulate from the garden through the door at the right, back and forth throughout the act.* BABAKINA *comes in through the door on the right and makes her way toward* ZINAIDA SAVISHNA.)

ZIANIDA SAVISHNA (*joyously*). Darling, Marfa Yegorovna . . .

BABAKINA. How are you, Zinaida Savishna! Let me congratulate you on your daughter's birthday! (*They embrace.*) May God grant . . .

ZINAIDA SAVISHNA. Thank you, darling. I'm so happy. . . . Well, how have you been?

BABAKINA. Fine, thank you. (*Sits down on the sofa next to* ZINAIDA SAVISHNA.) Hello, all you young people! (*Guests rise and bow.*)

FIRST GUEST (*laughing*). "Young people" . . . as if you were so old?

BABAKINA (*sighing*). I'm not used to all you young people. . . .

FIRST GUEST (*a deferential laugh*). For goodness' sake, why you . . . you're the only widow among the guests, and you're the best of them all.

(GAVRILA *serves* BABAKINA *tea.*)

ZINAIDA SAVISHNA (*to* GAVRILA). Why do you serve tea like that? Serve a little jam. Some gooseberry, or something. . . .

BABAKINA. Don't bother. Thank you so much. (*Pause.*)

FIRST GUEST. Did you come by way of Mushkino, Marfa Yegorovna?

BABAKINA. No, through Zimishche. The road's better there.

FIRST GUEST. Yes, of course.

KOSICH. Two spades.

YEGORUSHKA. Pass.

AVDOTYA NAZAROVNA. Pass.

BABAKINA. Zinaida Savishna, darling. Did you know that lottery tickets are going up again, and fast? Have you ever heard of such a thing? Tickets for the first drawing are already two-seventy, and for the second, nearly two-fifty. . . . It's never been like that before. . . .

ZINAIDA SAVISHNA (*sighs*). Those who got a few are in luck.

BABAKINA. Don't say that, darling; even though the price is high, they're not worth investing in. The insurance alone is enough to ruin . . .

ZINAIDA SAVISHNA. Well, that may be, but all the same, my dear, one can hope. . . . (*Sighs.*) God is good. . . .

THIRD GUEST. If you want my point of view, mesdames, I look at it this way. At the present time, there are no good investments. Blue-chip securities bring in practically no dividends, and speculation is very risky. My thoughts run this way, mesdames: anybody who has capital these days is in a more crucial position than the ones, mesdames, who . . .

BABAKINA (*sighs*). That's true! (FIRST GUEST *yawns*.) Now, is it nice to yawn in front of ladies?

FIRST GUEST. Pardon, mesdames. I didn't do it on purpose.

(ZINAIDA SAVISHNA *gets up and goes through the door on the right; a long silence.*)

YEGORUSHKA. Two diamonds.

AVDOTYA NAZAROVNA. Pass.

SECOND GUEST. Pass.

KOSICH. Pass.

BABAKINA (*aside*). Oh Lord, how boring, it's killing!

(*Enter* ZINAIDA SAVISHNA *and* LYEBEDEV.)

ZINAIDA SAVISHNA (*coming out of door at right; in a low voice*). What are you sitting out there for? What a prima donna! Sit with the guests! (*Resumes her seat.*)

LYEBEDEV (*yawns*). We certainly pay for our sins! (*Seeing* BABAKINA.) My goodness, here comes our little marmalade! Our rahat-loukoum! (*Greets her.*) How's your precious self?

BABAKINA. Thank you so much.

LYEBEDEV. Well, thank the Lord for that! . . . Thank the Lord! (*Sits down in armchair.*) Well, well. . . . Gavrila! (GAVRILA *serves him a small glass of vodka and a little pitcher of water. He drinks vodka first, then the water.*)

FIRST GUEST. To your good health! . . .

LYEBEDEV. What do you mean, my good health! . . . I'm not dead yet and for that I'm thankful. (*To his wife.*) Zhuzhushka, where's our little girl?

KOSICH (*tearfully*). Tell me: why didn't we take a single trick? (*Jumps up.*) Why did we play? Why the devil did we lose?

AVDOTYA NAZAROVNA (*jumps angrily*). You want to know the reason why? If you don't know how to play, then why sit in? What right do you have to follow suit? So you got stuck with your ace! . . . (*Both leave their table and run forward.*)

KOSICH (*tearful voice*). Allow me, my friends. . . . I had, in diamonds: the ace, king, queen, jack, and eight, the ace of spades and one, you understand, one little heart . . . and she, damn her, couldn't make a small slam. . . . I opened with notrump . . .

AVDOTYA NAZAROVNA (*interrupting*). I was the one who opened with notrump! You bid two notrump. . . .

KOSICH. This is outrageous! . . . Allow me. . . . You had . . . I had . . . you had . . . (*To* LYEBEDEV.) You be the judge, Pavel Kirilich. . . . My diamonds were the ace, king, queen, jack, and eight . . .

LYEBEDEV (*stopping up his ears*). Stop, be so kind . . . stop it. . . .

AVDOTYA NAZAROVNA (*yells*). It was I who bid notrump!

KOSICH (*furious*). Call me an idiot if I ever sit down to play anything again with that old octopus! (*Exits quickly into the garden.*)

(SECOND GUEST *goes out after him;* YEGORUSHKA *stays at the table.*)

AVDOTYA NAZAROVNA. Ai! He gives me a pain. . . . Old octopus! . . . *You're* an old octopus!

BABAKINA. You're not such a bargain yourself, Grandma. . . .

AVDOTYA NAZAROVNA (*seeing* BABAKINA, *throws up her hands*). My angel, my beauty! . . . She's here, and I, blind hen that I am, didn't see her . . . my darling . . . (*Kisses her on the shoulder and sits down beside her.*) What joy! Let me look at you, my white swan! Tsk, tsk, tsk . . . I won't hex you just by looking at you!

LYEBEDEV. Well, she's warming up. . . . Why don't you be nice and find her a husband . . .

AVDOTYA NAZAROVNA. Well, I will! Before I'm in my grave, sinner that I am, I'll have both Sanichka and her married! Before they put me in my grave! (*Sighs.*) Only, where are they to be found these days, these husbands? Here they are, our husbands, sitting around looking sullen, like a bunch of wet roosters.

THIRD GUEST. A highly unfortunate comparison! From my point of view, mesdames, if today's young men prefer to stay single, the fault lies, so to speak, with social conditions . . .

LYEBEDEV. Well, well! . . . Don't philosophize! . . . I don't like it! . . .

SASHA (*enters and goes to her father*). Such extraordinary weather, and you all sit where it's stuffy, people!

ZINAIDA SAVISHNA. Sashenka, don't you see Marfa Yegorovna is here?

SASHA. I'm sorry. (*Goes to* BABAKINA *and greets her.*)

BABAKINA. You're getting so stuck-up, Sashenka, so stuck-up, you haven't been to visit me once. (*They embrace.*) Congratulations, darling. . . .

SASHA. Thank you. (*Sits next to her father.*)

LYEBEDEV. Yes, Avdotya Nazarovna, it's not easy getting a fiancé these days. And not only the fiancé—where can you find a best man? Young people these days, no offense in-

tended, God help them, are a little flat, a little overdone.
. . . You can't even have a little dance with them, or a little
talk or a drink. . . .

AVDOTYA NAZAROVNA. They're all expert in the drinking
department . . . all you have to do is offer . . .

LYEBEDEV. What's so good about drinking—even a horse
can drink. . . . No, it's how you drink! When we were young,
we would be at our studies day in and day out, but as soon
as the evening started, we'd go right off to the first brightly
lit place, and spin around all night long like a top . . .
dancing around and amusing ourselves with the ladies, and
things like that. (*Flicks finger on neck to indicate enjoyment.*) And we'd tell big stories and philosophize until our
tongues almost fell off. . . . But these modern ones . . .
(*Waves his hands.*) I don't understand them . . . they're no
good to man or beast. In the whole district there's only one
decent fellow and he's married . . . (*Sighs.*) and he seems
to be going wild like the rest of them. . . .

BABAKINA. Who's that?

LYEBEDEV. Nikolasha Ivanov.

BABAKINA. Yes, he's a nice man. (*Grimaces.*) Only he's
not so happy!

ZINAIDA SAVISHNA. That's right, darling, but what do you
expect? (*Sighs.*) What a mistake he made, poor man! . . .
He got married to his Jewish girl, and the poor fellow calculated that her father and mother would give away a fortune with her, but it turned out quite the opposite. . . . From
the moment she changed her religion, her father and mother
didn't want to know her; they cursed her. . . . So he didn't
get anything. Now he's sorry but it's too late. . . .

SASHA. Mama, that's not true. . . .

BABAKINA (*excited*). Shurochka, why isn't it true? You
know everybody knows about it. If it wasn't in his interest,
why would he have married a Jewess? Is there a shortage of
Russian girls? He made a mistake, darling, he made a mistake. . . . (*Eagerly.*) Good God, doesn't he give it to her

now! It's a joke! He comes home from wherever he's been
and he says to her: "Your father and mother swindled me!
Get out of here, out of my house!" But where can she go?
Her father and mother won't take her back. She could get a
job as a maid somewhere, but she's not trained for that kind
of work . . . so he tortures her until even the Count has to
stand up for her. . . . If it weren't for the Count, she'd have
been worried into her grave long before this. . . .

AVDOTYA NAZAROVNA. And not only that, sometimes he
keeps her in the cellar, and says: "Come on, you so-and-so,
eat garlic." Eat-eat, until she's all blown up with it.

(*Laughter.*)

SASHA. Papa, you know that's a lie!

LYEBEDEV. Well, so what? Let them talk all they like. . . .
(*Shouts.*) Gavrila!

(GAVRILA *serves him vodka and water.*)

ZINAIDA SAVISHNA. So that's how he ruined himself, the
poor man. And business is bad, darling, so bad. . . . If
Borkin didn't look after the estate, then he and his Jewess
wouldn't have anything to eat. (*Sighs.*) As for us, darling,
we've suffered on account of that! We've suffered a great
deal, only God knows how much! Would you believe it, my
dear, for the past three years he's owed us nine thousand!

BABAKINA (*horrified*). Nine thousand rubles!

ZINAIDA SAVISHNA. Yes . . . it was my own Pashenka who
arranged to give it to him. He can't tell the difference between to whom you can give and to whom you can't. I'm
not talking about the capital—God keep him, if he'd only pay
the interest regularly.

SASHA (*hotheaded*). Mama, you've said that all a hundred
times!

ZINAIDA SAVISHNA. Is that your business? Why are you
standing up for him?

SASHA (*gets up*). How do you have the heart to say all that about a man who has never done you any harm? Well, what has he done to you?

THIRD GUEST. Alexandra Pavlovna, may I say a word? I respect Nikolai Alexeyevich and I have always been honored to know him, but let it be said *entre nous,* he's something of an adventurer.

SASHA. If that's how you feel, I congratulate you!

THIRD GUEST. As proof of what I've been saying, I'll confide to you the following fact which was related to me by his attaché, or as he's called, his cicerone Borkin. Two years ago, the time of the cattle episode, he bought some cows, insured them . . .

ZINAIDA SAVISHNA. Yes, yes, yes! I remember that. I've heard about that, too.

THIRD GUEST. He insured them and then you know, he infected them with the plague and claimed the insurance money.

SASHA. That's all nonsense! Nonsense! Nobody bought or infected any cattle! Borkin himself made up the whole thing and boasted about it everywhere. When Ivanov found out about it, Borkin had to beg his forgiveness for two whole weeks. Ivanov's only fault is that he has a weak nature and he hasn't the heart to throw Borkin out; it's his fault he trusts people too much! Everything he has has been pilfered and plundered; anybody could make a fortune taking advantage of his generosity if he only wanted to.

LYEBEDEV. Shura, you hothead! Control yourself!

SASHA. Why do they talk such nonsense? How boring it all is, so boring! Ivanov, Ivanov, Ivanov—there's nothing else they want to talk about. (*Goes to the door, then returns.*) It's astonishing! (*To the young people.*) I'm really astonished by your patience, people! Don't you get bored sitting here like this? The air is so thick with boredom! If only you'd say something, amuse the girls, make a move! Well, if you have nothing else to do but talk about Ivanov, then why don't you laugh, sing, dance, or something. . . .

LYEBEDEV (*laughing*). Go ahead, tell them off, tell them off good!

SASHA. Do me this favor! Listen! If you don't want to dance, laugh, or sing, if all that is boring to you, then I ask you, once in your life, just for the hell of it, why don't you surprise us, make us laugh, gather all your wits about you and make up something funny, sparkle a little, say something even if it's crude or vulgar, as long as it's fresh and funny! Or get together and do something, a little something, nothing special, but something out of the ordinary so that for once in our lives, we could look at you and ooh and ah about you a little. Don't you really want to please us? Then why don't you try? My God, you're all so sad, so sad, sad, sad! Just to look at you, I could give up. So sad, so sad! . . . I've told you a thousand times and I could go on telling you forever, that you're so sad, so sad, so sad!

SHABYELSKI (*comes in with* IVANOV *from the door on the right*). Who's making a speech? You, Shurochka? (*Laughs loud and shakes hands with her.*) Congratulations, my angel, and may God grant you long life and the luck not to be born again. . . .

ZINAIDA SAVISHNA (*joyous*). Nikolai Alexeyevich, Count . . .

LYEBEDEV. Well, who do I see . . . Count! (*Goes to meet him.*)

SHABYELSKI (*seeing* ZINAIDA SAVISHNA *and* BABAKINA, *stretching his arms out to them*). Two banks on one sofa! Beautiful to behold! (*They greet one another. To* ZINAIDA SAVISHNA.) How are you, Zhuzhushka? (*To* BABAKINA.) Hello, cutie.

ZINAIDA SAVISHNA. I'm so happy. You visit us so seldom! My dear count! (*Shouts.*) Gavrila, tea! Sit down, please! (*Gets up and goes out through the door on the right and returns at once; looks extremely preoccupied.*)

(SASHA *sits down where she sat before.* IVANOV *greets everybody in silence.*)

LYEBEDEV (*to* SHABYELSKI). Where have you been keeping yourself? What brought you? What a surprise! (*Kisses him.*) Count, you're such a rascal! Decent people don't behave this way! . . . (*Takes his arm and leads him to the front of the stage.*) Why don't you ever visit us? Are you angry or something?

SHABYELSKI. But how can I come to you? On a broomstick? I don't have any horses of my own, and Nikolai won't bring me with him. He makes me sit home with Sarah so she won't feel lonely. Send your horses for me and I'll come to see you.

LYEBEDEV (*waves hands*). Oh, yes, of course! Zhuzhushka would rather burst than send the horses. My darling boy, my dear, don't you know you're nearer and dearer to me than anybody else? Out of all our old friends there's only you and me now surviving! In you I love my suffering and the days of my lost youth. . . . Joking aside, I could almost cry. (*Embraces the* COUNT.)

SHABYELSKI. Let me go, let me go! You smell like an old wine cellar. . . .

LYEBEDEV. My dear fellow, you can't imagine how much I miss my friends! I could hang myself, I'm so depressed. . . . (*Quietly.*) Zhuzhushka and her stinginess have driven away all the nice people, and what remains, as you can notice, are only a few Zulus . . . lowlifes and fourflushers. . . . Well, have some tea. . . .

(GAVRILA *serves the* COUNT *tea.*)

ZINAIDA SAVISHNA (*preoccupied, to* GAVRILA). Well, what are you doing? Serving like that? Bring some jam. . . . Gooseberries, or something. . . .

SHABYELSKI (*laughs loudly. To* IVANOV). Well, didn't I tell you? (*To* LYEBEDEV.) I had a bet with him that when we arrived, Zhuzhushka would treat us right away to some goose-berry jam.

ZINAIDA SAVISHNA. Count, you're still the same old joker. . . . (*Sits down.*)

LYEBEDEV. Twenty barrels of it they've cooked up, so what can they do with it?

SHABYELSKI (*sits down beside the table*). Still hoarding it away, Zhuzhushka? Well, are you a millionaire yet, hm?

ZINAIDA SAVISHNA (*giving a deep sigh*). Yes, to an outsider it looks as if we're rich and others are not, but where's the money coming from? It's only talk. . . .

SHABYELSKI. Yes, yes, of course. We know! We know how badly you play the game. . . . (*To* LYEBEDEV.) Pasha, tell me with a clear conscience: have you made a million?

LYEBEDEV. I don't know. That's Zhuzhushka's department. . . .

SHABYELSKI (*to* BABAKINA). And our plump little pigeon here will soon be a millionaire! She gets prettier and plumper every day and in every way. . . . That's what a lot of money does for a woman. . . .

BABAKINA. Thank you very much, Your Excellency. I don't like your mocking ways.

SHABYELSKI. But my darling bank, do you call this mocking? It's a cry from the heart, from an excess of feeling. I talk too much. I love you and Zhuzhushka more than anything else in the world. (*Gaily.*) I'm ecstatic! Rapturous! I can't look at the two of you with indifference . . .

ZINAIDA SAVISHNA. You're the same as you always were. (*To* YEGORUSHKA.) Yegorushka, blow out the candles! Why let them burn if you're not playing!

(YEGORUSHKA *jumps up; then he blows out the candles and sits down.*)

(*To* IVANOV.) Nikolai Alexeyevich, how is your wife's health?

IVANOV. Bad. Today the doctor said that she's definitely tubercular. . . .

ZINAIDA SAVISHNA. Is it possible? What a pity! (*Sighs.*) And we're so fond of her. . . .

SHABYELSKI. Nonsense, nonsense, and more nonsense! She doesn't have t.b. . . . It's just the doctor's tricks . . . the charlatan! Aesculapius wants to wander about the house, so he thinks up t.b. Lucky the husband's not jealous. (IVANOV *makes an impatient gesture.*) As for Sarah, I don't trust a single word or action of hers. My whole life long I've never trusted doctors, lawyers, or women. Nonsense, nonsense, tricks and charlatanism!

LYEBEDEV (*to* SHABYELSKI). You're a remarkable fellow, Matvyey! . . . You've taken hold of some kind of misanthropic attitude and you carry it around with you like a child with a new toy. You're like anybody else, but once you start talking, it's like the plague, perpetual phlegm. . . .

SHABYELSKI. Well, do you want me to embrace all these scoundrels and rascals I meet? Do you?

LYEBEDEV. Where do you see all these scoundrels and rascals?

SHABYELSKI. Well, present company excepted, of course . . . but . . .

LYEBEDEV. Well, there comes the but. . . . It's all affected.

SHABYELSKI. Affected . . . it's a good thing for you that you don't have any *Weltanschauung*.

LYEBEDEV. What's my *Weltanschauung*? I'll tell you. I sit and moment to moment I wait to die. We haven't got time to think about *Weltanschauung*'s, my friend. And that's the truth. (*Shouts.*) Gavrila!

SHABYELSKI. You've had too much Gavrila. . . . Take a look at your nose . . . how dignified it looks!

LYEBEDEV (*sings*). "Never mind, my dear, I'm not going to be married today."

ZINAIDA SAVISHNA. Dr. Lvov hasn't been to see us for a long time. He's probably forgotten us.

SASHA. He's my nemesis. He's honesty personified. He can't ask for a glass of water or smoke a cigarette without showing off his extraordinary honesty. Walking or talking, it's written all over his forehead: "I'm an honest man!" He's a bore.

SHABYELSKI. He's a narrowminded, overdirect man, that doctor! (*Teasing.*) "Make way for human labor!" he pontificates, he lays down the law every moment, the parrot, and he thinks he's a great critic. Anyone who doesn't pontificate like him, he deems a scoundrel. His opinions are astonishing in their profundity. If a peasant earns his living and lives like a human being, that must mean he's a scoundrel and a thief. If I wear a velvet jacket and have a valet to help me dress—I am a scoundrel and a slavedriver. He's so honest that he's bursting with it. He can't stand still with it. I'm almost afraid of him. . . . I feel he might any moment, out of a feeling of duty, hit me in the face or call me names.

IVANOV. I find him terribly tiresome but all the same I find him *simpatico*; there's a great deal of sincerity in him.

SHABYELSKI. Marvelous sincerity! He came over to me last evening and, just like that, said to me: "Count, I find you deeply displeasing!" Well, thank you very much! All this isn't naïveté, you know. It's done with a purpose: his voice trembles, his eyes burn, he trembles and he shakes. . . . Damn his woodenheaded sincerity! . . . Well, I'm against him. He may find me repulsive and vile, that's all very well and good . . . and I know myself very well, but why should he say it to my face? I'm a good-for-nothing, but, be that as it may, he could have some respect for my gray hairs. . . . Miserable, merciless honesty!

LYEBEDEV. Now, now, now! You've been young yourself and you can understand.

SHABYELSKI. Yes, I've been young and foolish, and in my time I fancied myself another Chatsky, exposing scoundrels and villains; but never in my life have I called a thief a thief to his face or talked about a rope in the home of a condemned man. I was well brought up. Your stupid doctor would be in seventh heaven, on top of the world, if fate would give him the opportunity, in the name of principles and human ideals, to hit me in the face publicly.

LYEBEDEV. Young people all have habits like that. My uncle was a Hegelian . . . he filled up his house with guests and gatherings, and after a drink, he'd stand up on his chair and start: "You ignoramuses! You powers of darkness! The dawn of a new life is coming!" Ta-ta, te-tum, ta-ta. . . . And he'd go on and on lecturing them.

SASHA. And what did the guests do?

LYEBEDEV. Nothing. . . . They just listened and went on drinking. Once, however, I challenged him to a duel; my own uncle! It was on account of Bacon. I remember I was sitting . . . God help that memory of mine . . . right there, like Matvyey, and my uncle was with Gerasim Nilich, standing right there where Nikolasha was, or approximately . . . my friend, Gerasim Nilich, asked a question . . .

(*Enter* BORKIN, *dressed as a dandy, with a package under his arm, skipping and singing, coming from the door on the right. Roars of approval greet him.*)

YOUNG LADIES. Mikhail Mikhailovich!

LYEBEDEV. Mikhail Mikhailovich! I can tell he's here. . . .

SHABYELSKI. The life of the party!

BORKIN. Here I am! (*Runs up to* SASHA.) Most noble signorina, may I be so bold as to congratulate the universe on the birth of such a marvelous flower as yourself . . . as a tribute of my delight, I make bold to present this token . . .

(*Gives package.*) fireworks and Roman candles of my own manufacture. May they brighten the night as you brighten the shadows of this realm. (*Bows theatrically.*)

SASHA. I thank you. . . .

LYEBEDEV (*laughs loudly, to* IVANOV). Why don't you get rid of this Judas?

BORKIN (*to* LYEBEDEV.) Pavel Kirilich! (*To* IVANOV.) My patron. . . . (*Sings.*) "Nicholas *voilà* ha ha, ha ha!" (*Makes the rounds.*) Most honorable Zinaida Savishna . . . the divine Marfa Yegorovna . . . the venerable Avdotya Nazarovna . . . His Excellency, the Count . . .

SHABYELSKI (*laughs loudly*). The life of the party! . . . When he arrives, the atmosphere becomes more lively. Do you notice?

BORKIN. Oh, I'm weary. . . . I think I've greeted everybody. Well, people, what's the news? Anything special? Anything tantalizing? (*Promptly, to* ZINAIDA SAVISHNA.) So listen to this, Mama . . . as I was on my way here . . . (*To* GAVRILA.) Gavrila, give me some tea; and no gooseberry preserves! (*To* ZINAIDA SAVISHNA.) As I was on my way here, I saw some muzhiks down by the river stripping bark off the willows. Why don't you lease out those willows?

LYEBEDEV (*to* IVANOV). Why don't you get rid of this Judas?

ZINAIDA SAVISHNA (*alarmed*). Why not! It never occurred to me!

BORKIN (*moving his arms as if doing calisthenics*). I can't do without exercise. . . . Mama, isn't there something special we could play? Marfa Yegorovna, I'm in fine form . . . I feel exalted! (*Sings.*) "Again I stand before you . . ."

ZINAIDA SAVISHNA. Get something going, everybody's so bored!

BORKIN. People, really, why don't you cheer up? You're all sitting around like a bunch of criminal lawyers. Let's do something artistic! What will it be? Charades, skip-rope, dancing, fireworks?

YOUNG LADIES (*clapping their hands*). Fireworks! Fireworks! (*They run into the garden.*)

SASHA (*to* IVANOV). Why do you look so sad today?

IVANOV. My head aches, Shurochka, and I'm a little depressed. . . .

SASHA. Let's go into the living room.

(*They go out through the door on the right; all go out into the ~~~~, except for* ZINAIDA SAVISHNA *and* LYEBEDEV.)

ZINAIDA SAVISHNA. Now that's what I like . . . a real young man: he hasn't been here a minute and he's already cheered everybody up. (*Turns down the large lamp.*) While they're in the garden, there's no reason to burn expensive candles. (*Blows out candles.*)

LYEBEDEV (*following her*). Zhuzhushka, we should offer our guest some refreshments. . . .

ZINAIDA SAVISHNA. Look at those candles. . . . No wonder everybody thinks we're rich. (*Blows out candles.*)

LYEBEDEV (*following her*). Zhuzhushka, why don't we give the people something to eat. . . . They're young, they're most likely starving, poor things. . . . Zhuzhushka . . .

ZINAIDA SAVISHNA. Count didn't even empty his glass. Such a waste of sugar. (*Goes out through door on left.*)

LYEBEDEl (*with an expression of annoyance*). Tsh! (*Goes out to the garden.*)

SASHA (*entering with* IVANOV *from door on right*). They've all gone out to the garden.

IVANOV. That's how things are, Shurochka. In the past I worked a great deal and thought a great deal, but I never got tired; now I do nothing and think about nothing, and I'm tired in body and soul. Day and night my conscience troubles me. I feel deeply guilty, but how exactly I am to blame, I don't know. And then there's my wife's illness, my money troubles, the eternal bickering, gossiping, and super-fluous chatter of that stupid Borkin. . . . I'm sick of my home and living in it has become worse than torture for me. I tell you truthfully, Shurochka, even the company of my wife is unbearable, and she loves me. You're my old friend, so you won't be angry if I'm sincere. I've come here to you now to distract myself; but I'm depressed even here, and I'm longing to go home. Excuse me. I'll go home quietly now.

SASHA. Nikolai Alexeyevich, I understand you. Your mis-fortune is that you're lonely. You need someone near you whom you can love and who understands you. Only love can restore you.

IVANOV. Ha, you think so, Shurochka! It wouldn't do, if I, an old, wet rooster, would drag out a new love affair! God protect me from that misfortune! No, my clever one, it's not a love affair I need. I tell you, as God is my witness, I can bear anything: depression, anxiety, bankruptcy, the loss of my wife, premature old age, and solitude, but I can't bear, I cannot, the contempt I feel for myself. I'm dying of shame at the thought that I, a healthy, strong man, have turned into some kind of Hamlet, Manfred, or one of those super-fluous people . . . damn them. There are pitiful people who are flattered to be called Hamlets or superfluous, but I feel that's—a disgrace! It outrages my pride, I'm oppressed by shame and I suffer. . . .

SASHA (*jokingly, through tears*). Nikolai Alexeyevich, let's run away to America.

IVANOV. I'm too lazy to cross the threshold and you want to go to America. . . . (*They go toward the entrance to the garden.*) Really, Shura, it must be hard for you to live here! When I see the people around you, I become afraid. Who could you marry here? The only hope is to find some passing lieutenant or student to sneak you away and abduct you. . . . (ZINAIDA SAVISHNA *enters from the door on left with jar of jam.*) Excuse me, Shurochka, I'll catch up with you. . . .

(SASHA *exits to garden.*) Zinaida Savishna, I've something to ask you. . . .

ZINAIDA SAVISHNA. What is it, Nikolai Alexeyevich?

IVANOV (*hesitating*). You see, it's about the day after tomorrow when my promissory note comes due. I would be much obliged to you if you could give me some more time or permit me to add the interest to the principal. I don't have any money right now. . . .

ZINAIDA SAVISHNA (*scared*). Nikolai Alexeyevich, how is it possible? What kind of arrangement is that? No, and don't bring it up; for God's sake, don't torture me, I'm an unfortunate woman. . . .

IVANOV. I'm sorry. I'm sorry. . . . (*Goes out into the garden.*)

ZINAIDA SAVISHNA. My goodness, how he frightened me! Phew! I'm trembling all over. . . . (*Goes out by the door at right.*)

KOSICH (*entering from the door on left and crossing the stage*). I had the ace, king, queen, jack, and eight of diamonds, the ace of spades and one . . . one little heart, and she, damn her, couldn't make a small slam! (*Exits by the door at right.*)

AVDOTYA NAZAROVNA (*entering with the first guest from the garden*). I'd like to tear her to pieces, the old miser . . . tear her bit by bit! It's no joke, I've been sitting here since five o'clock, and she hasn't treated me even to some stale herring! Is this a home! Well, that's what you call hospitality!

FIRST GUEST. I'm so bored, I could bash my head against the wall! What people, God help them! I could howl from boredom and hunger and start gnawing on people.

AVDOTYA NAZAROVNA. I'd like to tear her to pieces, the old sinner.

FIRST GUEST. I'm going to have a drink, old lady—and

then I'm going home! Not even the fiancées you've promised me could keep me here! How the hell can you think of love if you haven't had anything to drink since dinner?

AVDOTYA NAZAROVNA. Shall we go and have a look, what do you say? . . .

FIRST GUEST. Shhh! Quietly! There's some schnapps in the dining room, in the sideboard. We'll put the screws on Yegorushka. . . . Shhh! (*They go out through the door on the left.*)

ANNA PETROVNA (*entering, with* LVOV, *from the door on the right*). That's all right, they'll be happy to see us. Nobody's in here. They must be in the garden.

LVOV. Well then, let me ask you why you brought me here to this den of vipers? This place is not for you and me! Honest people can't breathe this atmosphere!

ANNA PETROVNA. Now listen to me, Mr. Honest Man! It's ungracious to accompany a lady and to talk about nothing all the way but your own honesty! It may be honest, but to say the least, it's boring. Never talk to women about your virtues. Let them find that out for themselves. My Nikolai, when he was like that, like you, when he was in the company of women, he only sang songs and told stories, but among them each one knew what kind of man he was.

LVOV. Oh, don't talk to me about your Nikolai. I understand him only too well!

ANNA PETROVNA. You're a good man, but you don't understand anything. Let's go into the garden. He never expressed himself like that: "I'm honest! I'm suffocating in this atmosphere." He never talked about vipers, owl's nests, and crocodiles! He left the menagerie in peace and when he would be exasperated by something, all I ever heard from him was: "Oh, how unfair I was today!" or "Aniuta, I'm sorry for that man!" That's the way he was, but you . . . (*They go out.*)

FIRST GUEST (*entering from door at left, with* AVDOTYA NAZAROVNA). If it's not in the dining room, then it must be in the pantry somewhere. We should locate Yegorushka. Let's go through the living room.

AVDOTYA NAZAROVNA. I'd like to tear her from limb to limb. (*They go out through the door on the left.*)

(BABAKINA *and* BORKIN *run in from the garden, laughing; after them, laughing and rubbing his hands,* SHABYELSKI *minces in.*)

BABAKINA. I'm so bored! (*Laughs loudly.*) Bored out of my mind! They all walk around and sit like stiff pokers! I'm bored stiff as stone. (*Jumps up.*) I need to stretch my legs.

(BORKIN *grabs her by the waist and kisses her on the cheek.*)

SHABYELSKI (*laughs loudly and snaps his fingers*). Well, I'll be damned! (*Grunts.*) As it were. . . .

BABAKINA. Let me go. Keep your hands off me, you shameless fellow. God knows what the Count will think. Stop!

BORKIN. My little angel, my heart-throb. (*Kisses her.*) Let me borrow twenty-three hundred rubles!

BABAKINA. N-n-no . . . it's all very well, but when it comes to money—thank you very much—no, no, no! Oh, let go of my hands! . . .

SHABYELSKI (*mincing around them*). Little pigeon . . . she has her pleasing qualities. . . .

BORKIN (*seriously*). That's enough. Let's get down to business. Let's discuss it frankly, in a businesslike way. Answer me first, without fear and machinations: yes or no? Listen! (*Points to* COUNT.) He needs money over there, an income of three thousand a year, minimum. You need a husband. Would you like to be a countess?

SHABYELSKI (*laughs loudly*). A remarkable cynic!

BORKIN. Do you want to be a countess? Yes or no?

BABAKINA (*agitated*). You're inventing, Misha, really. . . . And these things just aren't done this way, so sudden. . . . If it pleases the Count, he can do it by himself, and . . . I don't know, all of a sudden, like this, in a minute. . . .

BORKIN. Well, don't complicate things! . . . It's business. . . . Yes or no?

SHABYELSKI (*laughing and rubbing his hands*). Really? Hm? I'll be damned, I'd better do something about this little piece of malice all by myself. Hm? My little pigeon . . . (*Kisses* BABAKINA *on the cheek.*) My little treasure! My little cucumber!

BABAKINA. Please wait, wait, you've upset me enough. . . . Go away, go away! . . . No, don't go away!

BORKIN. Quickly! Yes or no? We've no time to waste. . . .

BABAKINA. You know what, Count? You come to my house as my guest for two or three days. . . . It's a gay place, not like here. . . . Come tomorrow. . . . (*To* BORKIN.) No, you were joking, weren't you?

BORKIN (*angrily*). Who'd want to joke about serious matters?

BABAKINA. Stop, stop. . . . Oh, I feel faint! I feel faint! A countess . . . I'm fainting! I'm falling . . .

(BORKIN *and the* COUNT *run laughingly to take her by the arm and kiss her cheek, leading her out through the door at the right.* IVANOV *and* SASHA *run in from the garden.*)

IVANOV (*desperately clutching his head*). It can't be! You shouldn't, you shouldn't, Shurochka! . . . Oh, you shouldn't!

SASHA (*abandoned*). I love you . . . madly. . . . Without you my life has no meaning, no happiness, no joy! For me . . . you're everything. . . .

IVANOV. But why, why! My God, I don't understand any-thing. . . . Shurochka, you shouldn't!

SASHA. When I was a child, you were my only joy. I loved you and everything about you . . . as I did myself . . . but now I love *you*, Nikolai Alexeyevich. I'd go with you to the ends of the earth, Nikolai, to the grave and beyond; only for Heaven's sake, make it soon, or I'll suffocate. . . .

IVANOV (*bursts into happy laughter*). What is all this? Does it mean my life is beginning all over again? Yes, Shurochka? My happiness! . . . (*Drawing her close.*) My youth, my freshness . . .

(ANNA PETROVNA *enters from the garden, and, seeing her husband with* SASHA, *stops as if rooted to the spot.*)

Does it mean, to live? Yes? To work again? (*They kiss; after the kiss,* IVANOV *and* SASHA *look around and see* ANNA PETROVNA.)

IVANOV (*terrified*). Sarah!

CURTAIN

Act III

IVANOV's *study. Writing desk, on which papers, books, business letters, knickknacks, revolvers lie in disorder; beside the papers, a lamp, a carafe of water, a plate with herring, slices of bread and cucumbers. On the walls, maps, pictures, guns, pistols, sickles, whips, etc. It's midday.*

(SHABYELSKI *and* LYEBEDEV *are seated at the desk.* BORKIN, *center stage, astride a chair.* PYOTR *stands at the door.*)

LYEBEDEV. The French policy is clear and definite. . . . The French know what they want. They want to slit open the sausage eaters, and that's all; but Germany, my friend, is playing a different tune. Germany has many other fish to fry besides France. . . .

SHABYELSKI. Nonsense! In my opinion, the Germans are cowards and the French are cowards. . . . They don't give one damn about each other; they'll keep their hands in their pockets. Believe me, they may point at each other, but they won't fight.

BORKIN. And in my opinion, why should they fight? What's the use of all those armaments, congresses and expenses? You know what I'd do? I'd gather together all the dogs in the country, inject them with Pasteur's poison, a good dose, and let them loose in enemy country. All my enemies would go mad in a month.

LYEBEDEV (*laughs*). To look at him, he has a small head, but there are big ideas inside—countless thousands of them, like fish in the sea.

SHABYELSKI. He's a genius!

LYEBEDEV. God bless you, you make us laugh, Michel Michelich! (*Stops laughing.*) Well, gentlemen. We talk on endlessly, but not a word about vodka. *Repetatur.* (*Fills three glasses.*) We should live and be well! (*They drink and eat.*) Salt herring, Matushka, is of all snacks, *the* snack.

SHABYELSKI. Well, no. Cucumber's better. . . . Scientists since the creation of the world have been racking their brains and found nothing better than pickled cucumber. They didn't think up the cucumber. (*To* PYOTR.) Pyotr, go and get us some more cucumbers, and tell them in the kitchen to fry up four pirozhki with onions. See that they're hot.

(PYOTR *goes out.*)

LYEBEDEV. Vodka is nice to have with caviar, too. Only you know what? You need to know how. . . . Take a quarter pound of pressed caviar, two little green onions, olive oil, mix it all up, and then, you know . . . squeeze a little lemon juice on top. . . . It'll kill you! The smell alone will drive you out of your mind.

BORKIN. After vodka, it's also nice to eat fried gudgeons. But you have to know how to prepare them. You have to clean them, then crumble them in bread crumbs and fry them till they're golden-brown, until they're crunchable between the teeth . . . crunch, crunch, crunch . . .

SHABYELSKI. Yesterday Babakina had some nice hors d'oeuvres—white mushrooms.

LYEBEDEV. You don't say. . . .

SHABYELSKI. Only they were prepared in a special way. You know, with onion and bay leaves, and all kinds of spices. When you took the lid off the pan, the steam, the odor that came forth—pure joy!

LYEBEDEV. Shall we? *Repetatur,* gentlemen! (*They drink.*) May we live and be well. . . . (*Looks at his watch.*) It doesn't look like I'll get to see Nikolasha. It's time for me to go. You said you had mushrooms at Babakina's, but you haven't seen any here yet. Will you be so good as to tell me why the hell you're such a continual visitor at Marfutka's?

SHABYELSKI (*pointing to* BORKIN). Well, he's the one; he wants me to marry her. . . .

LYEBEDEV. Marry? How old are you?

SHABYELSKI. Sixty-two years old.

LYEBEDEV. Just ready to get married. And Marfutka's just what you've been waiting for.

BORKIN. Marfutka's not the reason, it's Marfutka's millions.

LYEBEDEV. Is that what you want: Marfutka's millions . . . maybe you want the moon, too?

BORKIN. When he's a married man and his pockets are stuffed, there won't be any talk about the moon. Then you'll be sorry. . . .

SHABYELSKI. He's really serious. Our genius is sure that I'll listen to him and get married. . . .

BORKIN. Well, what then? Aren't you sure?

SHABYELSKI. Have you gone out of your mind? . . . When was I sure? Sssss . . .

BORKIN. Thank you very much! . . . Thank you so very much! So that means you want to let me down? First you'll marry, then you won't . . . who the hell knows what you want? And I gave my word! So you won't marry?

SHABYELSKI (*shrugs shoulders*). He's serious! . . . An astonishing person!

BORKIN (*scandalized*). In that case, why did you get an honest woman all excited? Now that she's possessed by the idea of being a countess, she can't sleep or eat. . . . Is that something to joke about? Is that honest?

SHABYELSKI (*snaps his fingers*). Well, what if I do this malicious thing? Well? To spite them! I might just do it. My word of honor. . . . What fun!

(*Enter* Lvov.)

LYEBEDEV. Aesculapius, our humble one . . . (*Shakes* Lvov's *hands and sings.*) "Doctor, my saviour, saints above, I'm afraid of my dying day . . ."

LVOV. Nikolai Alexeyevich isn't back yet?

LYEBEDEV. No, I've been waiting for him for more than an hour myself. (Lvov *impatiently paces the stage.*) My dear boy, how is Anna Petrovna?

LVOV. Not well.

LYEBEDEV (*sighs*). May I go and present my respects to her?

LVOV. No, please, don't. I think she's asleep. . . . (*Pause.*)

LYEBEDEV. A sweet, nice woman. . . . (*Sighs.*) On Shurochka's birthday, when Anna Petrovna fainted, I looked at her face and then I knew that she wouldn't live long, poor thing. I don't understand why she fainted that time. I ran in and looked: there she was, lying on the floor, pale, with Nikolasha on his knees beside her, just as pale. Shurochka was crying. After that Shurochka and I went around for a whole week like we were crazy.

SHABYELSKI (*to* Lvov). Tell me, most esteemed priest of science, what scientist discovered that ladies suffering in the chest were helped by frequent visits from young doctors? It's a great discovery! A great one! How do we classify it— as allopathy or homeopathy?

(Lvov *tries to answer, but goes out after making a gesture of contempt.*)

What a withering glance. . . .

LYEBEDEV. What's got into you! Why did you insult him?

SHABYELSKI (*exasperated*). Why does he tell lies? Consumption, no hope, she's going to die. . . . He's lying! I can't stand it!

LYEBEDEV. Why do you think he's lying?

SHABYELSKI (*gets up and walks about*). I can't get it into my mind that a living being, suddenly, and for no reason at all . . . should die. Let's stop talking about it!

KOSICH (*runs in, out of breath*). Is Nikolai Alexeyevich at home? How are you all! (*Quickly shakes hands with everybody.*) Is he home?

BORKIN. No, he's not.

KOSICH (*sits down and then jumps up*). In that case, good-by! (*Drinks a glass of vodka and quickly has a bite.*) I better go. . . . Business. . . . I'm worn out . . . I can hardly stand on my feet. . . .

LYEBEDEV. What ill wind brought you?

KOSICH. I was at Barbanov's! We played cards all night and we just finished. . . . Ach! I lost everything playing. . . . That Barbanov plays like the old shark that he is. (*Tearful voice*). Listen: I was holding hearts the whole time . . . (*Turns to* BORKIN, *who jumps away from him.*) He bids diamonds. I play hearts again; he bids diamonds. . . . Well, I didn't make a single trick. (*To* LYEBEDEV.) He played the four of clubs. I had an ace, queen, six in my hand; ace, ten, three of spades . . .

LYEBEDEV (*stops his ears*). Spare me, spare me, for Christ's sake, spare me!

KOSICH (*to the* COUNT). You understand: ace, queen, six of clubs; ace, ten, three of spades . . .

SHABYELSKI (*pushes him aside*). Go away. I don't want to hear.

KOSICH. And suddenly, bad luck: my ace of spades was trumped right away . . .

SHABYELSKI (*snatching revolver from desk*). Go away or I'll shoot you!

KOSICH (*waving hands*). Darn it! . . . Can't I even talk to somebody? It's like living in Australia: no common interests, no togetherness. . . . Everybody living by himself. . . . But I have to go . . . it's time. (*Snatches up his cap.*) My time is valuable. . . . (*Taking* LYEBEDEV'S *hand.*) Pass! . . .

(*Laughter.* KOSICH *goes to the door and collides with* AVDOTYA NAZAROVNA.)

AVDOTYA NAZAROVNA (*shrieks*). Damn you, you almost knocked me down!

EVERYBODY. Here she comes again!

AVDOTYA NAZAROVNA. There you are. I've been looking for you everywhere. How do you do, my darlings. Eating well? (*Greets everybody.*)

LYEBEDEV. What are you doing here?

AVDOTYA NAZAROVNA. I'm here on business, my dear friend! (*To the* COUNT.) Concerning you, Your Excellency. (*Bows.*) She told me to send you her best regards and ask about your health. . . . And she also told me—my little sweetheart, to say that if you didn't come to see her this evening, she'd cry her little eyes out. "My dear," she said like that, "take him aside and whisper it secretly into his ear." But why secretly? We're all friends here. Such doings. We're not stealing chickens. We're arranging everything according to the laws of love, with mutual consent. Old sinner that I am, I never drink, but, as this is an occasion, I'll have one snort.

LYEBEDEV. And I will, too. (*Pours.*) And you, you old reprobate, you're holding up pretty well. I've known you for thirty years and you were old even then. . . .

AVDOTYA NAZAROVNA. And I've lost count of the years. . . . I've buried two husbands, and I'd have married a third, but no one wanted me without a dowry. I've had eight children . . . (*Takes a glass.*) Well, with God's help, we've begun a good thing, and with God's help we'll finish it! They'll live happily ever after, and we'll look on them with joy in our hearts. We'll give them advice and love . . . (*Drinks*.) Powerful vodka!

SHABYELSKI (*laughs, loudly, to* LYEBEDEV). Well, you know, it's curious; they think seriously that I— Astonishing! (*Gets up.*) And all the same, Pasha, what if I did go through with this vile business? For spite. . . . Well, what do you say to that, you old dog. . . . Eh, Pasha?

LYEBEDEV. You're talking nonsense, Count. Our business, my brother, is to think of dying. As for Marfutka's money, it's passed you by long ago. Our time has come.

SHABYELSKI. All right, I'll go through with it! On my honor, I will!

(*Enter* IVANOV *and* LVOV.)

LVOV. I want you to give me just five minutes of your time.

LYEBEDEV. Nikolasha! (*Goes to meet* IVANOV *and embraces him.*) How are you, my dear friend. . . . I've been waiting for you for a whole hour.

AVDOTYA NAZAROVNA (*bows*). How do you do, sir!

IVANOV (*bitterly*). Well, people; my study has again been turned into a bar. . . . I've asked you all a thousand times not to do this. . . . (*Goes to the table.*) Look, there, you've spilled vodka on my papers . . . crumbs . . . cucumbers. . . . It's disgusting!

LYEBEDEV. I'm sorry, Nikolasha, I'm sorry. . . . Forgive me. I've got to have a talk with you, my friend, about a very important matter. . . .

BORKIN. And so do I.

LVOV. Nikolai Alexeyevich, may I have a word with you?

IVANOV (*points at* LYEBEDEV). He wants me, too. Wait a minute, right after . . . (*To* LYEBEDEV.) What is it?

LYEBEDEV. People, I'd like to talk with him privately. Please. . . .

(*The* COUNT *goes out with* AVDOTYA NAZAROVNA; *after them,* BORKIN; *then* LVOV.)

IVANOV. Pasha, you can drink as much as you like. It's your weakness, but I ask you not to make a drunkard out of my uncle. He never used to drink in my home before. It's bad for him.

LYEBEDEV (*frightened*). My dear fellow, I didn't know. . . . I didn't pay any attention. . . .

IVANOV. If that silly old baby dies, God forbid, you wouldn't be blamed, I would. . . . What do you want? . . . (*Pause.*)

LYEBEDEV. You see, my dear friend . . . I don't know how to begin. I don't know how to begin so that it doesn't sound cruel. Nikolasha, I'm ashamed, I'm blushing. I'm tongue-tied, but my dear fellow, put yourself in my position, understand; I'm in a dependent position, I'm a slave, a nothing. . . . Forgive me. . . .

IVANOV. What is it?

LYEBEDEV. My wife sent me. . . . Be good, be a friend, pay her the interest! You wouldn't believe it. She's nagged me, worn me out, tormented me! Settle it, for God's sake!

IVANOV. Pasha, you know I don't have any money now.

LYEBEDEV. I know, I know. But what can I do? She doesn't want to wait. If she asks for payment, how can Shurochka and I ever look you in the face?

IVANOV. I'm ashamed myself, Pasha. I wish the earth would open up and swallow me, but . . . but where can I get some money? Tell me: where? There's only one thing to do: to wait till autumn when I sell the grain.

LYEBEDEV (*shouts*). She doesn't want to wait! (*Pause.*)

IVANOV. Your position is not a pleasant one; it's delicate,

but mine is far worse. (*Walks and ponders.*) I can't think of anything . . . I don't have anything I can sell . . .

LYEBEDEV. Why don't you go to Milbach and ask him; you know he owes you sixteen thousand.

(IVANOV, *in despair, waves his hand.*)

There it is, Nikolasha. . . . I know you'll explode . . . but oblige an old drunkard! For friendship's sake. . . . Look on me as a friend. We've both been students and liberals. . . . We have ideas and interests in common. . . . We both studied at Moscow University . . . our Alma Mater . . . (*Takes out his wallet.*) I have some money hidden in here and not a soul at home knows about it. Take it for your needs. . . . (*Takes out money and puts it on table.*) Forget your pride and look on it as a friendly gesture. . . . I'd take it from you, my word of honor. . . . (*Pause.*) Here it is on the table: one thousand one hundred. Go and see her today and give it to her personally. And say: "Here you are! Zinaida Savishna, now go choke on it!" Only, see to it you don't let her know you saw me, or God help you! She'd give it to me, that old gooseberry jam! (*Scrutinizing* IVANOV's *face.*) There, there, it's not necessary! (*Quickly picks up the money from the table and stashes it away in his pocket.*) You don't need to! I was joking. . . . Forgive me, for Christ's sake! (IVANOV *waves hand.*) Yes, what a business. . . . (*Sighs.*) You're going through a sad time and much sorrow. My friend, a man, you know, is like a samovar. You can't always put him on the shelf cold; he gets some coal pushed into him here and there . . . psh! . . . psh! . . . That's a hellish comparison, not suitable at all, but, well, I couldn't think of anything cleverer. . . . (*Sighs.*) Misfortune tempers the soul. . . . I'm not sorry for you, Nikolasha. . . . You'll turn out all right . . . things will come out right in the end, but it offends me, my friend, it annoys me that people— Be so good as to tell me, where does all that gossip come from? My friend, there's gossip circulating about you all over the district. It's enough to make the local police come and investigate you . . . they call you a murderer, a bloodsucker, a robber . . .

IVANOV. That's all nonsense and I have a headache.

LYEBEDEV. It's all because you think too much.

IVANOV. I'm not thinking anything.

LYEBEDEV. Never mind, Nikolasha. Come and visit us. . . . Shurochka likes you, she understands you and she thinks highly of you. She's a good, honest person, Nikolasha. She doesn't take after her mother and father; maybe it was a dashing passer-by. . . . I look at her sometimes, my friend, and I don't believe that she's mine, a red-nosed drunkard with such a treasure. Come over and have a talk with her about something clever—you'll have a good time. She's a true, sincere person. . . . (*Pause.*)

IVANOV. Pasha, my dear, leave me alone. . . .

LYEBEDEV. I understand. I understand. . . . (*Hurriedly looks at his watch.*) I understand. (*Kisses* IVANOV.) Good-by. I have to go to the dedication of a school. (*Goes to the door, then stops.*) She's an intelligent girl. Yesterday Shurochka and I started talking about gossip. (*He laughs.*) And she came out with an aphorism: "Papa," she said, "the glow-worms shine at night only so that the birds can see them easier and eat them up in the night, and good people exist so that they can be eaten up by gossip and slander." How do you like that? She's a genius. A George Sand! . . .

IVANOV. Pasha! (*Stops him.*) What's the matter with me?

LYEBEDEV. I've wanted to ask about that myself. But I admit I felt too shy to do so. I don't know, my friend! On the one hand, it seems to me that you've been overcome with so much misfortune; on the other hand, I know you're the kind that misfortune wouldn't defeat. . . . It must be something else, Nikolasha; but what it is, I don't know!

IVANOV. I myself don't understand. It seems to me . . . but it couldn't be that! (*Pause.*) You know what I meant to say. I used to have a worker named Semyon, whom you must remember. Once, at threshing time, he wanted to show off his strength to some girls; he hoisted two sacks of rye on his back and strained himself. He died soon after. It seems to me I've strained myself, too. High school, then university, then farming, schools, projects. . . . I didn't have the same beliefs as everybody else. I didn't marry like everybody else. I had a bad temper, I took risks; as you know, I took my money and threw it around, left and right. I've been happy and I've suffered as no one else in the district has. Those are my sacks, Pasha. . . . I put a heavy burden on my back and my back gave way. At twenty we're all heroes, we're ready for anything, we can do anything; at thirty we're already tired, and we're good for nothing. How do you explain such fatigue? However, it might be that it's not that. . . . Not that, not that! . . . Go now, Pasha. God be with you. You must be tired of me.

LYEBEDEV (*eagerly*). You know what? It's your surroundings that are killing you!

IVANOV. That's stupid, Pasha, and an old story. Go away!

LYEBEDEV. Yes, really, it's stupid. I see it myself, now. It's stupid. I'm going. I'm going! (*Exits.*)

IVANOV (*alone*). I'm a poor, pitiful, worthless person. You need to be a pitiful, played-out drunkard like Pasha to be able to love and respect me still. How I despise myself, my God! How I hate the sound of my own voice, my footsteps, my hands, these clothes, my thoughts. Well, isn't it ridiculous? Isn't it maddening? It's not even been a year since I was healthy and strong. I was cheerful, in good spirits, tireless, passionate. I worked with these same hands and I talked in such a way that I could move even idiots to tears; I could weep at the sight of suffering, I was filled with indignation when I encountered malice. I knew what inspiration was. I knew the charm and poetry of those quiet nights, when from dusk till dawn I sat working at my desk or enjoying myself, dreaming my own thoughts. I believed. I looked into the future, as if it were my own mother's eyes. . . . And now, oh, my God! I'm tired. I don't believe. I idle away my days and nights. I don't pay attention to my mind, my hands, or my feet. The estate is going to seed, the forests are being cut down. (*Weeps.*) My land looks at me like an orphan. I expect nothing, I regret nothing. I tremble for tomorrow. And the business with Sarah? I swore to love her forever. I predicted great happiness, opened up a future be-

fore her eyes which was better than she'd ever dared dream.
She believed me. For those five years I saw her wasting away
under the burden of her sacrifices, exhausted by the struggle
with her conscience. God knows she never looked askance at
me, not a word of reproach! And what happened? I stopped
loving her. . . . How? Why? For what? I don't understand.
Now she's suffering, her days are numbered, and I, like a
complete coward, run away from her pale face, her sunken
chest, her imploring eyes. . . . I'm so ashamed, ashamed!
(*Pause.*) Sasha, a child, is touched by my unhappiness. To
me, almost an old man, she speaks of love; and I get drunk
on that. I forget everything else in the world, like someone
bewitched by music, and I shout: "A new life! Happiness!"
But the next day I believe in this new life and happiness
just as little as I did in my wife. What's the matter with
me? What is this precipice I'm pushing myself over? Where
does all this weakness come from? What's become of my
nerves? If my poor sick wife pricks my vanity or the servants
don't please me or if my gun misfires, how rude I become,
how hot-tempered; not at all like myself. . . . (*Pause.*) I
don't understand. I don't understand. I don't understand! I
almost wish I'd put a bullet through my head! . . .

Lvov (*entering*). I must have a talk with you, Nikolai
Alexeyevich!

Ivanov. If we both keep talking things over every day,
Doctor, we won't have enough strength to keep it up!

Lvov. Will you listen to me?

Ivanov. I listen to you every day but I still don't understand: what, exactly, do you want from me?

Lvov. I've said it clearly and definitely, and anyone who
doesn't understand me has no heart.

Ivanov. My wife is near death—I know; I'm irrevocably
guilty before her—I know that too; you're an honest, direct
man—I also know that! What else do you want?

Lvov. It pains me to see human cruelty. . . . A woman is
dying. She has a father and mother whom she loves and
would like to see before she dies; they know perfectly well

that she is going to die soon and that she still loves them, but—the damnable cruelty, they only think of their religious heritage: they still curse her. You, the man for whom she has sacrificed everything—her own family and her peace of mind —openly and with obvious intentions, go over every day to visit the Lyebedevs!

IVANOV. Why, I haven't been there for two weeks now. . . .

LVOV (*not listening to him*). With people like you, one needs to speak directly and without beating about the bush; but if you don't want to listen to me, then don't listen! I'm accustomed to calling things by their real names. You want her death so that you can go on to new adventures; so be it, but why couldn't you wait? If you were to let her die naturally without gouging her with your obvious cynicism, do you really think you'd lose the Lyebedev girl and her dowry? Not now, but in a year or two, you marvelous Tartuffe, you'd have ample time to turn the head of a girl and take possession of her dowry, as well as now. What's your hurry? Why do you want your wife to die right now, and not in a month or a year?

IVANOV. Torture. . . . Doctor, you're a poor doctor, indeed, if you think a man can restrain himself endlessly. It's costing me a terrible effort not to answer your insults.

LVOV. That's enough. Why do you want to make a fool of me? Stop this pretense!

IVANOV. Listen, you clever man, think: in your opinion, there's nothing simpler than understanding my motives! Yes? I married Anya, expecting to receive Anya's big dowry . . . they didn't give me the dowry, I missed out, and now I'm hastening her death so I can marry another and get her dowry. . . . Yes? How simple and uncomplicated. . . . Man is such a simple and wondrous machine. . . . No, Doctor, each of us has too many wheels, screws, and valves to be judged by one another on first impressions or by two or three external symptoms. I don't understand you. You don't understand me, and we don't understand each other. It's possible to be an excellent physician—and at the same time not to know anything about people. Don't be so sure of yourself —admit I'm right.

Lvov. Do you really think you're so difficult to see through and that I have so few brains that I can't distinguish between meanness and honesty?

Ivanov. It's obvious we'll never drink together. . . . For the last time, I ask you . . . answer me, please, without beating about the bush: what, exactly, do you want of me? What are you getting at? (*Exasperated.*) And whom do I have the honor of addressing: the prosecuting attorney or my wife's doctor?

Lvov. I'm a doctor, and as a doctor, I demand that you change your conduct. . . . It's killing Anna Petrovna!

Ivanov. What can I do? What? If you understand me better than I understand myself, then say something definite: what can I do?

Lvov. Curb your actions and don't be so open about everything.

Ivanov. Oh, my God! Do you really understand yourself? (*Drinks water.*) Leave me alone. I'm a thousand times at fault. I'll answer before God, but nobody authorized you to torment me every day. . . .

Lvov. And who authorized you to insult what I think right? You've exhausted me and poisoned my mind. Until I came to this district, I admitted the existence of people who were stupid, mad, easily carried away, but I never believed that there were criminal people who were intelligent, consciously directing their will toward evil. I respected and loved human beings, but when I saw you . . .

Ivanov. I've already heard all about that!

Lvov. You've heard? (*Sees* Sasha *who has just come in; she is dressed in riding clothes.*) Well, now, I hope we understand each other perfectly! (*Shrugs his shoulders and goes out.*)

Ivanov (*frightened*). Shura, is it you?

SASHA. Yes, it is. Hello. Weren't you expecting me? Why haven't you been to see us for so long?

IVANOV. Shura, for God's sake, don't be so thoughtless! Your coming might have a terrible effect on my wife.

SASHA. She won't see me. I came in through the back. I'll go in a moment. I'm worried; are you well? Why haven't you come for so long?

IVANOV. My wife has already been insulted enough, she's near dying and you come here. Shura, Shura, that's thoughtless and unfeeling of you!

SASHA. What could I do? You haven't been to see us in two weeks; you didn't answer my letters. It was unbearable. I imagined you suffering unbearably, ill, or dead; I haven't been able to sleep at night. . . . I'll go in a minute. . . . At least tell me, are you all right?

IVANOV. No, I'm exhausted, everybody's torturing me . . . endlessly . . . my strength is gone! And now you! It's unhealthy! It's abnormal! Shura, it's all my fault, my fault!

SASHA. How you enjoy saying terrifying and pathetic things! Your fault? Yes? Is it your fault? Well, tell me why it is. Why?

IVANOV. I don't know. I don't know. . . .

SASHA. That's not an answer. Every sinner must know what his sin is. Have you been forging checks, or something?

IVANOV. That's not amusing!

SASHA. Is it your fault you don't love your wife any more? It may be that a man is not the master of his own feelings; you didn't want to stop loving her. Is it your fault she saw me telling you I loved you? No. You didn't want her to see . . .

IVANOV (interrupting). And so on and so forth. . . . Fell

in love, out of love, not a master of his own feelings—all this is so banal, trite phrases that don't help anything . . .

SASHA. It's tiring talking to you. (*Looks at paintings on wall.*) How beautifully that dog is painted! Was it painted from life?

IVANOV. Yes, from life. And this love affair of ours—commonplace, trite: "He lost his nerve and his ground. She appeared, of good cheer, strong, and held out a helping hand." It's lovely, but it resembles the truth only as it is in novels; in real life. . . .

SASHA. In real life it's the same.

IVANOV. I see you understand the little subtleties of life! My torment inspires you with reverence and awe; you imagine that you've found a second Hamlet in me; but, in my opinion, this nervous nature of mine and all of its symptoms would make good material for humor and nothing else! They could laugh till their sides split at all my clowning, but you . . . my guardian angel! You want to save me, to accomplish a heroic gesture. Oh, how angry I am with myself today. I have a feeling that I'm reaching some sort of climax with it all. . . . Either I'll break something or I'll . . .

SASHA. That's it! That's exactly what you need. Break something, smash something or start shouting. You're angry with me. I did something foolish by deciding to come here. Well then, be angry, shout at me, stamp your feet. Well? Start being angry . . . (*Pause.*) Well?

IVANOV. You're so funny!

SASHA. Good. Now we've smiled! Now be good and deign to smile just once more!

IVANOV (*laughing*). I've noticed that when you begin to save me and drive some sense into me, your face gets all naïve and the pupils of your eyes get much bigger, as if you were looking up at a comet. Wait, your shoulder's got a little dust on it. . . . (*Whisking dust off her shoulder.*) A naïve man—is a fool. You women manage to be naïve in such a becoming way; it's nice and wholesome and warm and not quite as silly as it seems. You know something else about your ways? As long as a man is healthy, strong and cheerful, you don't pay any attention to him, but as soon as he starts slipping and playing Lazarus, you hang round his neck. Is it really worse to be the wife of a strong and brave man than to be a sick-nurse to some tearful failure?

SASHA. It's worse!

IVANOV. Why should that be? (*Laughs loudly.*) It's a good thing Darwin didn't hear you say that or he'd tell you a thing or two! You're spoiling the human race. Thanks to you the world will soon be giving birth to nothing but whiners and neurotics.

SASHA. Men don't understand a lot of things. Every girl prefers a failure to a lucky man because she's tempted to live love actively. Do you understand? Actively. Men are busy with their work and love is only secondary to them. Talking with their wives, strolling with them in the garden, passing time pleasantly with them, weeping by their graves a little— and that's that. But for us, love—is life. I love you and that means I dream of ways of curing you of your melancholy and following you to the ends of the earth. . . . If you climbed a mountain, then I'd climb a mountain; if you fell into a ravine, so would I. For instance, it would be a great happiness for me to spend an entire night copying out your notes or keeping watch over you and seeing that no one wakes you up. Or walking with you for hundreds of miles. I remember, once, three years ago, you came to our house at threshing time, all covered with dust, all tanned with the sun, exhausted; and you asked for something to drink. I brought you the glass and you were already lying on the couch sleeping like a log. You slept there for half a day and I stood outside the door all the time and guarded it so that nobody should come in. And I was so glad! The greater the effort, the better the love; I mean, you understand, the stronger it is felt.

IVANOV. Active love. . . . Hm. . . . Infatuation . . . girlish ideas, or perhaps that's the way it ought to be. . . . (*Shrugs his shoulders.*) Who the hell knows! (*Gaily.*) Shura, honestly, I'm a decent person! . . . You can judge: I always loved to philosophize, but never in my life did I say "Our women are depraved" or "That woman's come to a pretty pass!" I was only thankful and nothing else! Nothing more! My little girl, so good, how priceless! and I, what a ridiculous blockhead I am! I upset good people; every day I play Lazarus. (*Laughs.*) Boo-hoo! Boo-hoo! (*Quickly pulls away.*) Now go, Sasha! We've been forgetting ourselves. . . .

SASHA. Yes, it's time I did. Good-by. I'm afraid your honest doctor may inform Anna Petrovna that I'm here. Listen to me: go to your wife and sit with her, sit, sit, sit . . . if necessary, sit . . . sit for a year. If ten years, then sit for ten. Do your duty. Show your grief and ask her forgiveness and cry—all as it should be. And the main thing is—don't forget your work.

IVANOV. I have that feeling again, as if I'd eaten some toadstools. Again!

SASHA. Well, God keep you! Don't think about me at all! Scribble me a note in about two weeks. And I'll write to you. . . .

(BORKIN *looks through the door.*)

BORKIN. Nikolai Alexeyevich, may I? (Seeing SASHA.) I'm sorry, I didn't see you. . . . (*Comes in.*) Bonjour! (*Bows.*)

SASHA (*embarrassed*). How do you do. . . .

BORKIN. You're plumper and prettier.

SASHA (*to* IVANOV). I'll be going now, Nikolai Alexeyevich. I'm going. (*She goes.*)

BORKIN. Marvelous vision! I came for prosaic reasons and I stumbled on poetry. . . . (*Sings.*) "You appeared, as the birdie to the light . . ."

(IVANOV, *agitated, paces back and forth onstage.*)

(*Sits down.*) She has something, Nicolas, something the

others don't have. Isn't that the truth? Something special, something phantasmagoric. . . . (*Sighs.*) As a matter of fact, she's the richest catch in the district, but her mother's such a horse-radish that nobody wants to get hooked with her. After her death, it will all be left to Shurochka, but until then, she'll only be given ten thousand, a few old dishes, a flatiron, and her mother will want Sasha to jump up and down with gratitude for that. (*Rummages through his pockets.*) Have a smoke—*de los mejoros.* Don't you want one? (*Extends his cigar case.*) They're good . . . very smokable.

IVANOV (*walks up to* BORKIN, *suffocating with anger*). Get out this minute and never set foot in this house again! This very minute! (BORKIN *half-rises and lets his cigar fall.*) Get out this minute!

BORKIN. Nicolas, what does this mean? Why are you angry?

IVANOV. Why? And where did you get those cigars? You think I don't know where and for what you take the old man every day?

BORKIN (*shrugs shoulders*). What do you mention that for?

IVANOV. Scoundrel that you are! Your crooked ventures have spread through the whole district, and have given me a reputation for dishonesty with everyone! We have nothing in common. I ask you to leave this house this very minute! (*Paces back and forth quickly.*)

BORKIN. I know you're saying all that because you're irritated about something, and for that reason I'm not angry with you. Insult me as much as you like. . . . (*Picks up cigar.*) It's time you stopped all this melancholia. You're not a schoolboy any more. . . .

IVANOV. What did I tell you? (*Trembling.*) Are you playing with me?

(*Enter* ANNA PETROVNA.)

BORKIN. Well, Anna Petrovna's here . . . I'm going. (*Goes out.*)

(IVANOV *stands beside his desk with his head downcast.*)

ANNA PETROVNA (*after a pause*). Why did she come here just now? (*Pause.*) I asked you: why did she come here just now?

IVANOV. Don't ask, Aniuta. . . . (*Pause.*) I'm very much to blame. . . . Think up whatever punishment you wish. I'll bear it all, but don't ask. . . . I have no strength left.

ANNA PETROVNA (*angrily*). Why was she here? (*Pause.*) Oh, so that's what you are! Now I understand you. Finally I see what kind of man you are. Dishonorable, low. . . . Do you remember how you came and lied to me that you loved me? . . . I believed you and I left my father, mother, religion, and followed you. . . . You lied to me about truth and goodness, about all your noble aspirations. But I believed every word. . . .

IVANOV. Aniuta, I never lied to you.

ANNA PETROVNA. I've lived with you for five years. I've suffered, gotten sick, but I loved you and never left you for a minute. . . . You were my idol. . . . And what came of it? All this time you were deceiving me in an outrageous way. . . .

IVANOV. Aniuta, don't say untruths. I made mistakes, yes, but I never lied once in my life. You wouldn't dare to reproach me with that. . . .

ANNA PETROVNA. Now everything's clear. . . . You married me and thought my father and mother would pardon me, give me money. . . . You thought that . . .

IVANOV. Oh, my God! Aniuta, don't try my patience so. . . . (*Weeps.*)

ANNA PETROVNA. Be quiet! When you saw there was no money, you tried a new game. . . . Now I remember everything and I understand. (*Weeps.*) You never loved me and you never were true to me . . . never! . . .

IVANOV. Sarah, that's a lie! Say what you like, but don't insult me with a lie. . . .

ANNA PETROVNA. Dishonorable, mean man. . . . You owe money to Lyebedev and now, to keep from paying your debt, you want to turn his daughter's head, to deceive her as you did me. Isn't it true?

IVANOV (*suffocating*). Quiet, for God's sake! I can't answer for myself. . . . I'm choking with rage, and I . . . I might insult you. . . .

ANNA PETROVNA. You've always deceived me outrageously, and not me alone. . . . All your dishonorable acts: you've shifted the blame for them on Borkin, but now I know . . . who it was. . . .

IVANOV. Sarah, quiet, go away, or I'll say something, it's on the tip of my tongue! I can hardly keep from saying something terrible and insulting! (*Shouts.*) Be quiet, you Jewess!

ANNA PETROVNA. I won't keep quiet. . . . You deceived me too long for me to keep quiet. . . .

IVANOV. You won't keep quiet? (*Struggles with himself.*) For God's sake . . .

ANNA PETROVNA. Now go and deceive the Lyebedev girl. . . .

IVANOV. Then you should know that . . . you're going to die soon. . . . The doctor told me that you would die soon. . . .

ANNA PETROVNA (*sits down. In a disappointed, failing voice*). When did he say that? (*Pause.*)

IVANOV (*clutching his head*). What have I done! God, what have I done! (*He sobs.*)

CURTAIN

Between the third and fourth acts, a period of a year passes.

Act IV

One of the drawing rooms in the LYEBEDEV *house. In the
center stage there is an arch separating the drawing room
from the ballroom. Doors at right and left. Antique bronze,
family portraits. Festive decorations. An upright piano with a
violin on top and a cello standing beside it. Throughout
the act, visitors dressed in evening clothes pass through the
ballroom.*

LVOV (*enters, looks at his watch*). It's almost five. It will
soon be time for the ceremony . . . the blessing and then the
wedding after that. The triumph of virtue and justice. He
didn't succeed in robbing Sarah so he sent her packing to
her grave; now he's found another! He'll play the hypocrite
for this one, too, until he's robbed her; and once he has, she'll
be going to the same place where poor Sarah lies. It's the
old money, money story. . . . (*Pause.*) He's so happy, he's
in seventh heaven. He'll live to a nice ripe old age and die
with a clear conscience. No, I'll show you up for what you
are! When I tear away that damned mask of yours and
everybody knows what kind of bird you really are, you'll fly
from your seventh heaven down into a pit from which even
devils won't be able to resurrect you! I'm an honest man; it's
my business to stand forth and open their blind eyes to the
truth. I'll fulfill my duty and tomorrow I'll get out of this
damned district! (*Ponders.*) What should I do? Explain it
to Lyebedev—a waste of breath. Challenge him to a duel?
Start trouble? My God, I'm as unnerved as a child. I've lost
the ability to think things out. What should I do? Duel him?

KOSICH (*comes in; joyfully, to* LVOV). Yesterday I bid a
small slam in clubs, but ended up with a grand slam. Only
that Barbanov spoiled the whole business for me again. We
start playing. I bid notrump. He passes. Two clubs; he passes.
I say two diamonds . . . three clubs . . . and imagine:

76

you can imagine—I bid slam, but he doesn't show his ace. If the idiot had shown his ace, then I would have had a grand slam in notrump. . . .

Lvov. Excuse me, I don't play cards and so I cannot share your joy. When will the blessing take place?

Kosich. It must be soon. Zhuzhushka is being revived. She's raving mad to lose that dowry.

Lvov. And not her daughter?

Kosich. The dowry. She's vexed. He's marrying her and that means he's not going to pay his debt. You can't try to collect on your own son-in-law's promissory note.

Babakina (decked out, with an air of importance, walks across the stage past Lvov and Kosich; the latter bursts out laughing; she turns around). Stupid fool! (Kosich touches her waist with his hands and laughs loudly.) Muzhik! (She goes out.)

Kosich (laughs loudly). That woman's off her nut! Until she became a nuisance trying to shine all over the place—she was a woman, just like any other. Now you can't get near her. (Mimics her.) Muzhik!

Lvov (agitated). Listen, tell me sincerely: what is your opinion of Ivanov?

Kosich. He's no good. He plays cards like a butcher. Last year, at Easter, it was like that. We sat down to play: I, the Count, Borkin, and he. I dealt . . .

Lvov (interrupting). Is he a good man?

Kosich. You mean him? He's a clever man. He can go through fire and water. He and the Count—birds of a feather. They smell the money where it is. He ran up against the Jewess and ate humble pie. Now he's making for Zhuzhushka's money bags. I'll bet you, curse him, that he'll turn Zhuzhushka right out into the street. Zhuzhushka and him, Babakina and the Count. They'll get their hands on the money and then go on living happily ever after. Doctor, why are you so pale today? Your face is a total blank.

Lvov. Nothing, nothing at all. I drank too much last night.

Lyebedev (*enters with* Sasha). We'll talk here. (*To* Lvov *and* Kosich.) Step into the ballroom with the ladies, my boys. We need to have a private little talk.

Kosich (*going past* Sasha, *enthusiastically snapping his fingers*). A picture! The queen of trumps!

Lyebedev. Go away, cavemen, go away! (Lvov *and* Kosich *go out.*) Sit down, Shurochka . . . right there. . . . (*Sits down and looks around.*) Listen attentively and with the proper respect. Here's the story: your mother ordered me to tell you the following . . . do you understand? I'm not telling you this from me, but on your mother's orders.

Sasha. Papa, quickly!

Lyebedev. Your dowry consists of fifteen thousand rubles in silver. . . . There. . . . Look, so later there won't be any argument! Wait, stay quiet! That's only the flower, the fruit will come later. Your dowry consists of fifteen thousand, but, I call your attention to a discount; Nikolai Alexeyevich owes your mother nine thousand; subtract that from your dowry. . . . Well, and besides that . . .

Sasha. Why are you telling me all this?

Lyebedev. Your mother ordered me to!

Sasha. Leave me alone! If you had the least respect for me and for yourself, you wouldn't allow yourself to talk to me this way. I don't need your dowry! I didn't ask for it, and I'm not asking for it now!

Lyebedev. Why are you casting aspersions on me? In Gogol's play the two rats started to sniff and then ran away; but you, you emancipated creature, you cast aspersions on me without even sniffing. . . .

SASHA. Leave me alone; don't insult my ears with your cheap calculations.

LYEBEDEV (*flaring*). Phew! You'll end up by making me stick a knife into myself or cut somebody's throat! That one's day to day howling, nagging and pestering, counting every kopeck, and this one's clever, humane, and so damned emancipated she can't understand her own father! I insult her ears! You can't understand that before I came here to insult your ears, I was . . . (*Points to the door.*) being cut into pieces, drawn and quartered. She can't understand! My head is swimming, I'm losing my mind. . . . That's what you've done! (*Goes to the door and stops.*) I don't like it; I don't like anything about it!

SASHA. What don't you like about it?

LYEBEDEV. I don't like anything about it! Anything at all!

SASHA. What do you mean, anything?

LYEBEDEV. Do you want me to sit down with you and tell you? I don't like it and I don't want to see your wedding! (*Comes to* SASHA *tenderly.*) Please forgive me, Shurochka, it may be that your wedding is intelligent, honest, noble, and full of high principles, but something about it isn't right, not right! It's not like other marriages. You—young, fresh, clean as a pane of glass, lovely—and he—a widower, worn out, used. I don't understand him, either, God keep him. (*Kisses his daughter.*) Shurochka, forgive me, there's something not clean about this. Too many people are talking. His wife Sarah died at his house, and then he wants to marry you all of a sudden. . . . (*With animation.*) Oh, I'm just an old woman, an old woman. I've become an old woman, like an old crinoline. Don't listen to me. Only listen to yourself.

SASHA. Papa, I myself feel there's something wrong . . . not right, not right, not right. If you only knew how it hurts me! It's unbearable! I feel uncomfortable and awful about admitting it. Papa, darling, for God's sake, cheer me up . . . tell me what to do.

LYEBEDEV. What? What are you saying?

SASHA. I feel worse than I've ever felt! (*Looks around.*) It seems to me I don't understand him and never will understand him. All the time I've been engaged to him, he's never once smiled, not once has he looked me straight in the eyes. All the time he's complaining, repenting for something, hinting about some guilt, trembling. . . . I'm tired of it. There were moments when it seemed to me that I . . . I didn't love him as much as I should. And when he comes to see us or talks to me, I start feeling bored. What does it all mean, Papa? It's terrible!

LYEBEDEV. My darling, my only child, listen to your old father! Give him up!

SASHA (*alarmed*). You, too! You, too! Don't!

LYEBEDEV. Really, Shurochka. There'll be a scandal. All the neighbors' tongues will wag like churchbells, but you'll see that it's better to live through a scandal than ruin yourself for a whole lifetime.

SASHA. Don't say that, don't say it, Papa! I don't want to listen. You have to struggle against these gloomy thoughts. He's a good, unhappy, misunderstood man. I will love him, understand him, put him back on his feet. I'll fulfill my task. That's decided!

LYEBEDEV. That's not a task, it's just neurotic.

SASHA. That's enough. I've confessed to you what I didn't even want to confess to myself. Don't tell anybody. Let's forget it.

LYEBEDEV. I don't understand anything. Either I've grown dull with age, or you've gotten too clever for me. I'll be a monkey's uncle before I understand any of it!

SHABYELSKI (*entering*). To hell with everybody, myself included! It's revolting!

LYEBEDEV. What's the matter with you?

SHABYELSKI. I'm serious. I'm going to have to go through with something so vile and mean that not only I but everybody will be against me. I'll go through with it. I give you my word! I've already told Borkin to announce my engagement today. (*Laughs.*) Everybody's mean, so I'll be mean, too.

LYEBEDEV. I've had enough of you! Listen, Matvyey, if you go on talking like that, then, pardon the expression, they'll take you off to the madhouse.

SHABYELSKI. Is the madhouse any worse than a brothel or any other kind of house? Do me a favor and take me there now. Be so kind. Everybody is so mean, petty, worthless, dull, and I disgust myself so. I don't believe a word I've said. . . .

LYEBEDEV. You know what, my friend? Put a candle in your mouth, light it, and breathe fire on people. Or better still: take your hat and go home. There's a wedding on here, everybody's enjoying himself, and you're going around croaking, like an old crow. Yes, really . . . (SHABYELSKI *leans on the upright piano and sobs.*) Good heavens, Matvyey! Count! . . . What's wrong? Matiusha, my own dear friend . . . my angel. . . . Did I hurt you? Excuse me, I'm an old dog. . . . Forgive a drunkard. . . . Have a drink of water. . . .

SHABYELSKI. I don't want it. (*Raises head.*)

LYEBEDEV. Why are you crying?

SHABYELSKI. No reason at all. . . .

LYEBEDEV. No, Matiusha, don't lie. . . . Why? What's the cause?

SHABYELSKI. I took a look just now at this cello . . . and I remembered the little Jewess. . . .

LYEBEDEV. Ai, what a time to remember! May she rest in peace, eternal peace, but this isn't the time to be thinking of her. . . .

SHABYELSKI. We used to play duets together. . . . A wonderful, excellent woman!

(SASHA *sobs*.)

LYEBEDEV. You too? Stop it! Lord, now they're both howling . . . and I . . . I . . . why don't you go where the guests can't see you!

SHABYELSKI. Pasha, when the sun shines you can feel cheerful in a cemetery. And when there's hope, even old age is good. But I have no hopes, not even one.

LYEBEDEV. Yes, really, it's true, you're badly off. . . . You have no children, no money, nothing to keep you occupied. . . . Well, what can you do! (*To* SASHA.) And what's the matter with you?

SHABYELSKI. Pasha, gave me some money. We'll settle it in the next world. I'll go to Paris and have a look at my wife's grave. In my life I've given away a great deal. I've given away half my fortune, that's why I have a right to ask. And why I'm asking it of a friend . . .

LYEBEDEV (*embarrassed*). My darling, I have no money! But, all right, all right! Anyway I don't promise; and you understand that . . . Of course, I will! Of course! (*Aside*.) They're tormenting me!

BABAKINA (*enters*). Where's my cavalier? Count, how do you dare leave me alone? You naughty boy! (*Beats the* COUNT *on the hand with her fan*.)

SHABYELSKI (*disgusted*). Leave me alone! I hate you!

BABAKINA (*struck dumb*). What? Hm?

SHABYELSKI. Get away from me!

BABAKINA (*falls into armchair*). Ai! (*Weeps*.)

ZINAIDA SAVISHNA (*comes in, weeping*). Somebody's just arrived . . . I think it's the best man. It's time for the ceremony. . . . (*Sobs*.)

SASHA (*imploring*). Mama!

LYEBEDEV. There, now they're all howling! It's a quartet! As if there wasn't enough wet weather lately! Matvyey! . . . Marfa Yegorovna! . . . If you keep this up, I'll . . . start crying, too! (*Weeps.*) Oh, my God!

ZINAIDA SAVISHNA. If you don't want to listen to your mother, if you have no obedience in you . . . then do what you please. I give you my blessing. . . .

(*Enter* IVANOV, *wearing a frock coat and gloves.*)

LYEBEDEV. That's all we needed! What now?

SASHA. What are you here for?

IVANOV. Excuse me, ladies and gentlemen. Please let me have a word with Sasha alone.

LYEBEDEV. It's not right to see your bride before the wedding! It's time you were in church!

IVANOV. Pasha, please. . . .

(LYEBEDEV *shrugs his shoulders; he,* ZINAIDA SAVISHNA, *the* COUNT, *and* BABAKINA *exit.*)

SASHA (*severely*). What do you want?

IVANOV. I'm filled with anger but I can speak with composure. Listen to me. Just now, as I was dressing for the wedding, I looked at myself in the mirror and I saw gray hair on my temples. Shura, let's not! Before it's too late, we must stop this senseless comedy. . . . You're young, pure, you have your life ahead of you, and I . . .

SASHA. All this is not new; I've heard it a thousand times already, and I'm sick of it! Go to the church and don't keep people waiting.

IVANOV. I'll be going home in a minute. You tell your people the wedding is off. Tell them anything you want. It's time we came to our senses. I've played Hamlet, and you the exalted young lady—but we can't continue like this.

SASHA (*blushing*). What kind of tone is that? I won't listen.

IVANOV. I'm talking and I'll go on talking.

SASHA. What have you come for? Your whining is becoming a mockery.

IVANOV. No, I'm not whining any more! A mockery? Yes, but I'm doing the mocking! And if I could mock myself a thousand times more strongly and make the whole world laugh at me—I'd do that, too! I took a look at myself in the mirror—and inside my consciousness it was like a cannonball bursting! I laughed at myself and I almost went out of my mind with shame. (*Laughs.*) Melancholy! Noble yearning! Uncontrollable grief! Only one thing is missing: I should write poetry. Whining, playing Lazarus, making everybody miserable, being conscious that my life energy is sapped forever, become rusted, outlived my time, given way to weakness of character and stuck up to my ears in this disgusting melancholia. When the sun shines brightly, you become aware that even the ants drag their burdens and are satisfied with themselves doing it—no, thank you! You know, when somebody thinks of you as a charlatan and a second person feels sorry for you, and a third lends a helping hand, and a fourth—which is worst of all—listens to your complaints with awe and looks on you as if you were the second Mohammed, waiting for you to reveal a new religion . . . no, thank God, I still have some pride and conscience! As I was coming here, I laughed at myself, and it seemed to me that the birds were laughing at me, the trees were laughing. . . .

SASHA. This isn't anger, it's madness!

IVANOV. You think so? No, I'm not mad. Now I see things in their true light, and my thoughts are as clear as your conscience. We love each other but our wedding will not take place! I can rave and rant as much as I like, but I have no right to ruin other people's lives! I poisoned my wife's last year of life with my whining. Since you've been my fiancée, you've forgotten how to smile and you've gotten

five years older. Your father, for whom everything in life
was clear, has now, thanks to me, stopped understanding people. Whether I'm at a meeting, on a visit, or off hunting,
wherever I go, I bring boredom, dejection, discontent. Stop,
don't interrupt me! I'm being sharp and fierce, but forgive
me, I'm choked by spite, and I cannot speak in any other
way. I never lied. I didn't slander life, but I've become a
grumbler, and, against my will, without noticing, I curse it,
I grumble against fate, I complain and all those who listen
to me are contaminated by an aversion to life; and they
begin to curse it, too. What a tone to take! As if I were
doing nature a favor by living. Devil take me!

SASHA. Wait. . . . From what you've just been saying, it
follows that you're tired of your whining, and it's time to
begin a new life! That's excellent!

IVANOV. I see nothing excellent about it. And what new
life is there? I'm ruined—irrevocably! It's time we both understood that! A new life!

SASHA. Nikolai, come to your senses! How do you know
you're ruined? What kind of cynicism is that? No, I don't
want to talk or listen. . . . Go to the church!

IVANOV. I'm ruined!

SASHA. Don't shout so, the guests will hear!

IVANOV. If a sensible, well-educated, and healthy man
without any apparent cause starts playing Lazarus and slipping downhill, without stopping, there's no saving him!
Well, where is my salvation? Where? I can't drink—wine
gives me a headache; write bad verses—that I can't do;
pray for my idle soul and see something exceedingly noble
in the prayers—I can't. Idleness is idleness, weakness is
weakness—I have no other names for them. I'm ruined—
ruined—there's no use talking about it! (*Looking around.*)
They might disturb us. Listen, if you love me, then help me.
Give me up right away, this minute! The sooner the better. . . .

SASHA. Oh, Nikolai, if you only knew how you tire me out!
You've worn me down! You're a good, intelligent man, you

can judge: is it right to set me such problems? There isn't a day without problems, each more difficult than the next. . . . I wanted to love actively . . . but this is not love, it's martyrdom!

IVANOV. And when you're my wife, the problems will be even more complicated. So give me up! Please understand: it's not love you feel, it's the obstinacy of your honest nature. You've set yourself a goal to resurrect the man in me; to save me, you flattered yourself that you were accomplishing a great feat . . . now you're ready to retreat, and you're prevented from doing so by a false emotion! Please understand!

SASHA. What strange, primitive logic you have! How can I give you up? How can I do it? You haven't a mother, a sister, or a friend. . . . You're ruined, your estate has been whittled away, everyone in your circle says terrible things about you . . .

IVANOV. It was stupid of me to come here. I should have done as I wanted to. . . .

(*Enter* LYEBEDEV.)

SASHA (*runs to meet her father*). Papa, for God's sake, he ran in here like a madman and he's torturing me! He demands that I give him up, that he doesn't want to ruin me. Tell him I don't want his magnanimity! I know what I'm doing.

LYEBEDEV. I don't understand anything. . . . What magnanimity?

IVANOV. There'll be no wedding!

SASHA. There will be! Papa, tell him that there will be a wedding!

LYEBEDEV. Wait, wait! . . . Why don't you want there to be a wedding?

IVANOV. I explained why but she doesn't want to understand.

LYEBEDEV. No, not to her, explain it to me. Explain it so I can understand! Oh! Nikolai Alexeyevich! God be your judge! You've brought so much confusion into our lives that for me it's like living in an art museum. I look and I don't understand anything I see . . . it's simply a punishment. . . . Well, what do you want an old man to do about it for you? Shall I challenge you to a duel, or something?

IVANOV. There's no need for a duel. All you need is to have a head on your shoulders and understand plain language.

SASHA (*paces stage with agitation*). This is dreadful! Dreadful! Just like a child!

LYEBEDEV. Wash your hands of the whole thing, that's all. Listen, Nikolai! According to you, this is very intelligent, subtle and conforms to all the rules of psychology, but in my opinion, it's a scandal and dishonest! Listen to me, an old man, for the last time! This is what I have to say to you: calm your mind! Look at things simply, like everybody else! In this world everything is simple. The ceiling is white, boots are black, sugar is sweet. You love Sasha, she loves you. If you love her, stay with her. If you don't, go—there will be no repercussions. That's how simple it is! You're both healthy, intelligent, moral, well-fed, thank God, and well-clothed. . . . What more do you need? You have no money! Of what great importance is that! Happiness doesn't come from money. . . . Naturally, I understand. . . . Your estate has been mortgaged, there's no money to pay off the interest. I, as a father, can understand. . . . Mother can do as she likes, God keep her; if she won't give you money, she doesn't have to. Shura says she doesn't need a dowry. Principles, Schopenhauer. . . . All that's nonsense. . . . I have ten thousand hidden in the bank. (*Looks around.*) Not a soul knows about it in the house. . . . It's Grandma's . . . it's for you both. . . . Take it, only on the condition that you do some good with the money: give Matvyey two thousand. . . .

(*Guests gather in the bedroom.*)

IVANOV. Pasha, this is worthless talk. I'm acting according to my conscience.

SASHA. And I'm acting according to my own. You can say what you please, I won't give you up. I'll go call Mama. (*She goes out.*)

LYEBEDEV. I don't understand anything. . . .

IVANOV. Listen, poor fellow. . . . I'll explain it to you. I'm . . . honest or dishonest, healthy or neurotic, I won't try. You wouldn't understand. I used to be young, passionate, sincere, sensible; I used to love, to hate and have my beliefs like everybody else, I worked like ten men and I had the same big hopes; I battled windmills, rammed down walls with my head; not knowing my strength, not reasoning, not knowing about life, I took up a burden which broke my back, pulled my tendons; I rushed to spend myself in my one and only youth; I got drunk, I became excited, I overworked; I didn't know the meaning of moderation. And tell me: could I have done otherwise? There are so few of us and so much work to be done, so much! God, how much! And how cruelly life has avenged itself on me, the life I fought against! I've strained myself! At thirty-five I have a hangover, I'm old, I've put on my dressing gown. With a heavy head, a lazy soul, I've gotten tired and strained, broken, without faith, without love, without aim; I loiter among the young people like a shadow and I don't know who I am, why I'm living, what I want. Already it seems to me that love is nonsense, caresses are saccharine, work is meaningless, songs and passionate speeches are old and dated. And wherever I go, I bring with me misery, a cold boredom, discontent, aversion to life. . . . I'm ruined, irrevocably! Before you stands a man, at thirty-five years of age, already tired, disenchanted, overwhelmed with his own insignificance; he's bursting with shame, taunting his own weakness . . . oh, my pride is outraged, I'm suffocated with fury! (*Reeling.*) You see how tired I am! I'm reeling . . . I'm weak. Where is Matvyey? Let him take me home.

(*Voices in the ballroom: "The best man's arrived!"*)

SHABYELSKI (*entering*). In somebody else's frock coat . . . without gloves . . . and for that they give me mocking glances, they make stupid jokes, they scoff at me . . . disgusting, small-minded people!

BORKIN (*entering quickly, with a bouquet; wears a frock coat, a best man's flower in his buttonhole*). Phew! Where is he? (*To* IVANOV.) They've been waiting for you in the church, and you're here talking philosophy. What a funny boy! By God, a funny one! Don't you know you're not supposed to be with the bride; you're to go with me, separately. Then I have to come from the church to get the bride. Really, can't you even understand that? It's positively comical!

LVOV (*comes in. To* IVANOV). So you're here? (*Loudly.*) Nikolai Alexeyevich Ivanov, I wish to declare publicly that you are a cad!

IVANOV (*coldly*). Thank you very much.

(*General confusion.*)

BORKIN (*to* LVOV). My dear sir, this is low! I challenge you to a duel!

LVOV. Mr. Borkin, I count it humiliating not only to fight with you, but even to have to talk to you! As for Mr. Ivanov, he may receive satisfaction whenever he wishes.

SHABYELSKI. My dear sir, I'll fight you myself! . . .

SASHA (*to* LVOV). Why did you do this! Why did you insult him? My friends, please, make him tell me why: why did he do it?

LVOV. Alexandra Pavlovna, I insulted with sufficient reason. I came here as an honest man in order to open your eyes and I beg you to listen to me.

SASHA. What can you say? That you're an honest man? The whole world knows that! You'd be much better off telling me honestly whether you understand yourself or not! You came here just now, as an honest man, and hurled a terrible insult at him which almost killed me; and you've pursued him like a shadow and interfered with his life, always confident that you were doing your duty as a honest person. You meddled in his private life, you slandered and judged him; whenever it was possible, you bombarded me and all my friends with anonymous letters—and all the time you thought of yourself as an honest man. You thought it was honest, Doctor, not even to spare his sick wife; you didn't allow her any peace with your suspicions. And whatever violence, whatever cruelty you accomplish, you still think that you're an honest and direct person!

IVANOV (*laughing*). This is not a wedding; it's a debate! Bravo, bravo. . . .

SASHA (*to* LVOV). Just think it over: do you understand yourself or not? You stupid man! (*Takes* IVANOV's *hand*.) Let's get out of here, Nikolai! Father, let's go!

IVANOV. Where shall we go? Wait, I'll put an end to all of this! My youth is awakening in me. The old Ivanov lives again! (*Takes out a revolver.*)

SASHA (*shrieks*). I know what he wants to do! Nikolai, for God's sake!

IVANOV. I've been going downhill long enough! Now I'll stop! One should not abuse hospitality! Stand aside! Thank you, Sasha!

SASHA (*shouts*). Nikolai, for God's sake! Stop him!

IVANOV. Leave me alone! (*Runs out and shoots himself.*)

CURTAIN

THE WOOD DEMON

A Comedy in Four Acts

CHARACTERS

ALEXANDER SEREBRYAKOV (SASHA), *a retired professor*

ELENA, *his young wife*

SOFIA, *his daughter by a first marriage, age twenty*

MARYA VOINITSKY, *mother of his first wife, widow of a privy councillor*

GEORGE VOINITSKY, *her son*

LEONID (LENYA) ZHELTOUKHIN, *a wealthy young man*

JULIA, *his sister, age eighteen*

IVAN ORLOVSKI, *a landowner*

FYODOR, *his son*

MICHAEL KRUSHCHOV, *the "Wood Demon," a landowner who is also a doctor*

ILYA DYADIN ("WAFFLES")

VASSILI, *Zheltoukhin's servant*

SEMYON, *a laborer at Dyadin's water mill*

Act I

The garden of ZHELTOUKHIN's *property. A house with a terrace. On the lawn, in front of the house, two tables: one big one, set for lunch, and another smaller one on which some hors d'oeuvres have been placed. Three o'clock in the afternoon.*

(ZHELTOUKHIN *and* JULIA *come out of the house.*)

JULIA. You would have done better to wear your gray suit. This one doesn't become you at all.

ZHELTOUKHIN. What does it matter? How stupid!

JULIA. Lenya, why are you so gloomy? What a face—on your birthday! You're really not very nice. (*She leans her head on* ZHELTOUKHIN's *chest.*)

ZHELTOUKHIN. Not so much love, please!

JULIA (*tears in her eyes*). Lenya!

ZHELTOUKHIN. Instead of showering me with sour kisses and lovesick looks . . . and embroidered gadgets, which are all of no use to me at all, you would do better to tell me what I want to know. Why haven't you written to the professor? Tell me.

JULIA. I *did* write, Lenya.

ZHELTOUKHIN. To whom?

JULIA. To Sofia. I insisted that she come today, *insisted* that she come at one o'clock. My word of honor, I wrote to her! I *did*.

93

ZHELTOUKHIN. And meanwhile it's almost three o'clock, and they're not here! Well, let them do as they please. We don't need them all that much! It is better to let go, nothing good can come of it. Humiliation, hypocritical feelings, nothing more. . . . She doesn't even know I exist. I'm not handsome, I'm not interesting, there's no romance in me; if she marries me, she'll do it for only one reason . . . my money.

JULIA. *Not* handsome . . . you can't see yourself!

ZHELTOUKHIN. Come come, I'm not blind! My beard is lopsided, not like everybody else's, my mustache is . . . oh, hell . . . my nose . . .

JULIA. Why are you so cruel to yourself?

ZHELTOUKHIN. I've been having that pain again, right here, under my eye.

JULIA. Yes, it's swollen just a little. (*Pause.*) Come, let me kiss it and it will be all better!

ZHELTOUKHIN. Oh, how stupid!

(ORLOVSKI *and* GEORGE VOINITSKY *enter.*)

ORLOVSKI. When are we going to have lunch, my dear? It's almost three o'clock!

JULIA. But, Godfather dear, the Serebryakovs haven't arrived yet.

ORLOVSKI. And until when must we wait for them? I'm hungry, little girl, and so is George!

ZHELTOUKHIN (*to* GEORGE VOINITSKY). Is your family really coming?

VOINITSKY. When I left the house, Elena was dressing.

ZHELTOUKHIN. Does that mean that you're absolutely certain they're coming?

VOINITSKY. One can never say anything absolutely. If our

professor were suddenly to be taken ill with an attack of gout—or a whim of some sort—well then, they'd stay at home.

ZHELTOUKHIN. In that case, we will eat. Why wait any longer? (*He shouts.*) Waffles! Guests!

(*Enter* DYADIN *with several guests.*)

Come come, help yourselves to some food, make yourselves at home! (*At the hors d'oeuvre table.*) The Serebryakovs haven't arrived, Fyodor has not come, the Wood Demon isn't here either, so . . . we have been forgotten! Eat!

JULIA. Godfather dear, will you have some vodka?

ORLOVSKI. A taste. (*Pause.*) Yes, that's fine . . . that's quite enough.

DYADIN (*tying a napkin around his neck*). Your property is remarkably well managed, Julia! Whether I wander through your fields, or stroll in the shade of your garden, or look at this table, everywhere I discover the supreme dexterity of your magic little fingers. (*Pause.*) To your health!

JULIA. We have our share of worries, Waffles. Yesterday, for example, Nazarka forgot to bring the turkeys back into the shed; they spent the night in the garden, and as it was a bit chilly this morning, five of them are now dead.

DYADIN. That's not a very nice thing to do; the turkey is a very delicate bird.

VOINITSKY. Waffles, cut me a slice of ham.

DYADIN. A pleasure. This ham is superb. The magic of a thousand and one nights! (*He cuts the ham.*) I'm carving it for you, George, according to all the rules of the art. Beethoven and Shakespeare themselves would not have done as well. . . . Except that this knife doesn't cut very well! (*He sharpens the knife on another knife.*)

ZHELTOUKHIN (*shuddering*). Vvvvvv! That's enough, Waffles! I can't bear that sound.

ORLOVSKI. Tell us, George, what's happening at home.

VOINITSKY. Nothing is happening.

ORLOVSKI. What's new?

VOINITSKY. Nothing; nothing new. As things were last year, so they are now. As is my wont, I talk too much and I don't get much accomplished. My old parrot of a mother is still babbling on about the emancipation of women. She has one eye on the grave, and with the other she studies learned tomes for traces of the dawn of a new life.

ORLOVSKI. And Sasha?

VOINITSKY. Unfortunately, the professor has not yet been eaten up by the termites. As ever, from morning till late at night, he is seated in his study writing. "Forcing our thoughts, we frown and write poems; and no praise, either for us or for them, comes." Poor paper. I'm sorry for the paper he writes on. And also, as before, Sofia reads intelligent books and keeps up a very intelligent journal.

ORLOVSKI. The darling!

VOINITSKY. Keen observer that I am, I really should write a novel. The subject needs only to be spread out on a piece of paper. A retired professor, dry as dust, a wise old owl . . . gout, rheumatism, migraine, liver, and other pleasantries . . . as jealous as Othello . . . lives against his will on his first wife's property, because he lacks the means to live in the city . . . complains incessantly of his troubles, although he is actually extraordinarily happy.

ORLOVSKI. Well!

VOINITSKY. Yes, that's what I said: extraordinarily happy. Think of it! Let's set aside the fact that as a scholarship winner, son of an ordinary sacristan, he obtained a degree from a university and a professorship; that he is "His Excellency," son-in-law of a senator, et cetera. That's not of much importance. But, note this: this man, for exactly twenty-five years, has been chewing and digesting other people's ideas of realism, the various "movements," and other such nonsense; for twenty-five years he has been reading and writing things that intelligent men have known about for a very long time, and which wouldn't interest imbeciles. In other words for twenty-five years he has been decanting nothing into nothing. And for all this, what success, what fame! But how? Why? For what reason?

ORLOVSKI (*laughing heartily*). You envy him! You envy him!

VOINITSKY. Yes, I envy him! . . . And what success he has with the women! No Don Juan ever enjoyed more complete success. His first wife, my sister, a sweet and marvelous creature, pure as the blue sky, noble, generous, with more admirers than he had pupils, loved him as only the divine angels can love beings as beautiful and pure as themselves. My own mother, his mother-in-law, adores him now; even now he inspires a sacred terror in her. His second wife, beautiful, intelligent—married him when he was already old; she gave him her youth, her beauty, her freedom, her brilliance. Why? Why? She has talent, she's an artist! How she can play the piano!

ORLOVSKI. All in all, it's quite a talented family. Quite an exceptional family.

ZHELTOUKHIN. Yes. Sofia has a splendid voice. An astounding soprano. I have never heard anything like it, not even in Petersburg. But she forces her top notes too much. What a shame! If only she didn't force, if only! Yes, without those top notes, I swear to you, on my honor, that she would be the most extraordinary singer. . . . Do you understand? . . . Excuse me, my friends, I must say a few words to Julia. (*Taking* JULIA *aside.*) Send them a word. Write and say that if they can't come at once . . . that they should at least be here for dinner. (*In a lower tone.*) And don't be stupid. Don't shame me. Write more legibly. "Arrive" is not written with one r! (*Louder, in a nicer tone of voice.*) Please.

JULIA. Very well. (*She goes out.*)

DYADIN. They say that the professor's wife, Elena, whose acquaintance I have not yet had the honor of making, distinguishes herself not only by her moral qualities, but also by her physical attributes.

ORLOVSKI. Yes, she is a charming woman.

ZHELTOUKHIN. Is she faithful to her professor?

VOINITSKY. Alas, yes!

ZHELTOUKHIN. Why alas?

VOINITSKY. Because that fidelity is false through and through. Full of rhetoric and very little logic. To be unfaithful to an old husband whom one cannot bear is immoral: to try and stifle one's youth and all human feelings in oneself, that is not immoral. What abominable logic!

DYADIN (*in a plaintive voice*). George! I don't like you to say such things. Yes, it's true . . . it makes me tremble. . . . Gentlemen, I have no talent, I don't know how to manipulate the flowers of rhetoric, but permit me, without uttering pompous phrases, to express to you in all seriousness . . . Gentlemen, whomsoever deceives his wife or his husband is an unfaithful person, and may just as well betray his country.

VOINITSKY. Shut up!

DYADIN. Permit me, George, Ivan, Lenya, my dear friends, to discourse on the strangeness of my fate. It's a secret to no one—therefore, no need to throw a veil of mystery over it all—that my wife ran away from my home, with her beloved, the very day after our marriage, and all because of my unattractive appearance.

VOINITSKY. She did the right thing!

DYADIN. Permit me, gentlemen! After that incident, I did not fail my duty. Even now I love her, I am faithful to her, I help her as much as I can, and I have willed all my goods to the children she had by her beloved. I have not failed my duty, and I am proud of it. Yes, proud! I have lost my happiness, but I have kept my pride. And she? Her youth has already passed, her beauty, conforming to the laws of nature, has faded; her beloved is dead, God rest his soul! And what does she have left? (*Sitting down.*) I speak seriously, and you laugh.

ORLOVSKI. You are a good man, you have a beautiful soul, but you talk too much, and you wave your arms about too much!

(FYODOR *comes out of the house; he is wearing a coat of the finest quality; high boots; on his chest, medals, decorations, and a massive gold chain, bearing trinkets; on his fingers he wears costly rings.*)

FYODOR. Hello, children!

ORLOVSKI. Fedya, my boy, my son!

FYODOR (*to* ZHELTOUKHIN). Congratulations on your birthday! May you finally become an adult! (*He greets everybody.*) Hello, Waffles! Good appetite!

ZHELTOUKHIN. What have you been up to? It isn't customary to arrive so late!

FYODOR. What heat! A little vodka is in order!

ORLOVSKI. (*proudly*). My darling bearded boy! Magnificent ornament of my old age! Gentlemen, isn't he a fine figure of a man? Look at him: a fine figure of a man, isn't he?

FYODOR. To the health of he who is reborn today! (*He drinks.*) Aren't the Serebryakovs here?

ZHELTOUKHIN. They haven't come.

FYODOR. Oh . . . and where is Julia?

ZHELTOUKHIN. I don't know. It's time to serve the pâté. I'll go and get her. (*He goes out.*)

ORLOVSKI. Our Lenya, our host, is out of sorts today. He's morose.

VOINITSKY. The brute!

ORLOVSKI. When one's nerves are shattered, there's nothing to be done about it.

VOINITSKY. It's his vanity that's shattering his nerves. Tell him to his face that his herring is tasty, and he'll immediately become offended: why isn't *he* being complimented? What a scoundrel! There he comes.

(ZHELTOUKHIN *enters with* JULIA.)

JULIA. Hello, Fyodor! (*She kisses him.*) Eat hearty, my little one! (*To* IVAN.) Look, Godfather dear, what a gift I gave Lenya today! (*She holds out the embroidered watchstand in the shape of a shoe-horn.*)

ORLOVSKI. My darling! A shoe-horn! Imagine!

JULIA. Gold braid all over. It cost eight and a half rubles. Look at the borders: little pearls, little pearls, little little pearls . . . and the inscription: "Leonid Zheltoukhin . . ." and there, embroidered in silk: "To the one I love, I give."

DYADIN. May I have a look at it? It's remarkable!

FYODOR. That's enough! Give it here! Julia, have the champagne served.

JULIA. But, Fyodor, the champagne is for tonight!

FYODOR. Tonight! What! Bring it here immediately, or I'm off! On my honor, I'll go! Where is it? I'll go get it myself.

JULIA. No, Fedya, you'd mess everything up, as you usually do. (*To* VASSILI.) Vassili, here's the key. The champagne is in the shed, you know, next to the raisins, in the basket. Now be careful not to break anything.

FYODOR. Vassili, bring us three bottles!

(VASSILI *goes out.*)

JULIA. You wouldn't make a good master, Fyodor! (*She brings out the pâté.*) Eat, gentlemen. . . . More! Take more. It's not yet dinnertime . . . you'll never amount to anything, Fyodor, you're a lost soul!

FYODOR. There we go, she's about to deliver a sermon!

VOINITSKY. I think someone's coming . . . can you hear . . .

ZHELTOUKHIN. Yes, it's the Serebryakovs . . . at last!

VASSILI (*returning*). Sir, the Serebryakovs have arrived.

JULIA (*shouting*). Sofia! (*She runs out.*)

VOINITSKY (*humming*). Let's go meet them! Let's go! (*He goes out.*)

FYODOR. Now they're all happy!

ZHELTOUKHIN. How little discretion people have! He's living with the professor's wife and he is incapable of hiding it.

FYODOR. Who is?

ZHELTOUKHIN. George, of course. He was singing her praises before you arrived. It was indecent!

FYODOR. How do you know he's living with her?

ZHELTOUKHIN. I'm not blind! Everybody in the district is talking about it. . . .

FYODOR. Lies! For the moment, no one is living with her, but very soon I will be living with her. . . . Me . . . do you understand?

(SEREBRYAKOV; MARYA; GEORGE, *giving his arm to* ELENA; SOFIA *and* JULIA *all enter together.*)

JULIA (*kissing* SOFIA). My dear! My dear!

ORLOVSKI (*going to meet them*). Hello, Sasha! Hello, my dear! Hello, little mother! (*He embraces the* PROFESSOR.) How's our health? God be praised!

SEREBRYAKOV. And you, Godfather? (*Pause.*) I find you hale and hearty. Glad to see you again. Been back long?

ORLOVSKI. Since Friday. (*To* MARIA.) Maria! How does Your Excellency feel? (*He kisses her hand.*)

MARYA. My dear friend . . . (*She places a kiss on his head.*)

SOFIA. Godfather dear!

ORLOVSKI. Sofia, my angel! (*He embraces her.*) My dove, my canary bird!

SOFIA. You look the same, sweet, tender, sentimental . . .

ORLOVSKI. And how she has grown, become more beautiful, a lady! My dear little girl!

SOFIA. How are you, all in all? Still in good health?

ORLOVSKI. In terribly good health.

SOFIA. You're a merry fellow, Godfather dear! (*To* FYODOR.) And I didn't even notice the big woolly bear! (*She embraces him.*) He's suntanned now and all hairy . . . a veritable spider!

JULIA. My dear!

ORLOVSKI (*to* SEREBRYAKOV). How are things, old fellow?

SEREBRYAKOV. Fair to middling. And how are they with you?

ORLOVSKI. How could they be? I'm existing. I have signed over my property to my son, I've married my daughters to responsible men, and now there isn't a man freer than myself. I go about as I wish.

YADIN. (*to* SEREBRYAKOV). Your Excellency has arrived a bit late; even the pâté is slightly warm. . . . Permit me to present myself: Ilya Ilyich Dyadin, and not, as certain people call me more or less jokingly, because of my pockmarked face, Waffles.

SEREBRYAKOV. How do you do!

DYADIN. Madame! Mademoiselle! (*He bows before* ELENA *and* SOFIA.) All these people are my friends, Excellency. Formerly I had an excellent position, but family circumstances, or, to speak as they do in intellectual circles, due to reasons of absolute necessity having nothing to do with the powers that be, resulted in my having to give up my own share to my brother, who, as a result of an unfortunate circumstance, lost seventy thousand rubles—belonging to the public funds. My profession: exploitation of the unchained elements. I see to it that the tempestuous waves turn the wheels of the mill—which I rent from my friend the Wood Demon.

VOINITSKY. Shut up, Waffles!

DYADIN. I always bow respectfully before the enlightenment of science, the ornament of our national horizon. Excuse my boldness, to dream of visiting Your Excellency, and of delighting my soul with a talk about the latest scientific discoveries.

SEREBRYAKOV. You flatter me! I would be only too happy . . .

SOFIA. Come, Godfather dear, tell us! Where have you spent the winter? Where did you disappear to?

ORLOVSKI. I was in Gmunden, I was in Paris, I was in Nice, in London, my dear. Finally, I was in . . .

SOFIA. That's enough, enough, you lucky devil!

ORLOVSKI. Will you come with me next autumn? Will you?

SOFIA. (*singing*). "Don't tempt me without reflecting . . ."

FYODOR. Please don't sing during lunch or your future husband will marry an idiot.

DYADIN. It would be so interesting to have a bird's-eye

view of this gathering at this moment. What a charming bouquet! A mixture of grace, beauty, erudition . . .

YODOR. What admirable speech! You sound like somebody was forcing it out of you.

(*Laughter.*)

ORLOVSKI (*to* SOFIA). And you, sweetheart, you're still not married?

VOINITSKY. For heaven's sake! Whom could she marry? Humboldt is dead, Lassalle as well, and Edison is in America. . . . The other day I found her diary on the table, right there! I opened it and I read: "No, I shall never fall in love. To love is to obey a selfish attraction of oneself to an opposite pole . . . and the devil only knows what else is to be found there! From a "transcendental" point of view, the culminating point of "parthenogenesis." . . . Ugh! (*To* SOFIA.) Where did you study?

SOFIA. Others can ridicule me all they like, Uncle George, but not you!

VOINITSKY. Why are you angry?

SOFIA. If you say one more word, one of us will have to go, you or me!

ORLOVSKI (*laughing heartily*). What a character!

VOINITSKY. Yes, a character that I shall define. . . . (*To* SOFIA.) Come, give me your paw! Give me your paw! (*He kisses her hand.*) Peace and reconciliation! . . . I won't do it again.

KRUSHCHOV (*coming out of the house*). Why wasn't I born an artist? What a picture!

ORLOVSKI (*joyous*). Michael! My dear godchild!

KRUSHCHOV. Greetings to the birthday boy! Good day, Julia! How lovely you look today! My dear Godfather! (*He and* ORLOVSKI *embrace.*) Sofia. . . . (*He greets everybody.*)

ZHELTOUKHIN. Is it really possible to arrive so late? Where were you?

KRUSHCHOV. At a patient's bedside.

JULIA. The pâté's been cold for hours.

KRUSHCHOV. No matter, Julia, we'll eat it cold! (*Pause.*) Where may I sit?

SOFIA. Sit here. (*She makes a place for him beside her.*)

KRUSHCHOV. It's a magnificent day today, and I'm devilishly hungry. But first, I will drink a little vodka. (*He drinks.*) To the birthday boy. . . . And now, a mouthful of pâté. . . . Julia, kiss the pâté and make it good! (*She kisses it.*) *Merci.* How are things, dear Godfather? I haven't seen you in a long time.

ORLOVSKI. Yes, a long time, a very long time. I was abroad.

KRUSHCHOV. I'd heard, I'd heard . . . and how I envied you! And you, Fyodor, how are you?

FYODOR. Not bad. We rely on your prayers as if they were pillars. . . .

KRUSHCHOV. And business?

FYODOR. I can't complain. We're making a go of it. Only, dear brother, I'm very tired. From here to the Caucasus, and from the Caucasus back here, again to the Caucasus, and back and forth indefinitely. . . . Yes, I run about like a madman. I have two properties there.

KRUSHCHOV. I know.

FYODOR. I am busy with colonization; I rid us of the scorpion and tarantula scourge. Business, all in all, could be considered booming, but, as for the "*grande passion,*" well, everything is as it was.

KRUSHCHOV. In love, of course?

FYODOR. On this occasion, my dear Wood Demon, we must drink! (*He drinks.*) Gentlemen, never fall in love with a married woman! Word of honor, it is still better to be wounded in the shoulder and stabbed in the leg, as your humble servant, than to love a married woman! It's not worth the . . .

SOFIA. Is it hopeless?

FYODOR. Hopeless? Listen to her. . . . Nothing in the world is hopeless! Despair, unhappy loves! Oh! ah! All that is childishness! It is sufficient to desire. If I want my gun to go off, it goes off; if I want the woman to love me, she will love me. And of course, if I so much as single a woman out, it will be easier for her to fly off to the moon than to escape me!

SOFIA. You're terrible!

FYODOR. No, she will never escape me! No sooner have I uttered a few words to her than she is already in my power. Yes, all I said was: "Madame, whenever you look at a window, any window at all, you will think of me, I command you." Thus she thinks of me a thousand times a day. Besides, I besiege her with letters daily.

ELENA. To write letters is a risky business. She receives them, but she may very well not read them.

FYODOR. You think so? Hmmm! I have been in the world for thirty-five years, and I have not yet met the woman remarkable enough to have the courage not to unseal a letter addressed to her.

ORLOVSKI (*admiringly*). What a merry fellow my son is! I was like him, exactly like him! Only I never went to war, I contented myself with drinking vodka and squandering money. Ah, that was something!

FYODOR. I love her, Michael; seriously, scandalously. . . . If she were to accept, I would give her everything; I would take her with me to the Caucasus, to the mountains; we would live there like fighting cocks. . . . I would guard her, Elena Andreyevna, like a faithful dog, and she would be for me, as the great master wrote, "queen of the world, my faithful love." Oh, she doesn't know how fortunate she is!

KRUSHCHOV. Who could this happy mortal be?

FYODOR. He who is too curious ages quickly! . . . But that's enough of that. Now, let's sing a different tune. I remember ten years ago; Lenya was still a schoolboy. We were celebrating his birthday just as we are now. We rode home on horseback; Sofia was at my right, Julia at my left, and both were trying to hold on to my beard. Gentlemen, let us drink to the good health of the friends of my youth, Sofia and Julia!

DYADIN (*laughing heartily*). That's wonderful! Wonderful!

FYODOR. One day, after the war, I got drunk with a Turkish pasha from Trebizond. He said to me . . .

DYADIN (*interrupting him*). Gentlemen, let us drink a toast to our harmonious relations. May our friendship prosper! *Vivat!*

FYODOR. Enough! Stop! Stop! A little attention, Sofia, please! Devil take me, I'm going to make a wager. There. I am putting three hundred rubles on the table. After lunch, we will go play croquet, and I wager that I'll get through all the hoops in one single round, back and forth.

SOFIA. I accept the wager, but I don't have three hundred rubles!

FYODOR. Well, if you lose, you will sing for me forty times!

SOFIA. Very well!

DYADIN. It's wonderful!

ELENA (*looking up at the sky*). What bird is that?

ZHELTOUKHIN. A vulture.

FYODOR. Gentlemen, to the health of the vulture!

(SOFIA *bursts out laughing.*)

ORLOVSKI. Well, she's off! (*Pause.*) What's the matter? (KRUSHCHOV *laughs.*) And what's got into you?

MARYA. Sofia, such unseemly behavior!

KRUSHCHOV. Excuse me, ladies and gentlemen. I shall stop it at once! (*Laughing.*) At once!

ORLOVSKI. That's what is known as stupid laughter.

VOINITSKY. All you have to do is point your finger at them if you want them to burst into laughter! (*Points his finger at* SOFIA.) There!

KRUSHCHOV. That's enough! (*He looks to see what time it is. To himself.*) My dear Michael, you have drunk and eaten. Now, farewell! It is time for me to leave.

SOFIA. Where to?

KRUSHCHOV. To pay a visit to a patient. (*Pause.*) Medicine disgusts me as much as bad-tempered women or a long winter.

SEREBRYAKOV. Excuse me. Medicine is, so to speak, your profession and also your livelihood.

VOINITSKY. He has another profession! He spends his time digging up the peat hidden under the ground on his property.

SEREBRYAKOV. What?

VOINITSKY. Peat. An engineer has calculated, as clear as the nose on your face, that the earth contains seven hundred twenty thousand rubles worth of peat. Don't laugh!

KRUSHCHOV. I don't dig up peat for the money.

VOINITSKY. Then why *do* you?

KRUSHCHOV. So that you won't cut down the forests.

VOINITSKY. Why not cut them down? To listen to you, one would think forests exist only as a meeting place for men and young ladies.

KRUSHCHOV. I never said that.

VOINITSKY. All that I have had the honor of hearing you say up until now about the conservation of the forests is old-fashioned, frivolous, and tendentious. Please excuse me. I don't make judgments lightly. I know almost all of your pleading by heart. For instance (*In an animated tone, gesticulating and imitating* KRUSHCHOV.): "You, you who destroy forests, though they embellish the earth, though they lead man to understand beauty and inspire him with elevated thoughts. . . . Forests mitigate the harshness of the climate. In countries which enjoy mild climates, one expends less energy struggling against nature, and that is why the people in these countries are more delicate and loving. The people there are beautiful, supple, sensitive. They speak elegantly, move gracefully. The sciences and the arts flourish among them. Their philosophy is not gloomy, and the feelings that they harbor for their women are full of a beautiful nobility, et cetera, et cetera. . . ." All that is very nice, but so unconvincing that I shall allow myself, my dear friend, to continue to burn wood in my stoves and to construct wooden sheds.

KRUSHCHOV. One can cut down forests when it is necessary, but it is time to put a stop to this annihilation. The Russian forests tremble under the hatchet, thousands of trees perish, the lairs of wild animals and the nests of birds are emptied. The rivers become sandy and dry up: and all that because men are too lazy to kneel down and pick up fuel. You have to be mad and barbarous to destroy that which you cannot create. Man was endowed with reason and creative strength in order to increase what was given to him, but up till now he has not created; he has been content with destroying. There are fewer and fewer forests, game has become more and more scarce, the climate becomes worse day by day, and each day the earth grows poorer and uglier. You look at me ironically, everything I say to you sounds old-fashioned and frivolous, but when I pass by a forest I have saved from deforestation, or I hear the hum of a young wood that I planted with my own hands,

I feel that the climate itself is somewhat in my power, and that if in a thousand years man succeeds in being happy, it will be in some little measure thanks to me. When I plant a young birch tree, and then I see it covered over with green leaves and swaying in the wind, my heart is filled with pride at the thought that I have helped God in his creation.

FYODOR (*interrupting*). To your health, Wood Demon!

VOINITSKY. That's all very well and good, but if you consider the matter from a scientific point of view . . .

SOFIA. Uncle George, you have a wicked tongue. Shut up!

KRUSHCHOV. She's right, George. Let's not speak of it any more, I ask you.

VOINITSKY. As you wish.

MARYA. Ah!

SOFIA. What is it, Grandmother?

MARYA (*to* SEREBRYAKOV). I forgot to tell you, Alexander . . . really, I'm losing my memory . . . that I received a letter from Kharkov today . . . from Pavel Alexeyevich. He sends you his best.

SEREBRYAKOV. I am very happy.

MARYA. He is sending me his latest pamphlet and he has asked me to show it to you.

SEREBRYAKOV. Interesting?

MARYA. Interesting, but quite strange. He denies what he advocated seven years ago. Typical, very typical of our times. Never have people changed convictions with as much ease as now. It's frightful!

VOINITSKY. There's nothing frightful about it. Eat some fish, Mother.

MARYA. But I want to talk!

VOINITSKY. But we have been speaking for the past fifty years about all these cliques and movements. It's about time we stopped!

MARYA. You really seem as if you can't bear for me to speak! Pardon me, George, but you've changed so much this past year that I absolutely cannot recognize you any longer. You were a man with definite convictions, an enlightened human being . . .

VOINITSKY. Ah yes! I was an enlightened human being, who enlightened no one. I was an enlightened being. How much wit, but also how much malice. I am forty-seven years old. Last year I sought as you do to veil my eyes by all sorts of abstractions and scholasticism, with the single purpose of not seeing life as it really is, and I thought I was doing the right thing. . . . It is only now, you see, that I understand how stupid I was to waste the moments when I could have had all that my old age now refuses me.

SEREBRYAKOV. Wait! One might actually say, George, that you are contradicting your former beliefs. . . .

SOFIA. That's enough, Papa! You're beginning to bore me!

SEREBRYAKOV (*to* VOINITSKY). Wait! One might really say that you are denying your former convictions. The fault is, however, not theirs, but yours. You have forgotten that convictions, when they have no purpose, are a dead issue. It was necessary to provide them with a purpose.

VOINITSKY. A purpose? Everybody can't be a *perpetuum mobile*.

SEREBRYAKOV. What do you mean by that?

VOINITSKY. Nothing. Let's finish this conversation. We're not at home.

MARYA. I've completely lost my memory. . . . I forgot to remind you, Alexander, that you must take your drops, before lunch. I brought them, but I forgot to remind you. . . .

SEREBRYAKOV. I don't need drops.

MARYA. But see here, you're ill, Alexander, very ill!

SEREBRYAKOV. Perhaps I am. But why shout it from the rooftops? Old, sick, old and sick. . . . That's all I ever hear. (*To* ZHELTOUKHIN.) Leonid, permit me to get up and go home. It's getting a bit warm here, and the mosquitoes are biting.

ZHELTOUKHIN. But, of course! The luncheon is over, so nothing need prevent . . .

SEREBRYAKOV. Thank you. (*He goes back into the house;* MARYA *follows him.*)

JULIA (*to her brother*). Go with the professor. It's not right. . . .

ZHELTOUKHIN (*to* JULIA). The devil take him! (*He goes out.*)

DYADIN. Julia, allow me to thank you from the bottom of my heart. (*He kisses her hand.*)

JULIA. For what, Waffles? You ate so little! (JULIA *is thanked by everyone.*) But it was nothing, my friends! You're quite welcome! You all ate so little!

FYODOR (*in the wings*). Well, what is everybody going to do? First we'll keep our wager, and play croquet. . . . But after that?

JULIA. After that, we'll have dinner.

FYODOR. And after that?

KRUSHCHOV. After that, you'll all come to my house. In the evening, we'll organize a fishing party on the lake.

FYODOR. Perfect!

DYADIN. Delightful!

SOFIA. If I understand correctly, my friends, we are now going to keep our wager and play a game of croquet. . . . Then we will dine with Julia rather early, and then at about seven o'clock we shall be ready to go into the woods . . . to Michael's house. Very well! Go fetch the croquet balls, Julia. (*She and* JULIA *enter the house again.*)

FYODOR. Vassili, take the wine to the croquet field. We will drink to the health of the winner. Are you coming, Father? We're going to indulge in noble sport.

ORLOVSKI. Wait for me, my boy, I have to spend five short minutes with the professor. It would be impolite. . . . Always observe the rules of etiquette! Play with my ball, while you wait. . . . I'll be right back. (*He re-enters the house.*)

DYADIN. Without another moment's delay I shall go in to listen to the great scholar . . . Alexander Serebryakov . . . in order to savor in advance the higher pleasures which . . .

VOINITSKY. You're boring us, Waffles! Now go!

DYADIN. I'm going! I'm going! (*He re-enters the house.*)

FYODOR (*going to the garden, singing*). "And you shall be queen of the world, my faithful love . . ." (*He goes out.*)

KRUSHCHOV. I shall sneak out at once, on the quiet. (*To* VOINITSKY.) George, I earnestly ask you, please . . . let us not speak again of forests or of medicine. I don't know why, but when you engage me in conversation on these two subjects, I have a strange feeling all that day; it's a little as if I had eaten from an unsterilized plate. I have the honor of bidding you good day. (*He goes.*)

VOINITSKY. Poor man. Everyone can utter stupidities, but I don't enjoy them when they're said with such pathos.

ELENA. You were impossible once again, George. Why did you have to speak to Marya and Alexander that way . . . *perpetuum mobile!* How petty!

VOINITSKY. How can I help it if I detest him!

ELENA. Alexander is not to be detested. He is . . . like everyone else.

(SOFIA and JULIA go to the garden with the croquet hoops and mallets.)

VOINITSKY. If only you could see your face, your movements. . . . How tired of living you seem! Oh, how tired!

ELENA. Yes, how tired and how bored. (Pause.) Everybody jumps down my husband's throat in front of me, without being upset by my presence. Everybody has compassion for me: the poor girl, she has an old husband! Everybody, even the good ones, wants me to leave Alexander . . . the ˍˍrest everyone takes in me, the tenderhearted looks, the sigh of pity, all for the same reason. As the Wood Demon said a while ago, you destroy the forests without thinking, and soon there will be nothing left alive on earth; in the same way, without further ado, you destroy human beings; so that it will be your fault if there is no longer any fidelity, purity, or possibility of sacrifice. Why can't you bear a faithful wife with composure when she isn't your own? The Wood Demon was right; the demon of destruction is in all of you! You have no pity either for forests, birds, women, or your fellow man.

VOINITSKY. I don't like this philosophizing.

ELENA. Tell Fyodor that he bores me with his impertinence. In the last analysis, it's quite repugnant! To look me straight in the eye and speak aloud in front of everyone about one's love for a married woman! It's astonishing, it's witty!

SEVERAL VOICES FROM THE GARDEN. Bravo! Bravo!

ELENA. On the other hand, the Wood Demon is very nice. He often comes to visit us but he intimidates me, and I've never really talked to him once as I should. Not once have I shown him any affection. He'll think I'm unpleasant or proud. (Pause.) Of course, George, if we're such good friends, both of us, it's because both of us are such boring and sad people. Quite boring! (Pause.) Don't look at me that way. I don't like it.

VOINITSKY. Can I look at you any other way if I love you? You're my happiness, my life, my youth! . . . I know the chances that my love may be reciprocated are less than none, but I don't ask for anything . . . allow me only to look at you, to hear the sound of your voice. . . .

SEREBRYAKOV (*at the window*). Lenotchka, where are you?

ELENA. Here.

SEREBRYAKOV. Come and sit with us, dear. (*He disappears.*)

(ELENA *goes toward the house.*)

VOINITSKY (*following her*). Sanction me to speak of my love, don't chase me away; that's all I need to keep me absolutely happy.

CURTAIN

Act II

The dining room of the SEREBRYAKOVS' *house. A sideboard. In the middle of the room, a table. Between one and two in the morning. The* NIGHT WATCHMAN *can be heard tapping his drum in the garden.*

> (SEREBRYAKOV, *installed in an armchair in front of the window, dozing.* ELENA, *seated beside him, also dozing.*)

SEREBRYAKOV. Who's there? Sofia, is that you?

ELENA. It's me.

SEREBRYAKOV. You, Lenochka. . . . If you only knew what an unbearable pain . . .

ELENA. Your footwarmer has fallen down. (*Wrapping it around his knees.*) I'm going to shut the window, Alexander.

SEREBRYAKOV. No, I'm stifling. I dozed off a while ago and I dreamed that my left leg didn't belong to me. A terrible pain awoke me. No, it's not gout; I'm sure it's rheumatism. What time is it?

ELENA. One-twenty. (*Pause.*)

SEREBRYAKOV. Tomorrow morning, find the Batiouchkov for me in the library. I think we have it.

ELENA. Oh?

SEREBRYAKOV. Tomorrow morning, find the Batiouchkov for me. I remember that we have it. Why do I have so much trouble catching my breath?

116

ELENA. You're tired. You haven't slept for two nights.

SEREBRYAKOV. They say that Turgenev had a stroke right after an attack of his gout. I'm afraid of having one, too, just as he did. Cursed, detestable old age! Devil take it! As I grow old, I am becoming an object of disgust to myself—and I must disgust all of you.

ELENA. To listen to you, one would think it was our fault that you're old.

SEREBRYAKOV. I disgust you above all.

ELENA. It's so exhausting! (*She goes away from him and sits further away.*)

SEREBRYAKOV. You are right, of course. I'm not stupid. I understand. You're young, healthy, beautiful, you want to live, and I'm almost a corpse. Do you think I'm not capable of understanding that? Of course, it's stupid that I'm still alive. But wait, soon I'll rid you of my presence. I don't have too much longer to drag myself about.

ELENA. Sasha, I'm exhausted. If I deserve something for all my sleepless nights, I ask for only one thing: keep quiet. For the love of heaven, keep quiet. That's all I ask.

SEREBRYAKOV. It seems it is my fault that everyone is dragging about, bored, ruining their lives. Only I profit from life, only I, only I am happy! Yes, yes, of course!

ELENA. Shut up! You're torturing me!

SEREBRYAKOV. I torture everybody!

ELENA (*crying*). It's unbearable! What do you want from me? Tell me!

SEREBRYAKOV. Nothing.

ELENA. Then shut up, please!

SEREBRYAKOV. It's bizarre. When George speaks, or that old mother of his, everybody listens. But if I utter one word, everybody begins to feel unhappy. Even my voice is repugnant. Very well, let us admit that I am repugnant, selfish, bossy. But haven't I, now that I am old, earned the right to some selfishness? Don't I deserve that? My life has been hard. Ivan Orlovski and I were students at the same time. Ask him! He had an easy time of it, consorted with gypsies; helped me a little bit; during all that time, *I* lived in a cheap, dirty garret; I slaved night and day like a beast of burden; I went hungry; I hurt from sponging on people. Then I went to Heidelberg, and I didn't see Heidelberg. I was in Paris, and I didn't see Paris; all the time I remained cooped up between four walls, and I worked. . . . And from that very day that I obtained my professorship, I have devoted my life to serving science with "truth and devotion," as they say—and I am still doing so. Is it possible, I ask you, that I don't deserve to have a tranquil old age and the loving care of my family and entourage?

ELENA. No one is contesting your rights. (*The wind beats against the window.*) It's windy. I'll shut the window. (*She shuts it.*) It's going to rain any moment. No one is denying your rights. (*Pause.*)

(*In the garden, the* NIGHT WATCHMAN *taps his drum and hums.*)

SEREBRYAKOV. To give one's entire life to science, to get used to the worktable and to one's audience, one's distinguished colleagues—and then, suddenly, without rhyme nor reason, to find oneself in the grave. Every day to be surrounded by imbeciles and listen to their silly chatter. . . . I want to live. I love success, I love fame, renown—and here, I am in exile. To cry over the past at every moment, to be confronted with the success of others, to fear death . . . I cannot bear it, I don't have the strength for it! And here, they don't even want to forgive me for my old age!

ELENA. Wait, be patient: in five or six years, *I* will be old, too.

SOFIA (*enters*). I don't know why the doctor is so late. I told them to go get the Wood Demon if they don't find the district doctor.

SEREBRYAKOV. What do you want me to do with your Wood Demon? He knows as much about medicine as I do about astronomy!

SOFIA. Would you want us to bring the entire medical faculty to treat your gout?

SEREBRYAKOV. I will not speak to this cretin.

SOFIA. As you wish. (*She sits down.*) It doesn't matter.

SEREBRYAKOV. What time is it now?

ELENA. After one.

SEREBRYAKOV. It's stifling here. . . . Sofia, give me the drops on the table.

SOFIA. Right away. (*She holds the bottle out to him.*)

SEREBRYAKOV (*irritated*). No, not one of those! One can never ask you for anything!

SOFIA. None of your nonsense! Some people enjoy it, but spare me, I don't. Do me that favor.

SEREBRYAKOV. That young lady has an impossible nature. (*Pause.*) Why are you angry?

SOFIA. Why do you whine so much? One could really believe you were unhappy, whereas there are very few people in the world as happy as you are.

SEREBRYAKOV. Oh, of course! I am very, very happy!

SOFIA. Perfectly happy! And if you have an attack of gout, you know perfectly well that the attack will be over in the morning. And that's that!

VOINITSKY (*enters, wearing his dressing gown, carrying a candle*). There's going to be a storm. (*Lightning.*) There now! Go to bed, Elena and Sofia, I've come to relieve you.

SEREBRYAKOV (*frightened*). No, no! Don't leave me alone with him! No! He'll . . . deafen me with his conversation!

VOINITSKY. They must rest. They haven't slept for two nights.

SEREBRYAKOV. They may go to sleep, but you go away too. Thank you very much, but I beg of you, in the name of our past friendship, don't protest. We will talk later.

VOINITSKY. Of our past friendship . . . I must admit that's something new. . . .

ELENA. Shut up, George.

SEREBRYAKOV. My dear, don't leave me alone with him! He'll talk me into the grave.

VOINITSKY. It's almost becoming comical.

KRUSHCHOV (*in the wings*). Are they in the dining room? Here? Please take care of my horse.

VOINITSKY. There, the doctor has arrived.

KRUSHCHOV (*comes in*). What weather, eh? The rain pursued me. I had a devil of a time getting away from it. Good morning. How is everyone? (*He greets everyone.*)

SEREBRYAKOV. Excuse us for having disturbed you. I didn't wish it.

KRUSHCHOV. Come come, it's of no importance! What's come over you, Professor Serebryakov? Aren't you ashamed of yourself—to be sick? That's no good. What's the matter with you?

SEREBRYAKOV. Why do doctors always speak to the sick in such a condescending manner?

KRUSHCHOV (*laughing*). You're much too observant! (*Gently.*) Come on, off to bed! You're not comfortable down here. It's warmer and more restful in bed. . . . Come, I'll examine you up there . . . and everything will be all right.

ELENA. Listen to him, Sasha; go on.

KRUSHCHOV. If you have difficulty walking, stay in your chair, and we'll carry you.

SEREBRYAKOV. No, I am perfectly able; I'll go. . . . (*He gets up.*) Only, they disturbed you for nothing. (KRUSHCHOV *and* SOFIA *lead him out, holding him under the arms.*) Besides, I don't believe in medicines. . . . Why are you leading me? I can manage by myself. . . . (*He goes out,* SOFIA *and* KRUSHCHOV *still supporting him.*)

ELENA. I've been torturing myself too much with him. I can't stand up any more!

VOINITSKY. He's torturing you. And I torture myself. I haven't slept for three nights.

ELENA. There's something wrong in this house. Your mother detests everything except her pamphlets and the professor; the professor is always irritated, he doesn't trust anybody, he is afraid of you; Sofia is angry with her father, with me, and she doesn't talk to me; you . . . hate my husband and openly despise your mother; and I, I get more and more nervous and upset every day; today I was on the verge of tears I don't know how many times. To put it bluntly, everybody is warring against everybody else; I wonder what it all means; where is it all leading?

VOINITSKY. That's enough philosophizing.

ELENA. Something is wrong in this house. Yes, George, you're cultivated, intelligent, and it seems to me you should understand that it isn't the highway robbers or thieves of this world that ruin everything, but secret envy and hate—that make good people despise each other; those who consider this house a "haven of the intelligence" cannot see it for what it is. Help me a little to reconcile them all to each other! I haven't the strength to do it alone.

VOINITSKY. Reconcile me first with myself. My dear! (*He leans over her hand.*)

ELENA. Please—leave me alone! (*She takes her hand away*.) Go away!

VOINITSKY. It will stop raining soon, and all of nature will be refreshed and breathe more easily. I'm the only one to whom the storm brings no consolation. Day and night, I am haunted by a familiar devil—the thought that my life is hopelessly lost. My past doesn't exist, it was stupidly consumed in foolishness, and the present is abominable in all its absurdity. You see before you my life and my love; what shall I do with them? What can I do? My feelings are gone, like a ray of sunshine swallowed up in a ditch; and I am losing myself.

ELENA. When you speak to me of your love, it puts me into a stupor and I don't know what to say. Forgive me, I don't really know what to say. (*She tries to leave*.) Good night!

VOINITSKY (*barring her way*). If you only knew how I suffer at the thought that I am not the only one in this house who is ruining his life: you're here! What are you waiting for? What cursed philosophy holds you here? Don't you understand that the highest morality does not consist in enslaving your youth and trying to stifle your enjoyment of life. . . .

ELENA (*looking at him intently*). George, you're drunk!

VOINITSKY. Perhaps, perhaps.

ELENA. Is Fyodor still in the house?

VOINITSKY. Yes, he's spending the night. . . . Perhaps . . . perhaps . . . everything is possible!

ELENA. You've been overdoing it again today! Why?

VOINITSKY. So that life may have some reality. Don't stop me from drinking, Elena.

ELENA. You never used to drink before, and you never spoke this way. Go to sleep. I'm tired of you. And tell your

friend Fyodor Orlovski that if he continues to annoy me,
I'll make sure to stop him. Now go!

VOINITSKY (*leaning over her hand*). My dear! My wonderful one!

KRUSHCHOV (*comes in and sees them*). Elena, the professor is asking for you.

ELENA (*taking her hand away from* VOINITSKY). I'm going.
(*She goes out.*)

(*to* KRUSHCHOV). Is there nothing sacred to you? You
should remember, you and that charming lady who has just
gone out, that her husband was once the husband of your
own sister, and also that there is a young lady living under
the same roof as you are. The whole district is talking about
your little idyll. What nerve! (*He goes off.*)

VOINITSKY (*alone*). She's gone. (*Pause.*) Ten years
ago I met her at my sister's house. She was alive then.
Elena was seventeen years old and I was thirty-seven. Why
didn't I fall in love with her then? Why didn't I ask to marry
her? Because it was possible then! Now she would be my
wife. . . . Yes, now the storm would have awakened us
both; she would have been afraid of the thunder; and I,
holding her in my arms, would have whispered: "Don't be
afraid of the thunder, I'm here." Wonderful dreams! How
beautiful that would be! I can laugh about it. . . . But, my
Lord, everything is spinning around in my head . . . why am
I old? Why doesn't she understand me? Her high-flown way
of talking, her lazy morality, her absurd, lazy notions about
a world that's headed for destruction, all that is odious to me.
(*Pause.*) Why am I made this way? How I envy that madman Fyodor, or that idiot Michael! They're spontaneous, sincere, idiotic . . . they don't live with that cursed irony which
poisons everything. . . .

FYODOR (*comes in, wrapped in a coverlet. At the door*).
You're alone? No ladies? (*He enters.*) The storm woke me.
What a downpour! What time is it?

VOINITSKY. Who the devil knows!

FYODOR. I thought I heard Elena's voice.

VOINITSKY. She was here a moment ago.

FYODOR. Wonderful woman! (*He examines the bottles on the table.*) What's this? Mint pastilles. (*He eats one.*) Yes, a wonderful woman. The professor is ill, isn't he?

VOINITSKY. Yes.

FYODOR. I don't know how he can live this way. They say the ancient Greeks got rid of the inferior weaklings among their children by hurling them off Mont Blanc. That's the kind of people they ought to get rid of!

VOINITSKY. It wasn't Mont Blanc, it was the Tarpeian rock. What filthy ignorance!

FYODOR. All right, rock . . . let's say rock. . . . That's not the question! Why are you so sad tonight? Are you feeling sorry for the professor perhaps?

VOINITSKY. Leave me alone. (*Pause.*)

FYODOR. Or are you perhaps in love with the professor's wife? Oh well, that's allowed! . . . You can pine away all you like! Only, listen here: if there's even a grain of truth in the gossip that circulates in the district, and I find out about it, don't ask me for help . . . I'll throw you off the Tarpeian rock!

VOINITSKY. She is my friend.

FYODOR. Already?

VOINITSKY. What do you mean by "already"?

FYODOR. A woman can only become a man's friend when she has already been his companion first, and then his mistress.

VOINITSKY. What a trivial philosophy!

FYODOR. In that case, let's drink. Come, I think I still

have some Chartreuse left; we will drink. And as soon as it's daylight, we'll go to my house. How about that? I have a steward, Louka; he never says, "How's that?"—only "How about that?" The rascal! Well then, how about that? (*Catching sight of* SOFIA, *who is entering.*) Heavens, excuse me; I'm not wearing a tie! (*He runs out.*)

SOFIA. Well, Uncle George, you've drunk some champagne with Fyodor, and you've gone driving in a troika. The two eagles have become friends; except that Fyodor is hopeless, he was born "fast," but it's not becoming in a man of your age.

VOINITSKY. Age has nothing to do with it. When one doesn't have a real existence, one lives with illusions. It's better than nothing.

SOFIA. The hay hasn't been brought in. The servants say it's going to rot in the rain, and you're upset about illusions! (*Suddenly frightened.*) Uncle, you have tears in your eyes!

VOINITSKY. What tears? It's nothing. Just foolishness . . . you looked at me the way your poor dead mother used to . . . my dear! (*He kisses her hands and face avidly.*) My sister . . . my dear sister. . . . Where is she now? If she knew! Oh, if she only knew!

SOFIA. What? If she only knew what, Uncle?

VOINITSKY. No, it would be too painful. It wouldn't be right. . . . Nothing.

(KRUSHCHOV *comes in.*)

Later. . . . Nothing. . . . I'm going. (*He goes out.*)

KRUSHCHOV. Your father doesn't want to listen to me. I tell him it's the gout, and he tells me it's rheumatism. I ask him to lie still; he sits up. (*He takes his cap.*) It's nerve-wracking!

SOFIA. He's too spoiled. Put your cap down. Wait for the rain to stop. Would you like to eat something?

KRUSHCHOV. I would, thank you.

SOFIA. I like to have a bite late at night. There must be something in the sideboard. (*She searches in the sideboard.*) Does he need a doctor? What he would need is a dozen ladies to attend him, looking him in the eye, moaning: "Oh, Professor!" There, have some cheese.

KRUSHCHOV. It's not right to take that tone when one talks of one's father. I agree. He has a difficult nature, but if you compare him with others, with all your Uncle Georges, with all those Ivan Orlovskis, you can easily see they're not worth his little finger.

SOFIA. Here's a bottle. (*Pause.*) I'm not speaking about my father, but about "the great man." I love my father, but great men bore me with their pretensions. (*They sit down.*) What a downpour! (*Lightning.*) Look!

KRUSHCHOV. The storm won't reach us, it will just pass right over.

SOFIA (*pouring*). Have a drink.

KRUSHCHOV. May you live a hundred years! (*He drinks.*)

SOFIA. Are you angry with us for having disturbed you in the middle of the night?

KRUSHCHOV. On the contrary. If you hadn't called me, I'd still be asleep right now, and I'd rather see you in reality than in dreams.

SOFIA. Then, why do you look so angry?

KRUSHCHOV. Because I am angry. (*Pause.*) Nobody's here, we can speak freely. Sofia, I would have taken you away from here a moment ago with great pleasure! I can't breathe the air you breathe in this house, and I think it's poisoning you, too. Your father devotes himself entirely to his gout and to his books, and doesn't want to know about anything else; while *Uncle* George and your stepmother . . .

SOFIA. My stepmother?

KRUSHCHOV. One can't talk about some things . . . one simply cannot! My dear friend, there are many things about people that I do not understand. In a human being, everything ought to be beautiful: the face, the clothes, the soul, the thoughts. . . . Sometimes I see a beautiful face and clothes to make one turn around and look, but the soul and the thoughts, my God! A beautiful exterior can sometimes hide a soul so black that no make-up could ever mask it. . . . Pardon me, if I annoy you. . . . It's because you're very dear to me.

SOFIA (*letting her knife fall*). I dropped it.

KRUSHCHOV (*picking it up*). It's not important. (*Pause.*) You see, when you've been walking in the forest of a dark night, and you see a little light far off in the distance, you feel, you don't know why, that your soul is so light that you notice neither your fatigue nor the darkness, nor the branches that slash against your face. . . . I work from morning till night, winter and summer; I never have any rest; I battle with those who don't understand me, I suffer sometimes in an unbearable way. . . . But I have finally found some light. I won't pretend to love you more than anything else in the world. I don't think love is everything in life. It is only my reward. My sweet, there is no greater reward for those who work, struggle, suffer . . .

SOFIA. I'm sorry, Michael, I have a question. . . .

KRUSHCHOV. What is it? Now tell me!

SOFIA. You see . . . you . . . come to our house very often, and I often visit your home with my parents. You must admit you can't forgive yourself for that.

KRUSHCHOV. What do you mean?

SOFIA. I mean . . . well . . . I mean that your feeling . . . your democratic sense is offended by the fact that you know us intimately. I was raised in a boarding school, Elena is an aristocrat, we dress fashionably, and you are a man of the people . . . a democrat.

KRUSHCHOV. Let's not talk of that. This isn't the time.

SOFIA. For you, the important thing is to dig up peat and plant trees. It's strange! To sum it up, you're a man of the people. . . .

KRUSHCHOV. A democrat, a man of the people! Sofia, can you say that seriously and still have a catch in your voice all the same?

SOFIA. Yes, yes, seriously, very very seriously.

KRUSHCHOV. No, no, you can't. . . .

SOFIA. I assure you. I swear to you on anything you like, that if I had, say, a sister, and you loved her and asked to marry her, you would never forgive yourself; because afterward you would be ashamed to show yourself to the other little doctors in the district and to their wives, ashamed to love a girl raised in a boarding school, a conceited thing who didn't go on to take courses in the university—and who dresses fashionably. I know it only too well. . . . I can see by your eyes that I'm telling the truth! All in all, your forests, your peat, your embroidered peasant blouse—all that is only a pose, putting on airs, a lie, that's all—nothing more.

KRUSHCHOV. But why? Why do you want to wound me, my dear? I'm a fool; serves me right. "Don't try to live in a world which isn't your own heritage." I suppose that phrase was meant for me. Good-by. (*He goes toward the door.*)

SOFIA. Good-by. . . . I was too harsh, I'm sorry. Forgive me.

KRUSHCHOV (*coming back toward* SOFIA). If you only knew how stifling it is here! What a place! Everybody is looked at askance, approached from a preconceived notion . . . they want to see you as a man of the people, as a psychopath, as a phrasemonger; to put it bluntly, they insist on seeing you as anything but what you are, a man. "Oh, that one, they say he's a psychopath!" and they're satisfied by that diagnosis. "That one, he's a phrasemonger," and they're as content as if they had just discovered America! And when they don't understand me nor what label to stick on my forehead, they don't blame themselves but me—and they say, "He's a strange man, very strange!" You're only twenty years old, but already you seem as old and levelheaded as your father and your Uncle George; I wouldn't be surprised if you sent for me to cure your gout! You can't live this way! Whoever I may be, look me straight in the eyes, sincerely, without preconceived notions, and above all, look for the human being in me, or else you'll never succeed in understanding anybody. Good-by! Remember what I've just told you: with eyes as sly and suspicious as yours, you'll never fall in love!

SOFIA. That's not true!

KRUSHCHOV. It *is* true!

SOFIA. It's not! There . . . just to contradict you . . . I am in love, I am in love, and it hurts, it hurts! Leave me alone. Go away, please, and don't come back here . . . any more. . . .

KRUSHCHOV. I have the honor to bid you good night. (*He goes off.*)

SOFIA (*alone*). He's angry. God help us from having a temper like that man! (*Pause.*) He speaks beautifully, but who can tell if he's saying anything more than words? He's a dreamer full of his forests and the trees that he plants. . . . That's fine, but maybe he is . . . a psychopath. . . . (*She buries her face in her hands.*) I don't understand. (*She cries.*) He studied medicine, but that's not what interests him. It's peculiar, peculiar! Oh God, help me to understand.

ELENA (*comes in. Opening a window*). The storm has passed. The air is clear. (*Pause.*) Where is the Wood Demon?

SOFIA. He's gone.

ELENA. Sofia?

SOFIA. Yes?

ELENA. How long are you going to keep sulking? We

haven't done each other any wrong—then why are we
enemies? That's enough of that. . . .

SOFIA. That's how I feel . . . (*She throws her arms around*
ELENA.) My dear!

ELENA. I'm so glad.

(*They are both moved.*)

SOFIA. Is Papa in bed?

ELENA. No, he's sitting up in the drawing room. . . . We
haven't said a word to each other for weeks, God knows
why! (*She looks at the table.*) What's that?

SOFIA. The Wood Demon had some supper.

ELENA. And even drank some wine. . . . Let's drink to our
friendship!

SOFIA. Let's!

ELENA. No, in the same glass. A loving cup. (*She fills
the glass.*) That's better. Shall we be friends?

SOFIA. Friends! (*They drink, and embrace one another.*)
I've wanted to make peace for some time now, but I didn't
dare. . . . (*She is in tears.*)

ELENA. Why are you crying?

SOFIA. Oh . . . nothing . . . nothing . . . just like that!

ELENA. That's enough! Come on. . . . (*She cries, too.*)
Now I'm crying, just like you, you little monster! (*Pause.*)
You were angry with me because people say that I married
your father for his money. . . . If you believe in solemn
oaths, I can swear to you that I married him for love. I fell
in love with him as one falls in love with a learned and
celebrated gentleman. It was not a true love, it was artificial,
but I believed at that time that it was a true one. I
haven't been unfaithful. . . . And, ever since our marriage,

you have been punishing me with your sly and suspicious looks.

SOFIA. All right, let's make peace! Peace! Let's forget! (*Pause.*) That's the second time today I've been told I give sly and suspicious looks.

ELENA. Don't! It's not becoming to you. You must believe in people or else it isn't possible to live.

SOFIA. A frightened crow is even afraid of a bush. I've been disappointed so many times!

ELENA. By whom! Your father is a distinguished man, a hard-working gentleman. Today you reproached him for his happiness. If he were really happy, occupied with his work, he wouldn't have paid attention. I haven't knowingly done any harm to you or your father. Your Uncle George is good, honest; but he's also a disappointed and unhappy man . . . then whom don't you trust?

SOFIA. Tell me sincerely, as you would a friend: are you happy?

ELENA. No.

SOFIA. I thought so. One more question: tell me sincerely: would you have wanted a young husband?

ELENA. What a child you are! Of course, I would have . . . (*She laughs.*) Well, ask me something else, go ahead and ask!

SOFIA. Do you like the Wood Demon?

ELENA. Yes, a great deal.

SOFIA (*laughing*). I act like an idiot, don't I? Well, he's gone, and I still can hear his voice, the sound of his footsteps; and when I look out the window, I think I see his face. . . . Let me tell you everything . . . but I can't say it out loud, I'm so ashamed. . . . Come into my room; we can talk better there. . . . I must seem like an idiot, admit it. . . . Is he a good man, do you think?

ELENA. Very good, very very good.

SOFIA. I find him . . . strange, with all his forest stories, and the peat. . . . I just don't understand it. . . .

ELENA. The forests don't matter. My dear, he has talent, that's what matters! Do you even know what talent is? It's daring, freedom of mind, the power to take off, to soar. . . . He plants a tree or digs up a few bushels of peat—and already he can foresee the future happiness of humanity. Men like that are rare. We must love them. May God help both of you; you are both pure, brave, genuine human beings . . . he is a little thoughtless, but you are sensible, wise . . . you'll make a fine match. (*She gets up.*) And I'm only a boring nonentity . . . a passing figure. . . . As a musician and as a housekeeper, as a woman, in everything, I was never anything but a passing figure. If you think about it, Sofia, I am without any doubt very very unhappy! (*She paces up and down nervously.*) There is no happiness for me in this world. None at all. Why are you laughing?

SOFIA (*laughing and hiding her face*). I am so happy, so happy!

ELENA (*wringing her hands*). I am really much too unhappy.

SOFIA. I am happy! Happy!

ELENA. I want to play the piano. I'd like to play something right at this moment. . . .

SOFIA. Play! (*She embraces ELENA.*) I can't sleep . . . so play!

ELENA. In a minute. Your father isn't sleeping, but when he is sick, music irritates him. Go and ask him . . . if he wouldn't be disturbed. . . . I'll play. Go ahead!

SOFIA. Yes. (*She goes out.*)

(*In the garden, the* NIGHT WATCHMAN *taps his drum.*)

ELENA. I haven't played for some time now. I'm going to

play and cry like an idiot. (*Calling out through the window.*)
Is it you who's tapping like that, Yefim?

VOICE OF THE NIGHT WATCHMAN. Yes, it is.

ELENA. Don't, please. The master is sick.

VOICE OF THE NIGHT WATCHMAN. I was on my way.
(*He whistles to his dogs. Pause.*) Malchik! Juchka! Juchka!

SOFIA (*returning*). He says no.

CURTAIN

Act III

A *"salon"* in the SEREBRYAKOV *house. Three doors: stage right, left, and in the middle. Early afternoon. In the wings, one hears* ELENA *playing Lenski's aria (before the duel scene, from* Eugene Onegin) *on the piano.*

(IVAN ORLOVSKI, GEORGE VOINITSKY, *and* FYODOR *are listening to the music.* FYODOR *is dressed in black, sheepskin cap in hand.*)

ORLOVSKI (*listening to the music*). It's she who's playing; yes, it's she, Elena . . . my favorite piece of music. (*The music stops.*) Yes, it's a beautiful thing. I think we've never been quite as bored here as we are now.

FYODOR. You've never known real ennui, my dear. When I was a volunteer in Serbia, I found out what real boredom was. It was hot, stifling, and the filth! . . . My head was bursting. . . . Once, I was sitting down—I remember—in a dirty little shed. With me—Captain Kachkinazi. We had already exhausted every subject of conversation; we had nowhere to go, nothing to do, and no desire to drink—we were nauseated, do you understand? We had only one desire—to hang ourselves. There we are, seated, like wild animals, looking at each other. He looks at me and I look at him; I look at him and he looks at me. . . . We look at each other and we don't know what's going on—you understand? One hour, two hours, and we're still there, looking at each other. Suddenly, without rhyme or reason, he jumps up, reaches for his sword, and jumps on me. . . . How about that! —Naturally, I reach for my sword; if I don't, he kills me—and there we are, in action: *chik, chak, chik, chak* . . . they had a hard time separating us. I got out of it in one piece, but Captain Kachkinazi is still walking around with

134

a scar on his cheek. . . . You see how easily people can lose their marbles!

ORLOVSKI. Yes, it happens.

SOFIA (*enters. Aside*). I don't know what to do with myself! (*She walks about, laughing.*)

ORLOVSKI. Where are you off to, my little kitten? Sit with us awhile.

SOFIA. Fyodor, come here! (*Dragging* FYODOR *aside.*) Come here!

FYODOR. What do you want? Why are you looking so radiant?

SOFIA. Fedya, give me your word of honor that you'll do it!

FYODOR. Do what?

SOFIA. Go to . . . the Wood Demon's place.

FYODOR. Why?

SOFIA. Just like that. Just go there. And ask him why he hasn't come to see us for such a long time. Already two weeks!

FYODOR. She's blushing! It's shameful! Gentlemen, Sofia is in love!

EVERYBODY. It's shameful! It's shameful!

(SOFIA *hides her face between her hands and runs off.*)

FYODOR. She prowls like a ghost from room to room and doesn't know what to do with herself. . . . She is in love with the Wood Demon.

ORLOVSKI. What a charming girl! I'm very fond of her. Fyodor, I dreamed you would marry her. It will all happen according to God's will, however . . . but how nice and

touching a thing that would be! I would have come to visit
you, and I would have found a young woman, a home, a
little samovar . . . steaming . . .

FYODOR. That's not in my power. If I ever get it into my
head to marry, it's Julia I'd have for my wife. At least she's
petite—and of all possible evils, one must choose the lesser.
And then, she's a good housekeeper! (*Hitting his finger
against his forehead.*) I have an idea!

ORLOVSKI. What?

FYODOR. We could be drinking champagne!

VOINITSKY. It's too early, and it's too hot. . . . Wait awhile.

ORLOVSKI (*full of admiration*). My boy, my wonderful
boy! . . . He wanted champagne, the little bugger!

(ELENA *comes in and is crossing the stage.*)

VOINITSKY. Admire her! She comes, she goes, back, forth,
she falls from place to place, so sluggishly. It's charming!
Completely charming!

ELENA. Stop it, George! Life is already boring enough
without your continual buzzing! (*She tries to leave.*)

VOINITSKY (*barring her passage*). "What a talent! What
an artist!" But do you look like an artist? No. You are
apathy personified, you are an Oblomov . . . you have so
many virtues—if you will pardon me—that I find this disgusting. . . .

ELENA. Don't look at me! . . . Let me be!

VOINITSKY. Why are you so languid? (*Sharply.*) Listen,
my darling, my splendid creature, be reasonable! In your
veins flows the blood of the water spirits; be an undine.

ELENA. Leave me alone!

VOINITSKY. Let yourself go, at least once in your life; fall

head over heels in love with another watersprite . . . anyone
at all . . .

FYODOR. Dive head first into the sea, both of you, so that
the Herr Professor and all of us may sit here dumfounded,
gaping!

VOINITSKY. A water spirit! Yes, a watersprite! (*Pause.*)
Love while the loving is good.

ELENA. What have I to learn from you? I know how I
should live! If I could, I'd fly away like a free bird, far, far
from you all, from your dead faces, your tedious conversa-
tions. I would forget that you exist, and nobody would dare
try and teach me anything. But I don't have any will of my
own. I am frightened, timid, and it seems to me always that
if I deceived my husband, all women would follow my example and leave theirs, and that God would punish me, and
my conscience would torture me. . . . If it weren't for that,
I would show you how one must live . . . freely! (*She goes
out.*)

ORLOVSKI. My darling, my beauty!

VOINITSKY. I think I shall despise that woman very soon.
She is as shy as a little girl, and she philosophizes like an
old priest, heavy with virtue. She makes me sick!

ORLOVSKI. That's enough, that's quite enough! . . . Where
is the professor?

VOINITSKY. Inside, in his study. He is writing.

ORLOVSKI. He sent for me about some business. Do you
know what it's all about?

VOINITSKY. It's not about business. He writes gibberish,
he grumbles, he envies everybody, and that's all he does,
nothing more.

(ZHELTOUKHIN *and* JULIA *enter at the door, stage right.*)

ZHELTOUKHIN. Good afternoon, my friends.

(*Exchange of greetings.*)

JULIA. Good afternoon, Godfather. (*They embrace.*)

ZHELTOUKHIN. Is the professor at home?

ORLOVSKI. In his study.

ZHELTOUKHIN. I must see him. He wrote to me about a business matter. . . . (*He goes out.*)

JULIA. George, did you get the barley you expected?

VOINITSKY. Thank you, I did. How much do I owe you? We also had some last spring; I don't remember how much. . . . You ought to keep accounts. I can't bear to neglect accounts or mix things up.

JULIA. In the spring you had eight kilos of wheat, George, two heifers, one young bull, and some butter.

VOINITSKY. How much do I owe you?

JULIA. How should I know? I can't count without an abacus, George.

VOINITSKY. Well then, if need be, I can bring you an abacus right away. . . . (*He goes out and comes back instantly with an abacus.*)

ORLOVSKI. How is your big brother, my dear?

JULIA. Well, thank God! (*Pause.*) Godfather, where did you buy that necktie?

ORLOVSKI. In town, at Kirpichov's.

JULIA. It's very pretty. I must buy one for Leonid.

VOINITSKY. Here is the abacus.

(JULIA *sits down and slides the little balls up and down.*)

ORLOVSKI. What a housekeeper God gave Leonid. A little snip of a creature, no bigger than a toadstool, and look how she works!

FYODOR. Yes, while all he does is walk about with his hands on his hips.

ORLOVSKI. Do you know she wears long pants? I passed the market place Friday, and there she was standing next to the wagons, in long pants. . . .

JULIA. You made me lose my count!

VOINITSKY. Let's go elsewhere, my friends. To the large drawing room, if you wish. I've had enough of it in here. . . . (*Yawns.*)

ORLOVSKI. Off to the drawing room! It's all the same to me. . . .

   (ORLOVSKI, VOINITSKY, *and* FYODOR *go out by the door at stage left.*)

JULIA (*after a pause*). Fodya's dressed in a Caucasian uniform. That's the way things are; his parents didn't know how to bring him up . . . there isn't a better-looking man in the province, and he's intelligent and rich, too . . . but as for good common sense . . . he's an idiot. . . . (*She moves the little balls noisily on the abacus.*)

SOFIA (*enters*). Is that you, Julia? I didn't know you were here.

JULIA (*kissing her*). My dear!

SOFIA. What are you doing here? Your accounts? What a good housekeeper you are! I get envious looking at you . . . Julia, why don't you get married?

JULIA. No reason. I've been asked, but I refused. I won't ever find the right one. (*Sighing.*) No, I won't!

SOFIA. But why?

JULIA. I'm too ignorant. I had to quit school before the second year.

SOFIA. Why did you have to quit?

JULIA. I was too ignorant. (SOFIA *laughs.*) Why are you laughing, Sofia?

SOFIA. I have a funny feeling. . . . Julia, I'm so happy today, so happy, happy, happy, that so much happiness is making me sad. . . . I don't know what to do with myself. . . . Let's talk about something. . . . Yes, let's talk about. . . . Have you ever been in love? (JULIA *nods her head yes.*) Was he interesting? (JULIA *whispers a few words in her ear.*) Who? Fyodor Orlovski?

JULIA (*after nodding her head yes*). And you're . . .

SOFIA. Yes. Only it's not Fyodor. (*Laughing.*) Tell me more.

JULIA. I've wanted to talk to you for some time now, Sofia.

SOFIA. I'm listening.

JULIA. I want to explain to you . . . you see . . . I have always been . . . very well disposed toward you. . . . I know many young ladies, but I prefer you to all of them. . . . If you had said to me, "Julia, give me ten horses, or, let's say, two hundred sheep," I would have answered, "With pleasure!" For you, I wouldn't have counted the expense.

SOFIA. Why are you so embarrassed, Julia?

JULIA. I'm ashamed . . . I . . . I . . . have always been very well disposed toward you. You're the best of all of them . . . not proud . . . and what a pretty little print dress you have on!

SOFIA. We'll talk about the print dress later. . . . Now tell me!

JULIA (*unnerved*). I don't know . . . how . . . to explain it to you intelligently. . . . Allow me to propose . . . to make

me happy . . . I mean . . . that is to say . . . marry Leonid!
(*She hides her face.*)

SOFIA (*getting up*). Let's not talk about that, Julia . . .
we mustn't . . . we mustn't. . . .

ELENA (*enters*). Nobody knows what to do with themselves. The two Orlovskis and George are going from room
to room; wherever one goes, one finds them. Boredom has
taken over, that's all there is to it! What are they doing here
anyway? They'd do better to go elsewhere.

JULIA (*tears in her eyes*). Good afternoon, Elena. (*Tries to
embrace* ELENA.)

ELENA. Good afternoon, Julia. I'm sorry, I don't like to be
kissed. Sofia, what is your father doing? (*Pause.*) Sofia, why
don't you answer me? I asked you what your father was doing.
(*Pause.*) Sofia, why don't you answer me?

SOFIA. Do you want to know? Then, come . . . (*Drawing
her aside.*) Very well, I'll tell you. . . . My soul is too pure
today to hide anything from you. Here! (*She hands her a
letter.*) I found it in the garden. . . . Julia, let's go.

(SOFIA *and* JULIA *go out by the door at stage left.*)

ELENA (*alone*). What's this? A letter from George, to me!
How difficult! How inhuman! What have I done to— Her
soul is so pure she cannot talk to me! My God, to wound
somebody that much! . . . My head is spinning . . . in a moment I'll faint.

FYODOR (*who has entered by the door at stage right,
crossing the stage*). Why do you all jump when you see me?
(*Pause.*) Hm! . . . (*He takes the letter out of her hands and
tears it up into little bits.*) Throw these things away; you
must think only of me. (*Pause.*)

ELENA. I beg your pardon?

FYODOR. When I've set my sights on someone, that someone doesn't slip through my fingers.

ELENA. You're stupid and insolent!

FYODOR. This evening, at seven-thirty, be at the little bridge, behind the garden; and wait for me. . . . You understand? That's all I have to say to you. . . . So, my angel, until this evening, at seven-thirty! (*He tries to take her by the hand;* ELENA *slaps him.*) That's a "striking" argument!

ELENA. Get out!

FYODOR. Your wish is my command. . . . (*He goes off, then returns just as quickly.*) Touché! Let's talk quietly. . . . You see, I've had every possible experience in this world. I've even eaten goldfish soup . . . twice. Only, look, I still haven't gone up in a balloon, and I haven't even once stolen a professor's wife.

ELENA. Get out!

FYODOR. I'm going . . . right away. . . . I've had every possible experience, and that's why I'm so insolent that you don't know how to react. . . . I'm telling you this because if you ever need a friend, or a faithful dog, you can always come to me. . . . Touché!

ELENA. I don't need dogs. . . . Get out!

FYODOR. I will obey. (*Moved.*) And yet I'm touched, yes, quite touched. (*He goes off, uncertainly.*)

ELENA (*alone*). My head hurts. . . . I have bad dreams every night. . . . I think something terrible is going to happen. . . . How despicable! All these young people were born and brought up together; they know one another, they spend their time embracing. They ought to live in peace and understanding, but soon they'll be devouring each other. . . . The Wood Demon saves the wood, but nobody saves human beings. (*She goes toward the door stage left, but, seeing that* ZHELTOUKHIN *and* JULIA *are about to enter that way, she goes out by the middle door.*)

JULIA. We're both so unhappy, Lenya! So unhappy!

ZHELTOUKHIN. Who authorized you to talk to her? You

put your finger in everything, just like a matchmaker! You spoiled everything! She'll think I'm incapable of speaking for myself. . . . How vulgar! I told you a thousand times not to meddle! Nothing good can come of it . . . only innuendoes, contemptible actions. . . . The old man has probably guessed that I'm in love with his daughter, and he's already taking advantage of my feelings. He wants me to buy his property!

JULIA. How much is he asking?

ZHELTOUKHIN. Shhh, here they come!

(SEREBRYAKOV, ORLOVSKI, *and* MARYA *enter by the door at stage left. The latter is reading a pamphlet while she walks.*)

ORLOVSKI. I don't feel perfectly well either, my dear. I've been having headaches for two days now, and pains all over my body.

SEREBRYAKOV. Where are the others? I don't like this house, it's a veritable labyrinth. Twenty-six enormous rooms, everybody dispersed and you can never find anybody. (*He rings.*) Call George and Elena.

ZHELTOUKHIN. Julia, you're not doing anything. Go get George and Elena. (JULIA *goes out.*)

SEREBRYAKOV. One can get used to illness if one has to, but what I cannot bear is my present state of mind. I have the feeling that I am already dead, or fallen from the earth onto another planet.

ORLOVSKI. That depends on one's point of view . . . which . . .

MARYA (*reading*). Give me a pencil! Still another contradiction! I must note it down.

ORLOVSKI. Here you are, Excellency. (*He gives her a pencil and kisses her hand.*)

VOINITSKY (*enters*). Do you need me?

SEREBRYAKOV. Yes, George.

VOINITSKY. And why do you need me?

SEREBRYAKOV. Why are you so angry? (*Pause.*) If I have offended you, I ask you to pardon me.

VOINITSKY. Don't take that tone. Let's go straight to the heart of the matter. What do you want?

(ELENA *enters.*)

SEREBRYAKOV. Ah, there is Lenochka. . . . Be seated, my friends. (*Pause.*) I have gathered you together, gentlemen, and ladies, to announce to you that the inspector general is arriving . . . (*Laughing at his own joke.*) Enough humor! The matter at hand is serious. I have gathered you here, my friends, to ask for your help and advice; knowing your habitual kindness, I hope that you will not refuse me. I am a scholar, a man who lives in his books, and who has never known anything of practical existence; so that I cannot do without the advice of competent people. That is why I ask you, Ivan, and you also, Leonid, and you, too, George . . . the fact is that . . . *manet omnes una nox.* In other words, we are all in the hands of God. I am old, sick, and consequently I think it expedient to put order into the material condition of my family. My life is finished; I no longer have thoughts for myself, but I have a young wife and a daughter who is not yet married. To continue to live in the country is impossible.

ELENA. It's all the same to me.

SEREBRYAKOV. We were not made for the country. To live in the city on the resources that we extract from this land is inconceivable. Two days ago, I sold a piece of this forest for four thousand rubles, but that was an unusual step to which one cannot have recourse every year. We must take steps to guarantee ourselves a more or less definite income. I have found such an expedient and I have the honor of submitting it to your judgment. Details aside, I intend to expose the general outlines to you. Our property does not bring us more than two percent revenue, on the average. I therefore propose to you to sell it. If we convert it into government bonds, the money will be realized, we will obtain four to five percent. I think that there will even be a surplus of several thousands of rubles which will permit us to purchase a villa in Finland.

VOINITSKY. One moment. . . . I must be hearing things. . . . Will you repeat what you just said?

SEREBRYAKOV. Convert the money into government bonds, and with the surplus, purchase a villa in Finland.

VOINITSKY. No, not about Finland. . . . You said something else.

SEREBRYAKOV. I propose to sell the property.

VOINITSKY. That's it, sell the property. What a rich, splendid idea! And where will you put us, my mother and myself?

SEREBRYAKOV. We will settle these questions at the proper time. We can't do everything at once.

VOINITSKY. One moment. . . . Of course, until this moment, I didn't have a grain of sense. Until this moment, I was stupid enough to believe that this property belonged to Sofia. My father had bought this property to give to my sister as a dowry. Until this moment, I was naïve enough to think our laws were not made in Turkey; I thought my sister's property belonged to Sofia.

SEREBRYAKOV. Yes, the property belongs to Sofia; who said anything different? Without Sofia's consent, I would not take it upon myself to sell it; and moreover, I am making this proposal in Sofia's interest.

VOINITSKY. It is inconceivable, inconceivable! Either I am mad, or else . . . or else . . .

MARYA. George, don't contradict the professor; he knows better than we do what is good and what is bad.

VOINITSKY. Give me some water. (*He drinks.*) Tell us what you want, what you want!

SEREBRYAKOV. I don't understand what is agitating you so

much, George. I don't maintain that my proposal is perfect. If everyone finds it untenable, I shall not insist.

(*Enter* DYADIN. *He is wearing a dress coat, white gloves, top hat with wide brim.*)

DYADIN. I have the honor to greet you one and all. I beg your pardon to have dared to enter without having myself announced. I am guilty, but I deserve your indulgence, for there were no servants in the waiting room.

SEREBRYAKOV (*taken aback*). I'm so glad. . . . But, of course! . . . Do . . . come in. . . .

DYADIN (*clicking his heels*). Your Excellency! Ladies! My intrusion in your midst has a double purpose. Firstly, I come to visit you and pay my respects; secondly, to invite you all, given this magnificent weather, to make a little expedition to my property. I live in a water mill rented to me by our mutual friend, the Wood Demon. It is an isolated little piece of land—very poetic, where one may listen to the water-sprites cavorting by night, and by day . . .

VOINITSKY. Wait, Waffles, we're talking business . . . you'll tell us later. (*To* SEREBRYAKOV.) Now, ask her . . . was this property bought from her uncle?

SEREBRYAKOV. Why do you want me to ask her that?

VOINITSKY. This property was bought at that time for ninety-five thousand rubles. My father spent only seventy thousand, thereby retaining a debt of twenty-five thousand. Now, listen . . . this property would never have been bought if I hadn't given up my share of the inheritance in favor of my sister, whom I loved. And besides that, I worked ten years like a beast of burden and I paid off my debt entirely.

ORLOVSKI. What do you want, my friend?

VOINITSKY. There is no mortgage on the property, and if everything is in good order it is due entirely to my own personal efforts. And now that I am old, they want to take me by the neck and throw me out.

SEREBRYAKOV. I don't understand what you're getting at.

VOINITSKY. For twenty-five years I've administered this property. I worked, I sent you the money like the most conscientious of stewards; and during all this time you have not thanked me once; during all this time—when I was young, and even now, you granted me—you granted me five hundred rubles a year; a starvation wage. And not once did the idea enter your head to give me a higher salary, not even one single ruble!

SEREBRYAKOV. George, how could I guess . . . I'm not a practical man. I don't understand these things. You could have raised your wages yourself as much as you liked.

VOINITSKY. Why didn't I steal? Why didn't you all scorn me for not having stolen? It would only have been just, and today I wouldn't be a beggar!

MARYA (severely). George!

DYADIN (unnerved). George, you mustn't! You mustn't! I'm upset. . . . Why poison good relations? (He embraces him.) You mustn't. . . .

VOINITSKY. For twenty-five years I remained with this mother of mine, shut in between four walls, like a rat. . . . All our thoughts, all our feelings belonged to you alone. In the daytime we spoke of you, of your work; we were proud of your fame, we pronounced your name with respect; and our nights were spent reading magazines and books which I now despise with all my being.

DYADIN. You mustn't, George, you mustn't. . . . I cannot . . .

SEREBRYAKOV. I don't understand what you want.

VOINITSKY. You were for us a being with a superior nature, and we knew your articles by heart. . . . But now my eyes are opened. I see everything! You write about art, but you don't understand anything about it! All your work, that I loved so much, isn't worth a kopeck!

SEREBRYAKOV. My friends, make him keep quiet! Please! I'm going!

ELENA. George, shut up, I insist! Do you hear?

VOINITSKY. I will not keep quiet. (*Barring* SEREBRYAKOV's *way.*) One moment, I'm not finished! You have destroyed my life. I have not lived, not lived! Because of you I have spoiled and annihilated the best years of my life. You are my worst enemy!

DYADIN. I cannot . . . I cannot . . . I'm going into another room! (*Very upset, he exits by the door at stage right.*)

SEREBRYAKOV. What do you want of me? And what right do you have to speak to me in that tone? Nonentity! If this property belongs to you, take it; I have nothing more to do with it.

ZHELTOUKHIN (*aside*). What a state of affairs! I'm going! (*He goes out.*)

ELENA. If you don't shut up, I'll leave this hell this very instant. (*She shouts.*) I can't stand it any longer. . . .

VOINITSKY. My life is lost! I had talent, intelligence, audacity. . . . If I had lived a normal life, I would perhaps have become a Schopenhauer or a Dostoyevsky. . . . But I'm digressing! I'm losing my mind! . . . Mama, I'm a desperate man! Mama!

MARYA. Obey the professor.

VOINITSKY. Mama, what shall we do? No, don't say anything, it's useless. I know what I must do! (*To* SEREBRYAKOV.) You'll remember me! (*He goes out by the middle door,* MARYA *following him.*)

SEREBRYAKOV. Gentlemen, what is happening? Get me away from this lunatic!

ORLOVSKI. It's nothing, it's nothing, Sasha! Let him calm down. Don't unnerve him any more.

SEREBRYAKOV. I cannot live under the same roof with him. He lives here . . . (*He points to the middle door.*) almost at my very side. Let him move, let him go to the village or to the annex, or I'll go. I cannot remain if he is here. . . .

ELENA (*to her husband*). If you're going to continue making these scenes, *I* will go.

SEREBRYAKOV. Don't try to frighten me, please!

ELENA. I am not trying to frighten you, but it's as if all of you had conspired to make my life a hell. . . . I'm going!

SEREBRYAKOV. Everybody knows perfectly well that you are young, that I am old, and that you are giving proof of great devotion by living here with me!

ELENA. Keep it up! Keep it up!

ORLOVSKI. Come, come! My friends!

KRUSHCHOV (*enters suddenly. Agitated*). I am very glad to find you at home, Professor. . . . Excuse me, I may not have come at the best moment, and I am perhaps disturbing you . . . but that's neither here nor there. . . . Good afternoon. . . .

SEREBRYAKOV. What do you want?

KRUSHCHOV. Excuse me, I'm upset. . . . I rode a little too fast . . . a while ago. . . . Professor, I heard that you sold your forest for timber to Kouznetsov two days ago. If that is true, and not just hearsay . . . then, I ask you not to do it. . . .

ELENA. Michael, my husband is not disposed at the moment to speak of business matters. Come to the garden.

KRUSHCHOV. But I must talk to him immediately!

ELENA. As you wish, but I cannot . . . (*She goes out.*)

KRUSHCHOV. Allow me to go to Kouznetsov and tell him

that you've thought it over . . . and changed your mind. . . . May I? Will you allow me to do that? To cut down thousands of trees, to destroy them for two to three thousand years, and all for a few rags, whims, sumptuous display . . . to annihilate them, so that those who come after, posterity, may curse your barbarism! If you, a cultivated, famous man, decide to do such a cruel thing, then what will people do who are much inferior to you? It's terrible!

ORLOVSKI. Michael, we'll talk about that later.

SEREBRYAKOV. Let's go, Ivan, there's no reason to hope that this will cease.

KRUSHCHOV (barring SEREBRYAKOV's way). In that case, this is what I have to say to you, Professor: wait; in two or three months I will receive money, and I'll buy it from you myself.

ORLOVSKI. Excuse me, Michael, but this is rather unusual. . . . You're a worthy, honorable gentleman, and we have great respect for you. (He bows.) But why make such a row?

KRUSHCHOV (boiling mad). Godfather of the whole human race! There are many benevolent people in the world, and they always seem to suspect me. They are only benevolent because they are . . . indifferent!

ORLOVSKI. Well, my dear, you've come here to pick a quarrel! That's not good! An idea is an idea, but, brother dear, one must have a little of this— (He indicates his heart.) Without this, my dear, your forests and your peat bogs aren't worth a kopeck. . . . Don't be offended, but you are still a greenhorn, what a greenhorn!

SEREBRYAKOV (cutting him short). Next time, please have yourself announced before coming in, and I beg of you to spare me your extravagant nature. You all want to put me out; well, you have succeeded! Please leave me alone. In all your forests and your peat bogs, I see only delirium and psychopathic behavior. That is my opinion. Come, Ivan. (He goes out.)

ORLOVSKI (*following him*). That's too much, Sasha! Why are you being so harsh? (*He goes out.*)

KRUSHCHOV (*alone, after a pause*). Delirium, psychopathic behavior . . . that means that according to the celebrated and erudite professor, I am only a madman. . . . I bow before the prestige of Your Excellency and I am going home immediately . . . to shave my head. No, no, it's the earth that's mad to think of supporting you any longer.

(*He goes toward the door at stage right; SOFIA runs in by the door at stage left; hidden behind the door, she has listened to the whole scene.*)

SOFIA. Wait! I heard everything. . . . Speak to me! Speak, or . . . I won't be able to hold myself back . . . and I'll be the one to speak first.

KRUSHCHOV. Sofia, I have already said everything I had to say. I begged your father to spare his forest and I was right to do so; but he offended me, he treated me like a madman. . . . I, mad!

SOFIA. That's enough! Enough!

KRUSHCHOV. Yes, those who succeed in passing off their indifference to life as wisdom—they're not mad; not mad, those who marry old men with the sole purpose of deceiving them publicly . . . and buying fashionable dresses with the money gotten from cut-down, destroyed forests!

SOFIA. Listen to me, listen to me. . . . (*She squeezes his hand.*) Let me tell you . . .

KRUSHCHOV. Let's end it all! I'm a stranger to you. I already know your opinion of me. I have nothing more to do here. Farewell. I'm sorry that after the brief but pleasant relations we've had, that all I will have to remember will be your father's gout and your opinion of my democratic tendencies. But the fault is not mine . . . not mine . . .

(*SOFIA cries, covers her face with her hands, and goes out very quickly by the door at left.*)

I had the foolishness to fall in love here; let that be a lesson to me! Let's go, let's get out of this tomb!

(*He goes toward the door at right;* ELENA *enters from the door at left.*)

ELENA. You're still here! Wait! A moment ago Ivan told me that my husband spoke to you harshly. Excuse him, he is in bad humor today, and he didn't understand you. . . . I feel very close to you, Michael. Please believe in my sincere esteem for you. I sympathize; I am moved. Please allow me to offer you my sincere friendship. (*She holds out her two hands.*)

KRUSHCHOV (*with disgust*). Get away . . . I scorn your friendship. (*He goes out.*)

ELENA (*alone, trembling*). Why? Why?

(*A shot rings out from behind the stage.* MARYA *arrives panting at the middle door, screams, and faints.* SOFIA *enters and runs out again through the middle door.* SEREBRYAKOV, ORLOVSKI, *and* ZHELTOUKHIN *can be heard outside.*)

EVERYONE. What's happened?

SOFIA (*can be heard lamenting; she comes back in and cries out*). Uncle George has shot himself!

(SOFIA, ORLOVSKI, SEREBRYAKOV, *and* ZHELTOUKHIN *run in and out.*)

ELENA (*trembling*). Why? Why?

DYADIN (*appears at the right. At the door*). What's happened?

ELENA (*to* DYADIN). Get me out of here! Cast me into the darkness, kill me, but I can't remain here any longer! Quick, help me! (*She goes out with* DYADIN).

(*The curtain falls on a stage empty of everyone but the unconscious* MARYA.)

JULIA (*alone*). He's probably sleeping. (*She sits down on the bench in front of the window and heaves a big sigh.*) Some sleep, others walk about, while all day long I torture myself, I torture myself. There's no rest for the weary. (*She sighs deeper yet.*) Lord, how is it that there are people in the world as stupid as Waffles? I passed by his warehouse just now and a little black pig came out of it. . . . He'll see, the pigs will eat up all the sacks of grain—and they don't even belong to him!

DYADIN (*enters*). Ah, it's you, Julia! Excuse my simple attire; I wanted to abandon myself a little to the arms of Morpheus.

JULIA. Good day, Waffles.

DYADIN. Pardon me for not inviting you in. There is such a disorder in my rooms, et cetera. . . . Would you like to come to the mill?

JULIA. I can stay right here. Waffles, Leonid and the professor are organizing a little picnic just for a little distraction . . . they'd like to come and have tea at the mill with you. . . .

DYADIN. An excellent idea!

JULIA. I came ahead to ask. They'll be here any moment now. Have the servants put a table right here, and a samovar, of course. . . . Also, tell Semyon to take my basket of provisions out of the carriage.

DYADIN. All that is feasible. (*Pause.*) And how is everything up at your place?

JULIA. Not good, Waffles. So many troubles. Even I have become ill over it all. You know, of course, that the professor and Sofia are living with us now?

DYADIN. I know.

JULIA. Since George put an end to his life, they haven't been able to live in their house any more. They're afraid. Not in the daytime, but when evening comes they gather together in the same room and sit up till dawn. They're all afraid. George might come back to them in the darkness.

DYADIN. They are superstitious! . . . And do they think of Elena?

JULIA. Of course, they think of her. (*Pause.*) She's run away.

DYADIN. It's a subject worthy of Aivazovki's brush. The desire to run away took possession of her, and . . . she ran away.

JULIA. Nobody knows where she is. . . . Perhaps she went far away, and perhaps, in despair . . .

DYADIN. God is merciful, Julia! Everything will be for the best!

KRUSHCHOV (*enters, carrying a portfolio and the box containing his materials. Looking in the other direction*). Anyone home? Semyon?

DYADIN. Look in another direction.

KRUSHCHOV. Ah, good afternoon, Julia.

JULIA. Good afternoon, Michael!

KRUSHCHOV. Here I am, Ilya. Here to do some work at your place again. I couldn't stay at home. Please give the order to put the table under this tree, as you did yesterday; and tell them to bring two lamps; the sun is setting.

DYADIN. At your orders, Your Excellency!

KRUSHCHOV. How are things, Julia?

JULIA. Not so good. (*Pause.*)

KRUSHCHOV. Are the Serebryakovs living at your place?

JULIA. They are.

KRUSHCHOV. Ah! and what is Leonid doing?

JULIA. He spends most of his time in the house. With Sofia.

KRUSHCHOV. I should think so. (*Pause.*) He ought to marry her.

JULIA (*sighing*). May God grant it! He is a cultivated man, an aristocrat; she comes from a good family as well. . . . I always hoped that he . . .

KRUSHCHOV. She's a dull creature!

JULIA. Don't say that!

KRUSHCHOV. And your Leonid takes the prize. All of your circle is the same. Each as clever as the next. Witty to their fingertips!

JULIA. Perhaps you got up on the wrong side of the bed today?

KRUSHCHOV. What makes you think that?

JULIA. Your bad humor.

(DYADIN *and* SEMYON *enter, carrying a medium-sized table.*)

DYADIN. At least you're not in a bad humor, Michael. You've found a magnificent place to work! It's an . . . oasis! That's it, an oasis! Imagine the trees all around to be palms, Julia is a gentle doe, you are a lion. . . . I am a tiger . . .

KRUSHCHOV. Ilya, you are a good and sensitive man, but what manners you have! All your insipid conversation, and clicking your heels, shrugging your shoulders! . . . If somebody were to observe you from afar, God knows what they'd take you for, certainly not a man! . . . Really, you're quite annoying!

DYADIN. In other words, it is my inevitable fate . . . it is written that . . .

KRUSHCHOV. There you are again . . . inevitable fate. . . .

Stop that kind of talk! (*He attaches his drawing to the table.*) I'm going to spend the night here.

DYADIN. That makes me very happy! You've done it, you've made me angry, Michael! But what of it? My soul remains nonetheless indescribably happy! One might say that a little bird is lodged in my chest and chirps its little plaint inside!

KRUSHCHOV. Well then, rejoice! (*Pause.*) You may have a little bird in your chest, but I have a toad! Twenty thousand scandals, Waffles! Shimanski has sold his forest for timber, that's number one; Elena is gone and no one knows where she is, that's number two; I feel I am becoming more and more stupid, petty, and useless with each day . . . that's number three! Yesterday, I meant to tell you, but I couldn't, I lacked the courage. . . . Congratulate me! The deceased left a journal; which journal, a few days after George's death, fell into Orlovski's hands; and as I was there, I read it . . . about a dozen times.

JULIA. They read it at our house, too.

KRUSHCHOV. The romance of George and Elena, gloated over by the entire district, was revealed to be nothing but a filthy, vile piece of gossip; and I believed in that gossip, and with the others I spread the slander, I hated, I scorned, I offended. . . .

DYADIN. That was not a nice thing to do.

KRUSHCHOV. The first person I talked to was your brother, Julia. That was the thing to do! I took your brother, for whom I have no respect, into my confidence; and this poor woman was sacrificing herself under my very nose. I believe in evil more easily than in good; I don't see any further than the end of my nose. In other words, I am a nonentity, like everybody else!

DYADIN (*to* JULIA). Come to the mill, my child. Let the bad man work here alone, we'll go walking. . . . Work, work, Michael! (*He goes out with* JULIA.)

KRUSHCHOV (*alone, thinning color in a saucer*). One evening I saw him lean his face toward Elena's hand. In his journal, he recounts that evening in detail; he describes my arrival, what I said to him. He quotes me and treats me like an idiot, says I am a bundle of prejudices. (*Pause.*) This color's too dark; I must lighten it. . . ." Further on, he scolds Sofia because she loved me. She never loved me. . . . (*His brush slips.*) I've smeared it. . . . (*He scrapes the paper with his knife.*) And even admitting there were some truth to it, we must put it out of our minds. It began stupidly and it ended stupidly.

(SEMYON *and another worker bring a large table.*)

What's that for?

SEMYON. We were told to bring it. The ladies and gentlemen are coming from the Zheltoukhin place to have tea.

KRUSHCHOV. Thank you! That means I'll have to interrupt my work. I'll gather all this up and go into the house.

(SOFIA *and* ZHELTOUKHIN *enter arm in arm.*)

ZHELTOUKHIN (*singing*). "Without knowing why, toward these sad shores / a mysterious force attracts me . . ."

KRUSHCHOV. Who's there? Ah! (*He hurries to arrange the material in his box.*)

ZHELTOUKHIN. One more question, Sofia dear. Do you remember? You were lunching at our house the day of my birthday. Something about the way I looked made you burst into laughter! Didn't it?

SOFIA. Leonid, how can you say such things? I laughed for no reason at all.

ZHELTOUKHIN (*seeing* KRUSHCHOV). Ah, what do I see? You here, too? Good afternoon!

KRUSHCHOV. Good afternoon.

ZHELTOUKHIN. Are you working? Perfect! Where is Waffles?

KRUSHCHOV. Down there.

ZHELTOUKHIN. Where, down there?

KRUSHCHOV. I thought it was quite clear. Down there, in the mill!

ZHELTOUKHIN. I'll go get him. (*He goes out humming.*) "Without knowing why, these sad shores . . ."

SOFIA. Good afternoon.

KRUSHCHOV. Good afternoon.

SOFIA. What are you drawing?

KRUSHCHOV. Nothing . . . it's of no interest.

SOFIA. A sketch?

KRUSHCHOV. No, the forestry map of our district. I myself surveyed it. The green color represents the places where there were forests in our grandparents' days and before that; the light green represents the forests which have been cut down in the last twenty-five years, and the light blue, the forests which still remain intact . . . yes . . . (*Pause.*) And you? Are you happy?

SOFIA. This is not the time to think of happiness, Michael.

KRUSHCHOV. Then what should we think about?

SOFIA. Our unhappiness came about only because we thought too much about happiness.

KRUSHCHOV. Oh, is that so! (*Pause.*)

SOFIA. It's an ill wind that blows nobody good. Unhappiness has taught me a great deal. Michael, one must forget one's happiness and think only of the happiness of others. All of life must be made up of sacrifices.

KRUSHCHOV. Yes, yes. . . . (*Pause.*) Marya Voinitsky's son shot a bullet through his head, and she still searches for contradictions in her pamphlets. A terrible thing happens to you, and you satisfy your vanity: you seek to distort your life and you think you are making sacrifices. Everyone is heartless, even you and I. We do exactly the opposite of what we should do, and our lives disintegrate into dust. I will go away now and not bother you any more, you and Zheltoukhin. . . . Why are you crying? I didn't want to make you cry.

SOFIA. It's nothing, nothing. . . . (*She wipes her eyes.*)

(JULIA, DYADIN, *and* ZHELTOUKHIN *come in together. The voice of* SEREBRYAKOV *is heard nearby.*)

VOICE OF SEREBRYAKOV. Hoo-ooo! Where are you, my friends?

SOFIA (*crying out*). Here, Papa!

DYADIN. They're bringing the samovar! Wonderful!

(JULIA *and* DYADIN *busy themselves with the table.* SEREBRYAKOV *enters with* ORLOVSKI.)

SOFIA. Here, Papa!

SEREBRYAKOV. I see you. . . .

ZHELTOUKHIN (*in a very loud voice*). Gentlemen, I declare the session opened! Waffles, uncork the liqueur bottles!

KRUSHCHOV (*to* SEREBRYAKOV). Professor, please forget everything that has passed between us. (*He holds out his hand.*) I beg your pardon.

SEREBRYAKOV. Thank you. Most gladly. You also: pardon me. The day after this incident, when I tried to reflect on everything that had happened, and I remembered our conversation, I felt a very disagreeable sensation indeed. . . . Let us be friends, henceforth! (*He takes* KRUSHCHOV *by the arm and leads him to the table.*)

ORLOVSKI. Things ought to have been like this for a long time now, my dear. A bad peace is much better than a good quarrel.

DYADIN. Excellency, I am so happy that you have deigned to come to my oasis. It's pleasant here, indescribably pleasant!

SEREBRYAKOV. Thank you, my dear Ilya Dyadin. It is a pleasant place. One feels it. It is exactly what you call it, an oasis.

ORLOVSKI. Do you like nature, Sasha?

SEREBRYAKOV. Infinitely. (*Pause.*) Let us not remain silent, my friends, let us talk. In the situation in which we find ourselves, that is best. One must look adversity straight in the face, courageously. I look at it more like a man, because I am unhappier than all of you.

JULIA. My friends, I won't put any sugar in; take it with some jam.

DYADIN (*busying himself with the guests*). Oh, I'm so happy! So happy!

SEREBRYAKOV. In these last weeks, Michael, I have undergone many trials and I have reflected in such great measure that I believe I could write a treatise on the way in which one must live—for the edification of posterity. You may live a century: it is only unhappiness that teaches you.

DYADIN. "He who remembers the past will have his eyes put out." God is merciful, and everything will turn out for the best.

(SOFIA *shudders.*)

ZHELTOUKHIN. Why did you shudder?

SOFIA. Someone cried out.

DYADIN. It's probably the peasants fishing crayfish in the river. (*Pause.*)

ZHELTOUKHIN. But we decided to spend the evening as if nothing had happened, gentlemen. . . . Yet there's a feeling of tension in the air. . . .

DYADIN. Excellency, my feeling for science is not just veneration, but a sentiment which is . . . familial. The brother of the wife of my brother Grigori Ilich—perhaps you know him—Konstantine Gavrilovich Novosyolov—was a professor of foreign literature.

SEREBRYAKOV. I didn't know him personally, but I have heard of him. (*Pause.*)

JULIA. It will be two weeks tomorrow that George is dead.

KRUSHCHOV. Let's not talk about that, Julia!

SEREBRYAKOV. Courage, courage! (*Pause.*)

ZHELTOUKHIN. All the same, there's a tension in the air. . . .

SEREBRYAKOV. Nature has a horror of the void. She has deprived me of two close friends, and to compensate for this desertion, she has immediately sent me new friends. I drink to your health, Leonid!

ZHELTOUKHIN. Thank you, dear Alexander. And let me be the first to drink to your productive intellectual endeavors. "Sow wisdom, goodness, *éternité*! / Sow! Sow! . . . Thank you, the Russian people will say to you / most cordially."

SEREBRYAKOV. I appreciate the compliment, and wish with all my heart that the time may come when our friendly relations will be transmuted into even more intimate relationships.

FYODOR (*enters*). There we are: a picnic!

ORLOVSKI. My boy! My beauty!

FYODOR. How do you do.

(SOFIA, JULIA, *and* FYODOR *embrace*.)

ORLOVSKI. We haven't seen each other for two entire weeks. Where were you? What have you been up to?

FYODOR. I was at Leonid's place. They told me you were up here—so I came by.

ORLOVSKI. Where have you been hiding yourself?

FYODOR. I haven't slept for three nights— Yesterday, Papa, I lost five thousand at cards. . . . And I've been drinking, playing cards. . . . I went into town at least five times. . . . I was in one of my moods. . . .

ORLOVSKI. Ah, youth! And now you're drunk?

FYODOR. Not in the least. Juliet, some tea! With lemon, as acid as possible. . . . George! That one! Without rhyme or reason, he goes *kkkkk!* right in the forehead! And with what does he do it? With a Lefauché! As if he couldn't have used a Smith and Wesson!

KRUSHCHOV. Shut up, you brute!

FYODOR. Brute perhaps, but thoroughbred brute! (*Caressing his beard.*) What a beard! Yes, I am a brute, an imbecile, a scoundrel—but if I so much as look at a girl, she consents to become my fiancée! Sofia, marry me! (*To* KRUSHCHOV.) Oh, my apologies!

KRUSHCHOV. Stop playing the idiot!

JULIA. You're a lost creature, Fyodor. There's not another drunkard or wastrel in the province like you. If I look at you it's enough to make me sick; it's agonizing!

FYODOR. There she goes! Come over here and sit beside me. . . . Yes, like this. I'll come and spend two weeks with you. One must rest. (*He kisses her.*)

JULIA. I'm ashamed for you in front of everybody. You ought to be a consolation to your father in his old age, and all you do is dishonor him. A stupid life, worthless!

FYODOR. No more drinking. Truce. (*He pours some liquor out.*) Is that plum or cherry liqueur?

JULIA. Don't drink! Now don't drink!

FYODOR. A little glass; one has the right to that. . . . (*He drinks.*) Wood Demon, I'm going to make you a gift of a pair of horses and a gun. I'll go to live with Julia. I'll spend about two weeks here.

KRUSHCHOV. You should be put in a stockade.

JULIA. Drink. Drink your tea.

DYADIN. Take some biscuits, Fyodor!

ORLOVSKI (*to* SEREBRYAKOV). As for me, my dear Sasha, I led the same life as my Fyodor until my fortieth year. Once, my dear, I set out to figure up the number of women I had made unhappy in my time. I counted and counted, and when I arrived at a total of seventy, I gave up. Well, when I turned forty, something suddenly happened to me. A sadness threatened to envelop me. I didn't know what to do with myself. I went hither and thither, I read books, I worked, I traveled—nothing would help. And one day, my dear, I went to visit my dear departed friend Dimitri Pavlovich. We dined together . . . and after dinner, in order not to go to bed, we decided to practice marksmanship in the courtyard. There was quite a crowd assembled; our friend Waffles was also there . . .

DYADIN. I was there, I was there . . . I remember!

ORLOVSKI. I felt sad, infinitely sad; it was unbearable. Then, suddenly, tears flowed from my eyes. I staggered. I cried out with all my strength: "My friends, good people, pardon me, in the name of Jesus Christ our Lord!" At that very instant, I felt a great warmth envelop my soul; I knew that everything was now peaceful and pure. And since that time, my friend, there is not a happier man in this district than I. (*Pause.*) Well, you must do the same.

(*A reddish glow from a fire lights up the sky.*)

SEREBRYAKOV. Do what?

ORLOVSKI. Well, the same thing, you must give in.

SEREBRYAKOV. Now there is a sample of your native . . .

philosophy! You urge me to ask forgiveness, but for what? Let them ask for my forgiveness!

SOFIA. But Papa, we're the ones at fault.

SEREBRYAKOV. Really? My friends, you are probably thinking at this present moment of my relationship with my wife. Do you really think that I am at fault? You know, the whole thing is really quite comical, my friends? She has neglected her duty by abandoning me at a particularly difficult moment.

KRUSHCHOV. Listen to me, Professor. You have served science for twenty years; you have been a professor for twenty years. I plant forests and occupy myself with medicine, but why—for whom do we do these things—if we do not spare those in whose interest we are working? We pretend to serve mankind and at the same time we destroy one another in a manner which is completely inhuman. Did we, for example, you and I, do something to save George? Where is your wife whom we have all offended? Is your daughter happy? Where is your own peace of mind? Everything is finished, destroyed, disintegrated into dust. My friends, you call me the Wood Demon, and yet I am not the only one who deserves that name: in each one of you there is a "wood demon"; all of you are wandering about in a dark forest, groping your way. Your intelligence, knowledge, and hearts serve only to ruin your lives and those of everyone else.

(ELENA *comes out of the house and sits on the bench in front of the window. No one sees her.*)

I thought I was a man of principles, filled with humanity, and yet I never pardoned anyone the slightest lapse. I put faith in slander, I joined with everyone—and when, for example, your wife offered me her friendship in all sincerity, I shouted down at her from the height of my noble character: "Get away from me; I despise your friendship!" That is what I am like! There is a demon inside of me. I am petty, devoid of talent, blind; but you are not an eagle either, Professor. And yet the whole district, all the women—see me as a hero, a man of progress; and you are celebrated in all of Russia. But if one really takes men of my kind to be heroes, and if men like you are truly celebrated, that just means that in the last analysis no true heroes exist—no geniuses, no men to lead us out of this dark forest, to repair what we spoil; there are no true eagles deserving of their honorable reputations. . . .

SEREBRYAKOV. You will excuse me! I did not come here to engage in polemics with you and to defend my right to fame!

ZHELTOUKHIN. Michael, let's stop this conversation!

KRUSHCHOV. I will stop it right away, and I'm going. Yes, I am petty; but you, Professor, I repeat, you're not an eagle, either. George was petty, too, but he didn't find anything better to do than put a bullet through his head. Everybody is petty! And as for the women . . .

ELENA (interrupting him). As for the women, they're not much better. (She comes over to the table.) Elena left her husband, but do you think she made sensible use of her freedom? No, don't worry, she'll come back. (Sits down at the table.) She has already returned.

(General confusion.)

DYADIN (laughing madly). It's wonderful! Gentlemen, don't blame me! Let me say just one word, only one: Excellency, it is I who abducted your wife, just as a certain Paris once abducted the beauteous Helen! I! Although there aren't any Parises in the world with pockmarked faces, there are more things in heaven and earth . . .

KRUSHCHOV. I don't understand any of this . . . is that really you, Elena?

ELENA. I've been spending two weeks at Ilya's house . . . Why are you all looking at me that way? Well, how do you do. . . . I was seated at the window and I heard everything. (Hugging SOFIA.) Let's make peace! Hello, dear girl. . . . Peace and harmony!

DYADIN (rubbing his hands). It's wonderful!

ELENA (to KRUSHCHOV). Good afternoon, Michael. (*She holds out her hand.*) He who remembers the past will have his eyes put out. . . . Good afternoon, Fyodor. . . . Julia!

ORLOVSKI. My dear, our "professor's wife," our lovable, beautiful— She has come back; she has come back to us!

ELENA. I missed you all. Good afternoon, Alexander. (*She holds out her hand to her husband, but he turns away.*) Alexander!

SEREBRYAKOV. You have neglected your duty.

ELENA. Alexander!

SEREBRYAKOV. I am not hiding it; I am very happy to see you and to speak with you, but not here; at home. (*He goes away from the table.*)

ORLOVSKI. Sasha! (*Pause.*)

ELENA. Good . . . that means, Alexander, that our problem is very simply resolved; that is to say, not at all. Well, it was meant to be this way. I am a passing figure, my happiness is that of a canary, the happiness of a good little woman . . . stay shut up all your life in the house, eat, drink, sleep, and listen to him speak about his gout every day, about his rights, his talent. Why are you all lowering your heads as if you were embarrassed? Come, let's drink some liqueur; why not?

DYADIN. Everything will be all right, it will all be patched up; everything for the best!

FYODOR (*agitated. Coming over to* SEREBRYAKOV). Professor, I am very touched. . . . I beg of you, be kind to your wife, say something to her, be it only a good word. If you do, I promise you my friendship for life. I will make you a present of my best troika.

SEREBRYAKOV. I thank you, but excuse me, I do not understand why.

FYODOR. Hmmm! You don't understand me. . . . Once I was returning from a hunt and I saw a great horned owl sitting on a tree. I aimed at him and I fired birdshot. There he was sitting. . . . I aim, I fire, I aim, I fire, I aim, I fire, nine times! and he's still sitting there. . . . Nothing reaches him! He just sits there and blinks. . . .

SEREBRYAKOV To what are you referring?

FYODOR. To a great horned owl! (*He comes back to the table.*)

ORLOVSKI (*listening attentively*). Gentlemen, please! Quiet, please . . . an alarm is being sounded somewhere. . . .

FYODOR (*who suddenly notices the glow in the sky*). Oh! Oh! Oh! Look up at the sky! What a glow!

ORLOVSKI. Lord! We've been sitting here and we can't see anything.

DYADIN. That's something!

FYODOR. Ta-ta-ta! We're having an illumination! It's coming from Alexeyevsk.

KRUSHCHOV. No, Alexeyevsk is further right. It's from Novopetrovsk.

JULIA. It's terrible! I'm so afraid of fires!

KRUSHCHOV. Of course, it's at Novopetrovsk!

DYADIN (*shouting*). Semyon, run to the breakwater and see what's burning. From there, you can most likely see . . .

SEMYON (*shouting*). It's the forest of Telibyevsk that's burning!

DYADIN. What?

SEMYON. The forest of Telibyevsk!

DYADIN. The forest . . . (*Long pause.*)

KRUSHCHOV. I must go down there where the fire is. Farewell. Pardon me if I am abrupt but I am overcome with grief today. My heart is heavy. . . . But it isn't that bad. One must be a man and stand firmly on one's two feet. I won't put a bullet through my head and I won't throw myself under the wheels of the mill. . . . Very well then, I am not a hero, but I shall become one! I'll grow eagle's wings, and neither the heat of the fire nor the devil in person will frighten me. Let the forests burn, it's of little importance since I'll plant new ones. It doesn't matter if she doesn't love me, I'll love another! (*He goes out rapidly.*)

ELENA. How brave he is!

ORLOVSKI. Yes. (*Pause.*) "If she doesn't love me, I'll love another!" How are we to take that?

SOFIA. Take me away from here. I want to go home.

SEREBRYAKOV. Yes, it's time to go home. The humidity is unbearable. . . . I must have left my footwarmer and my overcoat somewhere.

ZHELTOUKHIN. My footwarmer is in the carriage; here is the overcoat. (*He hands* SEREBRYAKOV *the overcoat.*)

SOFIA (*very nervous*). Take me away from here . . . take me away from here.

ZHELTOUKHIN. Yes, yes.

SOFIA. No, I'll go with Godfather. Take me with you, Godfather.

ORLOVSKI. Let's go, my dear; let's go then. (*He helps the* PROFESSOR *to put on his coat.*)

ZHELTOUKHIN (*aside*). Devil take it . . . nothing but humiliation and despicable actions. . . .

(FYODOR *and* JULIA *arrange the dishes and the napkins in the basket.*)

SEREBRYAKOV. The sole of my left foot hurts me. Rheumatism, no doubt. . . . I won't be able to sleep a wink all night again. . . .

ELENA (*buttoning her husband's coat*). Dear Waffles, will you please bring my cape from the house.

DYADIN. Right away! (*He enters the house and comes out again with the cape.*)

ORLOVSKI. Did the glow from the fire frighten you, my dear? Don't be frightened, it's already dying down. The fire is going out, little by little.

JULIA. There's a half a pot of cornelberry preserves. . . . Well, it will be for Waffles. (*To her brother.*) Leonid, take the basket.

ELENA. I'm ready. (*To her husband.*) Well, take me, my Commander's statue, and disappear with me into your twenty-six dreary rooms. That's where I must of course go.

SEREBRYAKOV. The statue of the Commander. . . . I would laugh at that comparison if the pain in my foot weren't preventing me. (*To everybody.*) Farewell, my friends. Thank you for the invitation and for your pleasant company. . . . A magnificent evening, delicious tea. . . . Everything is perfect, but, excuse me, there is one thing I cannot accept: your "native" philosophy and your way of looking at life. One must do something, my friends, work! One cannot remain like this . . . one must do something. . . . Oh yes . . . farewell! (*He goes out with his wife.*)

FYODOR. Let's go, Long Pants! (*To his father.*) Farewell, Papa! (*He goes out with Julia.*)

ZHELTOUKHIN (*following them basket in hand*). This basket is heavy! Devil take it! I can't abide these picnics!

(*He goes off shouting in the wings.*) Semyon, bring the horses!

ORLOVSKI (*to* SOFIA). Well, why are you sitting there? Come, my pet! (*He comes to her.*)

DYADIN (*aside*). Nobody is saying good-by to me! It's remarkable! (*He extinguishes the candles.*)

ORLOVSKI (*to* SOFIA). What's the matter?

SOFIA. I can't go away, Godfather. I can't. . . . I'm desperate, Godfather, desperate . . . my heart is too heavy!

ORLOVSKI (*uneasy*). What is it? What's the matter? My darling, my pretty girl . . .

SOFIA. Let's stay. . . . Let's stay here a little while.

ORLOVSKI. "Take me away," "Let's stay" . . . I can't make you out!

SOFIA. I lost my happiness here today. I can't— Oh, Godfather, why am I still alive? (*She hugs him.*) If you knew, if you only knew!

ORLOVSKI. You need some water. Let's sit down . . . or . . .

DYADIN. What's the matter, Sofia, my dear friend. . . . I cannot, I'm all atremble. . . . (*Tearfully.*) I can't see you like this . . . my child. . . .

SOFIA. Waffles, my friend, take me to see the fire, please!

ORLOVSKI. But why do you need to see the fire? What will you do down there?

SOFIA. Take me, please, or else I'll go by myself. . . . I'm desperate. Godfather, I'm desperate, my heart is so heavy; it's unbearable! Take me to see the fire.

KRUSHCHOV (*enters rapidly, shouting*). Waffles!

DYADIN. Yes. What do you want?

KRUSHCHOV. I can't go on foot. Give me a horse!

SOFIA (*recognizing* KRUSHCHOV, *shouting joyously*). Michael! (*She goes toward him.*) Michael! (*To* ORLOVSKI.) Go away, Godfather. I must speak to him. (*To* KRUSHCHOV.) Michael, you said that you would love another. . . . (*To* ORLOVSKI.) Go away, Godfather. (*To* KRUSHCHOV.) I am another, now. I only want the truth. . . . Nothing, nothing, nothing but the truth. I love, I love you . . . love . . .

ORLOVSKI. What a story! (*He bursts out laughing.*)

DYADIN. It's remarkable!

SOFIA (*to* ORLOVSKI). Go away, Godfather! (*To* KRUSHCHOV.) Yes, the truth, nothing else. . . . Speak to me, speak. . . . I've said everything I . . . !

KRUSHCHOV (*embracing her*). My darling!

SOFIA (*to* KRUSHCHOV). Don't go away now, Godfather. Each time you made declarations to me, I choked up with joy, but I was paralyzed by my prejudices. I was prevented from telling you the truth just as my father was prevented from smiling at Elena. Now, I'm free . . .

ORLOVSKI (*laughing wildly*). Together at last! Well, you've made it up between you, finally. You've done it! I have the honor of congratulating you. (*Bowing low.*) The shameless creatures! The shameless creatures! They were dawdling, hanging on to each other . . .

DYADIN (*embracing* KRUSHCHOV). Michael, my dear, how happy you make me! Misha!

ORLOVSKI (*hugging and kissing* SOFIA). My pet, my little canary . . . my little goddaughter . . .

(SOFIA *bursts out laughing.*)

Now she's off!

KRUSHCHOV. I don't understand any of this. . . . Let me . . . speak to her a little . . . don't bother us . . . please, go!

(JULIA *and* FYODOR *are entering but do not see the others.*)

JULIA. You're lying, Fyodor. Listen to me, you're lying! That's all you're doing, lying!

ORLOVSKI. Shhhhh! Not so loud, my children! There's my brigand down there, coming this way. Let us hide, my friends! Faster, come!

(ORLOVSKI, DYADIN, KRUSHCHOV, *and* SOFIA *hide.*)

FYODOR. I forgot my whip and a glove.

JULIA. You're just lying!

FYODOR. Very well, then, I'm lying. What of it? I don't want to go to your house now. Let's walk for awhile. Then we'll go.

JULIA. You are a trouble! A punishment! (*Raising her arms up to the sky.*) What an imbecile that Waffles is! He still hasn't cleared the table. Look, the samovar could have been stolen! . . . Oh, that Waffles! that Waffles! The older he gets, the more unreasonable he becomes . . . like a child.

DYADIN. I thank you humbly.

JULIA. I thought I heard something.

FYODOR. Peasants swimming, no doubt. (*Picking up his glove.*) Here it is, one glove . . . Sofia's. . . . Today, I thought she acted as if she had been bitten by a bug. That Sofia! She's in love with the Wood Demon. She's head over heels in love . . . and he, that dolt, doesn't see anything!

JULIA (*angry*). Where are we going?

FYODOR. To the breakwater. . . . Let's go walking. There's no better place in all the district. It's very beautiful there.

ORLOVSKI (*aside*). My boy, my beauty, my offspring!

JULIA. I just heard . . . a voice.

FYODOR. It's "wonderful," there are spirits everywhere, wandering about, watersprites sitting on the branches. . . . Yes, that's how it is, Uncle! (*He smacks* JULIA *on the back in comradely fashion.*)

JULIA. I'm not your uncle!

FYODOR. Let's calm down . . . and talk. . . . Listen, Julia . . . I've run the gamut. . . . I'm thirty-five years old and my only rank is lieutenant at the Serbian front, petty officer in the Russian reserve. I'm suspended between heaven and earth. . . . I must change my way of life . . . you understand, I have ideas in my head at this very moment that are so fantastic that if I get married, my entire life will be upset by them. . . . Marry me! I don't ask for anything more.

JULIA (*troubled*). Well— Reform yourself first, Fyodor.

FYODOR. Of course, but of course! I'm not a gypsy. Speak frankly to me!

JULIA. I'm embarrassed. (*Looking around her.*) Wait! I think somebody's coming, somebody's listening. . . . I think I saw Waffles looking out the window.

FYODOR. No, there's nobody at all.

JULIA (*throwing herself at him*). Oh, Fedya!

(SOFIA *bursts out laughing.* ORLOVSKI, DYADIN, *and* KRUSHCHOV *burst out laughing. Everybody applauds and shouts,* "Bravo! Bravo!")

FYODOR. Good Lord! You frightened us! Where were you?

SOFIA. Julia, I congratulate you! And me too . . . me too . . .

(*Laughter, embracing, general revelry.*)

DYADIN. It's wonderful! It's wonderful!

CURTAIN

ON THE HIGHROAD

A Dramatic Study in One Act

CHARACTERS

TIHON EVSTIGNEYEV, *proprietor of an inn on the highroad*
SEMYON SERGEYEVICH BORTSOV, *a ruined landowner*
MARYA YEGOROVNA, *his wife*
SAVVA, *an old pilgrim*
NAZAROVNA ⎫
YEFIMOVNA ⎬ *lady pilgrims*
FEDYA, *passing worker*
YEGOR MERIK, *a tramp*
KUSMA, *a passer-by*
POSTMAN
BORTSOV'S WIFE'S COACHMAN
PILGRIMS, CATTLE DEALERS, PASSERS-BY, *etc.*

The act takes place in one of the provinces of southern Russia.

The scene is set in TIHON's *inn. At the right is the counter and shelves with bottles. Backstage, a door, leading out. Over it, on the outside, hangs a red, soiled lantern. The floor and the benches, standing against the wall, are all filled with pilgrims and passers-by. Many of them, for lack of room, sleep sitting up. It is late at night. As the curtain rises, thunder is heard, and lightning is seen from the door.*

(TIHON *is at the counter.* FEDYA *quietly plays his concertina, sprawled out on one of the benches.* BORTSOV *sits near him, fully dressed in a shabby summer overcoat. On the floor,* SAVVA, NAZAROVNA, *and* YEFIMOVNA *recline near the benches.*)

YEFIMOVNA (*to* NAZAROVNA). Talk to the old man, dear! He's as quiet as death.

NAZAROVNA (*raising the edge of a coarse, heavy cloth from* SAVVA's *face*). Holy man, I say, holy man! Are you alive or are you already dead?

SAVVA. Why should I be dead? I'm alive, my dear! (*Raises himself on his elbow.*) Cover up my feet, will you, dear? There. A little more on the right one. That's it, dear. God be with us.

NAZAROVNA (*covering his feet*). Sleep, old man.

SAVVA. How can I sleep? If only I had the patience to bear this torment; sleep: as if it were possible, my dear. Can an

179

unworthy sinner hope for peace? What's that noise, pilgrim woman?

NAZAROVNA. God is sending a storm. The wind is howling and it's pouring, pouring. Down the roof and at the windows like pellets of peas. Do you hear? It's pouring. . . . (*Thunder.*) Hail Mary, hail Mary, hail Mary. . . .

FEDYA. It thunders and moans and howls and there's no end to it. *Hooooo* . . . like forest murmurs . . . *hoooo* . . . the wind howls like a dog. . . . (*Huddling away from it.*) It's cold! My clothes are wringing wet, the door is wide open. . . . (*Plays softly.*) My concertina is soaked, my good people, so there won't be any music, or I'd play you such a concert you'd take your hats off to me! Something splendid! A quadrille or a polka . . . or a Russian dance, a funny song. We could do all that. In the town, where I was a servant at the Grand Hotel, I didn't make any money, but I outdid myself playing on the concertina all night long. And how I can play the guitar!

VOICE FROM THE CORNER. There goes the fool, raving again.

FEDYA. Spoken by a fool. (*Pause.*)

NAZAROVNA (*to* SAVVA). If you'd only lie where it's warm and protect your feet. (*Pause.*) Old man! Holy man! (*Shakes* SAVVA.) Are you getting ready to die?

FEDYA. You should drink some vodka, Grandpa. Drink, and it will burn and burn in your tummy, go right to your heart and give you a little more time. Drink up!

NAZAROVNA. Don't brag, young man! The old man may be giving back his soul to God or repenting his sins; and you talk like that and play your concertina. . . . Stop playing! Shameless!

FEDYA. And what are you pestering him for? He's not up to much, and you, with your old wife's foolishness . . . he's a pious man and he can't utter a crude word to you; and you're all so content to let him listen to your nonsense. . . . Go on sleeping, Grandpa, don't listen! Let her chatter on, and don't give her any notice. . . . Old woman's tongue . . . like a devil's broom, sweeps away wise men and fools with a boom! Don't take any notice. . . . (*Throwing up his hands.*) You're so thin, my friend! It's awful! You're like a dead skeleton! No life in you! Are you really dying?

SAVVA. Why should I be? God's goodness saves me from dying in vain. . . . I'll suffer a little and then I'll get up with God's help . . . the Mother of God won't let me die in a strange land . . . I'll die back at home.

FEDYA. Are you from very far away?

SAVVA. From Vologda. The town of Vologda itself. . . . I'm a local citizen. . . .

FEDYA. And where is this Vologda?

TIHON. The other side of Moscow . . . in the country.

FEDYA. Well, well, well. . . . You've come a long way, you old billygoat! Was it all the way on foot?

SAVVA. Yes, on foot, my boy. I've been at Tihon on the Don and I'm on my way to the Holy Hills. . . . From the Holy Hills, if it be God's will, to Odessa. . . . From there, they say they'll take you to Jerusalem for twenty-one rubles . . . real cheap. . . .

FEDYA. And have you been to Moscow?

SAVVA. Have I? Five times. . . .

FEDYA. It's a good town, is it? (*Lights up a cigarette.*) And well worth seeing?

SAVVA. There are many holy places there, my boy. . . . Where there are many holy places, there it is always good. . . .

BORTSOV (*Goes to counter. To* TIHON). I'm asking you once more! Give me a drink, for Christ's sake!

FEDYA. The main thing about a town is that it should be

clean . . . if there is dust, they should water the streets; if it is dirty, they should clean it. There should be big houses . . . a theater, police . . . cabs, which . . . I've lived in a town myself; I know about them.

BORTSOV. A little glass . . . this little glass here. You'll see, I'll pay you! Let me have it!

TIHON. All right, all right! We know.

BORTSOV. Well, I'm asking you. Be kind!

TIHON. On your way!

BORTSOV. You don't understand me. . . . Understand me, you boor, if there's even a drop of brains in your wooden peasant's skull; it's not me that's asking, it's my inside, asking in your language, a peasant's language! My sickness is asking! Understand!

TIHON. We don't understand anything! . . . Get away!

BORTSOV. You see, if I don't have a drink right this minute, you must understand this; if I don't satisfy my craving, I may commit a crime! God only knows what I can do! You boor, you've seen a lot of drinking people in your days in this pothouse; is it possible that in all this time it never entered your mind what kind of people they are? They're sick! Put them in chains, beat them, stick knives in them, but give them vodka! I beg you, humbly! Be so kind! I'm humiliating myself! My God, how I'm humiliating myself!

TIHON. Give me the money, and then there'll be vodka.

BORTSOV. Where can I get the money? It's all drunk up! It's utterly used up! What can I give you? This overcoat is all that I have left, but I can't give it to you. . . . I'm wearing it over my naked body. . . . Do you want my cap? (*Takes off cap and gives it to* TIHON.)

TIHON (*examining cap*). Hm. . . . There are no two caps alike . . . it has holes like a sieve. . . .

FEDYA (*laughs*). A gentleman's cap! To walk in the street

with and take off in front of the ladies. How do you do? Good-by. How are you?

TIHON (*gives* BORTSOV *back his cap*). I wouldn't take it as a gift. Shit!

BORTSOV. You don't like it? In that case, give it to me on credit! I'll come back from town and bring you your five kopecks! You can go choke on those five kopecks! Choke! May it stick in your throat! (*Coughs.*) I hate you!

TIHON (*banging fist on counter*). Why do you keep it up? What kind of man are you? What kind of a swindler? Why did you come here?

BORTSOV. I want a drink. Not me, but my sickness! Can't you understand that!

TIHON. Don't try my patience! You'll find yourself on the outside!

BORTSOV. What am I to do? (*Moves away from counter.*) What shall I do? (*Lost in thought.*)

YEFIMOVNA. It's the devil. Don't pay any attention to him, sir. He keeps on whispering to you, curse him: "Drink! Drink!" And you say to him: "I won't drink! I won't!" He'll stop!

FEDYA. I'll bet it's going *boom-boom bam-bam* in his old noggin . . . his stomach's leading him on. . . . (*Laughs.*) You're a strange one, Your Honor! Lie down and go to sleep! It's no good standing up there in the middle of the inn like a scarecrow! This isn't a kitchen garden!

BORTSOV (*angrily*). Shut up! Who's asking for your opinion! You ass!

FEDYA. Go on, talk, talk, you don't fool us! We've seen the likes of you! There's a lot of your kind roaming around the highroad! And as for asses, wait till I box your ears for you, you'll howl worse than the wind. Ass yourself! Idiot! (*Pause.*) Lowlife!

NAZAROVNA. The old man is probably saying his prayers and giving his soul to God and those devils are bullying each other and saying all sorts of . . . shameless!

FEDYA. And you, you old cabbage, you're in a pothouse, so don't go complaining! In Rome we do as the Romans do!

BORTSOV. What is there for me? What can I do? How can I make him understand? What words shall I use? (*To* TIHON.) My blood is boiling in my chest! Uncle Tihon! (*Weeps.*) Uncle Tihon!

SAVVA (*moaning*). I've got shooting pains in my legs, like bullets of fire. . . . Good woman, pilgrim, my dear!

YEFIMOVNA. What, old man?

SAVVA. Who is that crying?

YEFIMOVNA. The gentleman.

SAVVA. Ask the gentleman to shed a tear for me, also, that I may die in Vologda. Tearful prayers are more welcome.

BORTSOV. I'm not praying, Grandfather! These are not tears! They're juice! My heart has burst and the juice is flowing out. (*Sits down at* SAVVA's *feet.*) Juice! But you wouldn't understand! You can't understand, Grandfather, in your ignorance. Ignorant people! Living in the dark!

SAVVA. Where are those who live in the light?

BORTSOV. There are some that have light, Grandfather. . . . They would understand!

SAVVA. Yes, they do exist, my son, they do . . . the saints lived in the light . . . they understood all sorrow. . . . Without your telling them, they understood. . . . They glanced into your eyes, and understood . . . and you had such comfort from their understanding, it was as if you had no grief —it was taken out of your hands.

FEDYA. Have you ever seen any saints?

SAVVA. On occasion, my boy. . . . On this earth there are all kinds of people, sinners and servants of God.

BORTSOV. I don't understand all this. . . . (*Rises quickly.*) One can't talk without understanding. What sense do I have left now? I only have instinct, thirst! (*Goes to the counter quickly.*) Tihon, take my overcoat! Do you understand? (*Wants to take his coat off.*) My coat . . .

TIHON. What do you have on under the coat? (*Looks inside* BORTSOV'S *coat.*) Your naked body? Don't take it off, I won't allow it. . . . I'll not take a sin on my soul.

(*Enter* MERIK.)

BORTSOV. Very well, I'll take the sin on myself. Agreed?

MERIK (*takes off heavy coarse coat in silence, remains in his long jerkin. He has an ax on his belt*). A man may be cold, but a bear and a man desired are always hot. I'm hot! (*Puts ax on floor and takes off his jerkin.*) By the time you lift your leg out of the mud, you sweat buckets. You get one leg out, and the other gets stuck.

YEFIMOVNA. Yes, that's true . . . my boy, has it stopped raining?

MERIK (*looking at* YEFIMOVNA). I don't waste words on old women. (*Pause.*)

BORTSOV (*to* TIHON). I take the sin on myself. Do you hear me or don't you?

TIHON. I don't want to hear you, get away!

MERIK. It's as dark as if they'd been smearing the sky with tar. You can't see your nose in front of your face. The rain beats into your face like a snowstorm! (*Picks up armful of clothes and ax.*)

FEDYA. Your kind has the easy life. You swindlers—the beast of prey hides while you have a holiday, you clowns.

MERIK. Who said that?

FEDYA. Look around . . . you're not blind, are you?

MERIK. We'll remember that . . . (*Goes up to* TIHON.) Hello, moonface! Don't you know me?

TIHON. If I remembered all you drunkards on the high-road, I'd need about ten eyes in my head.

MERIK. Take a good look. . . . (*Pause.*)

TIHON. I do know you. Well. I recognized you by your eyes. (*Offers his hand.*) Andrey Polikarpov?

MERIK. I was Andrey Polikarpov, but now, the honorable Yegor Merik.

TIHON. Why's that?

MERIK. Whatever passport God sends, I use. . . . I've been Merik now for the past two months. . . . (*Thunder.*) Rrrrr. . . . Thunder away, I'm not afraid! (*Looks around.*) No bloodhounds around?

TIHON. What bloodhounds! Just little midges and gnats . . . just good people. The bloodhounds are, I think, fast asleep in their feather beds. . . . (*Loudly.*) Good Christians, watch out for your pockets and your clothes, or you'll have cause for regret. He's an evil one! He'll rob you!

MERIK. Well, let them watch out for their money, if they have any; I won't touch their clothes. I wouldn't have any use for them.

TIHON. Where the devil are you going?

MERIK. To Kuban!

TIHON. You don't say!

FEDYA. To Kuban? Really? (*Sits up a little.*) A fine place. Such a land, my brothers, that you wouldn't dream about in your wildest dreams. Freedom. They say there are birds

and wild fowl and wild beasts of all kinds there . . . and
. . . my God! Grass grows all the year round, people love one
another and have too much land to know what to do with!
The government, they say . . . a soldier was telling me the
other day . . . gives away three hundred acres per head. Now
there's happiness, or God strike me dead!

MERIK. Happiness . . . happiness always walks behind . . .
you don't see it. When you can bite your elbow, you'll see
happiness. . . . It's all foolishness! (*Looks toward the
benches and the people.*) Like a bunch of convicts. . . .
Good evening, you poor people!

YEFIMOVNA (*to* MERIK). Such wicked eyes! There's evil
in you. . . . Don't look at us. . . .

MERIK. Good evening, poor people!

YEFIMOVNA. Turn away! (*Nudges* SAVVA.) Savvushka,
the wicked man is looking at us. He'll do us harm, my dear.
(*To* MERIK.) Turn away, I tell you, you serpent!

SAVVA. He won't touch us, Mother, he won't touch us. . . .
God won't allow it.

MERIK. Good evening, good Christians! (*Shrugs his shoulders.*) They keep silent! You're not asleep, are you, you
clumsy fools! Why don't you say something?

YEFIMOVNA. Turn your wicked eyes away! Turn away
your devilish pride!

MERIK. Be quiet, you old hag! It wasn't with devilish
pride, but with affectionate and kind words that I wanted to
honor your bitter fate! You're huddling like flies in the cold
—well, I felt sorry for you and wanted to say a few kind
words, pity your poverty; and you turn your noses up at
me! What a way to behave! There's no need for that kind
of behavior! (*Goes up to* FEDYA.) Where are you from?

FEDYA. From around here. From the Hamonyevsky factory . . . brickworks.

MERIK. Get up!

FEDYA (*sitting up a little*). Well?

MERIK. Get up. All the way up. I'm going to lie down here. . . .

FEDYA. What? Is this your place?

MERIK. It is mine. Go lie on the ground!

FEDYA. Go away, you tramp. . . . I'm not afraid of you! . . .

MERIK. You're a clever fellow . . . get going, no talking! You'll be sorry, you silly fellow!

TIHON (*to* FEDYA). Don't contradict him, my boy. Never mind.

FEDYA. What right do you think you have? You stare at me with those fishy eyes of yours and you think . . . I'm afraid! (*Gathers up his belongings in his arms and goes and spreads himself on the ground.*) Devil! (*Lies down and covers his head.*)

MERIK (*stretches out on the bench*). You can't ever have seen the devil if you call me one. Devils are not like me. (*Lies down, places his ax next to him.*) Lie there, my little ax, little brother . . . let me cover up your handle.

TIHON. Where did you get that ax?

MERIK. I stole it. . . . I stole it and now I fuss over it like a child over a new toy. I'm sorry to have to throw it away and I have nowhere to put it. . . . Yes. . . . Like a wife you're tired of. (*Covering himself.*) Devils aren't like me, brother. . . .

FEDYA (*thrusting his head out from under his coat*). Like what, then?

MERIK. They're like steam or vapor. Blow into the air . . . (*He blows.*) that's what they're like. You can't see them.

VOICE FROM THE CORNER. If you sit under a harrow, then you'll see one.

MERIK. I sat under one once. I didn't see one . . . old wives' tales and silly old men's. . . . You won't see a devil or a goblin or a corpse . . . our eyes weren't made to see everything. . . . When I was little, I went into the woods purposely at night to get a look at the wood goblins. I'd shout and shout to find out if there were any spirits. I'd conjure up a spirit without batting an eyelash: I'd see all sorts of little things but I saw no wood goblins. I went to the graveyard at night; I wanted to get a look at a ghost . . . old wives' tales. I've seen all sorts of wild animals, but as for something terrible . . . nonsense. . . . The eyes aren't made for that. . . .

VOICE FROM THE CORNER. It just so happens one can see . . . a peasant was disemboweling a wild boar . . . he cut open the entrails, and something jumped out at him!

SAVVA (sitting up). Children, don't speak of the evil one! It's a sin, my dears!

MERIK. Aaaaaa . . . graybeard! Skeleton! (Laughs.) No need to go to the graveyard, the corpses come up from the floor to give advice . . . a sin . . . don't teach people your silly notions! You're ignorant people, living in darkness. . . . (Lights his pipe.) My father was a peasant and he loved to preach to people. One night he stole a sack of apples from the priest, brought it to us, and admonished us: "Look children, before Easter! Don't touch an apple, because that's a sin. . . ." It's just like you, you mustn't mention the devil, but you can call somebody a devil. . . . Now take this old hag over here. (Points to YEFIMOVNA.) She saw the evil one in me, but in her time, with her female foolishness, she must have given her soul to the devil countless times.

YEFIMOVNA. Tsk, tsk, tsk. . . . The power of the cross be with you! (Covers her face with her hands.) Savvushka!

TIHON. Why are you scaring them? What pleasure do you get from that? (Door slams in the wind.) Jesus! What a wind!

MERIK (stretching). To cross swords with that wind! I can't tear the door down, but what if I pull the inn up by its roots! (Gets up and lies down again.) I'm upset!

NAZAROVNA. Say a prayer, heathen! Why are you so restless?

YEFIMOVNA. Don't touch him! Let him be! He's looking at us again! (*To* MERIK.) Don't look at us, wicked man! Those eyes are like the eyes of the devil before matins.

SAVVA. Let him look, pilgrim woman! Say a prayer and his eyes won't harm you.

BORTSOV. No, I can't! It's more than I can endure! (*Goes up to the counter.*) I'm asking you for the last time . . . a half a glass!

TIHON (*shakes his head no*). The money!

BORTSOV. My God, I've already told you! It's all been spent on drink! Where can I get it for you? You won't go broke if you give me a drop of vodka on credit. A glass of vodka costs you a half-kopeck piece, and it saves me from suffering! I'm suffering! It's not just a whim: it's agony! Understand me!

TIHON. Go tell that to somebody else, not me. . . . Go over and ask those good people; let them treat you, for Christ's sake, if they want to. I only give bread for charity.

BORTSOV. You can rob them yourself, poor people, but, oh no, I won't! Not me! Do you understand? (*Hits counter with fist.*) Not me! (*Pause.*) Hmm . . . just wait. . . . (*Turns to the pilgrim women.*) That's an idea, good people! Spare me five kopecks! My inside is asking. I'm sick!

FEDYA. How do you like that! Crook! Do you want some water?

BORTSOV. How I'm humiliating myself! How humiliating it is! I don't need it. I don't want anything . . . I was joking!

MERIK. You won't get it out of him, sir. . . . We all know he's a skinflint. Wait, I've got a five-kopeck piece lying around somewhere . . . we'll both have a glass between us. . . . (*Fumbles in his pockets.*) The devil . . . it's stuck somewhere . . . seemed to me there was a tinkle in my pocket

the other day . . . no . . . nothing . . . nothing . . . brother.
Your luck! (*Pause.*)

BORTSOV. If I can't drink, I'll commit a crime or commit
suicide. . . . What shall I do, my God! (*Looks toward the
door.*) Should I go? Go out into this darkness, as far as the
eye can see? . . .

MERIK. Why not give him a sermon, pilgrims? And you,
Tihon, why don't you turn him out? You see he hasn't
paid you for his night's lodging. Turn him out, take him by
the scruff of the neck, and give him a shovel. Ho-ho, people
are cruel nowadays! No gentleness and kindness in them.
. . . Cruel people! A man is drowning and they shout out
to him: "Hurry up and drown, there's no time to look, it's a
working day!" As for throwing him a rope, no use discussing
it. A rope costs money. . . .

SAVVA. Don't judge, my good man!

MERIK. Keep quiet, you old wolf! Cruel people! Herods!
Judases! (*To* TIHON.) Come over here. Take off my boots!
Quickly!

TIHON. Well, he's lost his temper! (*Laughs.*) It's terrible!

MERIK. Come on, do as you're told! Be quick about it!
(*Pause.*) Do you hear me or don't you? Am I talking to the
walls? (*Gets up.*)

TIHON. Come, now! That will do! . . .

MERIK. Listen, you fleecer, I want you to take my boots off
for me, a poor beggar.

TIHON. Well, well . . . now don't get all upset! Come and
have a glass. . . . Have a drink, will you?

MERIK. People, what do I want? To be treated to vodka,
or to have my boots taken off? Did I make a slip and say
something else? (*To* TIHON.) So you didn't catch what I
said? I'll wait a minute. Perhaps then you'll hear me?

(*Agitation among the* PILGRIMS *and* PASSERS-BY; *they*

raise up and look at TIHON *and* MERIK. *Silent expectation.*)

TIHON. An ill wind brought you here! (*Comes out from behind the counter.*) What a gentleman! All right, then, where are they? (*Pulls off* MERIK'S *boots.*) Son of Cain. . . .

MERIK. There we are. Put them side by side . . . that's it . . . you can go your way now!

TIHON (*after taking off* MERIK'S *boots, goes back to the counter*). You like to complicate matters a little too much! Complicate things a little more and you'll be flying out of this inn real quick! Yes indeed! (*To* BORTSOV, *who is approaching.*) Are you starting again?

BORTSOV. You see, I could give you a little thing made of gold, if you like . . . if you wish, I could give you . . .

TIHON. Why are you shaking? Talk sense!

BORTSOV. It may be mean and vile on my part, but what am I to do? I've decided to do this vile thing, without thinking of the future. They would excuse me for it in court. . . . Take it, only on condition that you return it to me after, when I come back from town. I'm giving it to you in front of witnesses. . . . People, you will be my witnesses! (*Takes a gold locket out of his breast pocket.*) Here it is. . . . I ought to take the portrait out, but I have nowhere to put it; I'm soaked through. . . . So, take it with the portrait! Only, mind you . . . you . . . don't touch the face with your fingers. . . . Please . . . I was rude to you, my dear fellow. . . . I was stupid, but you must please forgive me . . . and . . . don't touch it with your fingers. . . . Don't look on that face with your eyes. . . . (*Gives* TIHON *the locket.*)

TIHON (*examining the locket*). A stolen watch. . . . Well, all right, drink. . . . (*Pours out vodka.*) Guzzle it down. . . .

BORTSOV. Only don't put your fingers . . . on it. . . . (*Drinks slowly, convulsively.*)

TIHON (*opens the locket*). Hm . . . a lady. . . . Where did you pick such a thing up?

MERIK. Let's have a look! (*Gets up and goes to the counter.*) Let's have a look!

TIHON (*pushes his hand away*). Where are you shoving? Look while I hold it!

FEDYA (*gets up and goes to* TIHON). Let me have a look, too!

> (*To the counter on either side come the wanderers and wayfarers; they form a group.*)

MERIK (*strongly, with both his hands, holds* TIHON's *hand with the locket, and silently looks at the portrait. Pause*). Handsome she-devil. A lady. . . .

FEDYA. A lady . . . the cheeks, the eyes . . . your hand is in the way, I can't see. Hair down to her waist. . . . Just as if she were alive! and ready to speak. . . . (*Pause.*)

MERIK. A sure destruction for a weak man. Once you've got one like that saddled round your neck . . . (*Waves his hand.*) and . . . that's the end of you!

> (*Voice of* KUSMA *is heard:* "Trrrr . . . whoa, you deaf beasts.")

KUSMA (*enters*). There's an inn in my path. . . . Shall I drive away, walk past it? One can pass one's own father in daylight and not see him, but an inn can be seen miles away in the dark. Let me pass, if you believe in God! Hello there! (*Plunks a five-kopeck piece down on the counter.*) A glass of real Madeira! And be quick about it!

FEDYA. How do you like that, you devil!

TIHON. Don't wave your arms about! You'll knock something over!

KUSMA. That's what God gave them to me for, to wave! Are you made of sugar? I suppose you're melting? Poor little auntie, poor little chicken. Afraid of the rain, poor delicate things! (*Drinks.*)

YEFIMOVNA. One might well be afraid to be caught on the road on such a night. Thank God, this is a paradise where there are villages and many peasant households where one can get shelter from the weather. In the old days, the Lord knows what it was like! We could go for a hundred miles and not find a house or a village or even a stick to look upon. We had to sleep on the ground. . . .

KUSMA. Have you been around that long, old girl?

YEFIMOVNA. Nigh on eighty years, old man.

KUSMA. Eighty years! Soon you'll have lived as long as a carrion crow! (*Looks at* BORTSOV.) What kind of queer fish is that over there? (*Staring at* BORTSOV.) Sir!

(BORTSOV *recognizes* KUSMA *and, in his confused state, retreats to the corner and sits on a bench.*)

Semyon Sergeyevich, is that you, or isn't it? Hm? Why should you be in such an inn? It's not a place for you, is it?

BORTSOV. Be quiet!

MERIK (*to* KUSMA). Who is he?

KUSMA. A poor martyr. (*Paces nervously up and down in front of the counter.*) Eh? In a pothouse, imagine that! In rags! Drunk! I'm upset, brothers . . . I'm upset . . . (*To* MERIK.) It's our master, our proprietor, Semyon Sergeyevich, Mr. Bortsov. . . . You see what a state he's in? What has he come to? To drink to such an extent. . . . Fill my glass! (*Drinks.*) I'm from his village, from Bortsovka—you may have heard of it—it's a hundred and fifty miles from here, in the Yergovsky district. We were his father's serfs. . . . What a pity!

MERIK. Was he rich?

KUSMA. Very. . . . A great man.

MERIK. He wasted away his father's legacy?

KUSMA. No, it was fate, dear friend. . . . He was great, rich, sober . . . (*To* TIHON.) You yourself must have seen him sometimes riding past the inn on his way to town. Fine, high-spirited horses, a carriage with springs—the finest quality! He had five troikas, brother. . . . Five years ago, I remember, he came here from Mikishinsky ferry and threw down five rubles change. . . . Like that!

MERIK. So he went out of his mind?

KUSMA. His mind was still there. . . . It was cowardice that did it! Soft-heartedness. Yes, children, it was because of a woman. . . . He fell in love, from the heart, with a woman of the town, and it seemed to him there was no more beautiful creature in all the world. . . . Fall in love with a raven, worse than with a falcon. Oh, she came from a good family. She wasn't a bad girl or anything like that, but . . . flirtatious . . . a little too . . . frivolous! Frivolous! Screwing up her eyes! Flirting! And always laughing, always laughing! No sense at all. . . . The gentry like that; they think it's clever, but we peasants would turn that kind out. . . . Well . . . he fell in love, and he was done for. . . . Fate! He began fussing over her, one thing led to another, tea and sugar, et cetera . . . all night in a boat, playing the piano . . .

BORTSOV. Don't tell them, Kusma! What's the good of it? What business is my life of theirs?

KUSMA. Excuse me, Your Honor, I've told them only a little. . . . I've told them, and that's enough for them. . . . I told them a little, because I was nervous . . . I was very upset. Fill my glass! (*He drinks.*)

MERIK (*in a half-whisper*). And did she love him?

KUSMA (*in a half-whisper which gradually changes into his habitual voice level*). She certainly did! He was a gentleman of some consequence! . . . You can easily fall in love with a man who has three thousand acres and is rolling in money . . . and he himself so sober, dignified, reliable . . . he shook hands with all the authorities just like with you and me. . . . (*Takes* MERIK's *hand.*) "Hello and good-by, and you're welcome. . . ." Well, one evening I was walking along by myself, through the manorial garden . . . what a garden, brothers, well! acres of it. . . . I was walking along quietly, and I saw that they were sitting on a bench and (*Imitates sound of a kiss.*) kissing each other . . . he kisses her once, and she, the snake, gives him back two . . . he takes hold of her white little hand, and she, all ablaze, presses close, how she presses close to him. . . . I love you, Senya, she says, and Senya, like a damned fool, goes about bragging from place to place about his happiness, the fool. . . . To one he gives a ruble, to another, two. . . . He gave me money to buy a horse, pardoned everybody their debts, in his joy. . . .

BORTSOV. My God! . . . Why tell them about it? These people have no sympathy . . . it's painful, you know!

KUSMA. I haven't said much, sir! They keep prodding me! Why not tell them a little? There, there, I won't if you're angry . . . I won't . . . I don't give a damn about them. . . . (*Hears the post bells.*)

FEDYA. Don't shout; speak quietly. . . .

KUSMA. I am speaking quietly. . . . I'm not allowed to talk, so there's nothing to do. . . . And there's really nothing more to tell. They got married . . . that's all there was to the whole thing. . . . There was nothing more. Fill the glass for Kusma, the disinterested! (*He drinks.*) I don't like drunkenness! And after the wedding, when the people sat down to supper, she got away and took off in a carriage . . . (*In a whisper.*) To town, to the lawyer, to her lover. . . . So? What do you think of her now? At that very moment! For that, killing would be too little!

MERIK (*pensive*). Yes. . . . And what happened then?

KUSMA. He went off his head. . . . As you can see, he started drinking hard . . . it started with a drop and now it's the whole bucket, as they say . . . and he still loves her. Look: how he loves her! He'd probably crawl to town and back to get a single look at her. . . .

(*The post drives up to the inn. The POSTMAN enters and has a drink.*)

TIHON. The mail is late today!

(*The* POSTMAN *pays quietly and goes out. He drives off, bells ringing.*)

VOICE FROM THE CORNER. In this bad weather, the post could be robbed, as easy as spitting.

MERIK. I've been alive for thirty-five years and I've never robbed the post once. (*Pause.*) Now it's gone, too late . . . too late . . .

KUSMA. Do you want to smell of prison?

MERIK. People rob without getting the smell. And what if they do! (*Abruptly.*) Well, what then?

KUSMA. You mean, what happened to the poor gentleman?

MERIK. Well, who else?

KUSMA. The second reason, brothers, why he was ruined, was his brother-in-law, his sister's husband. . . . He took it into his head to act as security for his brother-in-law at the bank—for not more than thirty thousand or so . . . the brother-in-law liked to borrow . . . that rascal knew which side his bread was buttered on; you can't make a silk purse out of a sow's ear . . . he borrowed and he didn't pay back . . . so our master had to pay up the thirty thousand. . . . (*Sighs.*) A fool suffers for his foolishness. His wife had children by the lawyer and his brother-in-law bought an estate near Poltava; our master, like a fool, hung about in pothouses and complained to the likes of us: "I've lost my faith, brothers! I don't have faith in anybody any more!" Softheartedness! Every man knows his own grief, a snake sucking at his heart, but is that a reason to drink? Take our village elder, for example. His wife plays around with the schoolteacher in broad daylight, spends the husband's money on drink, but the elder walks about with a smile on his face. His cheeks are a little sunken in, though. . . .

TIHON (*sighs*). Men bear up as God gives them the strength. . . .

KUSMA. There are many kinds of strength, it's true. . . . Well? How much does it come to? (*Pays.*) Take your pound of flesh! Bye-bye, children! Good night to you, and pleasant dreams! . . . I'm off. It's time I went. . . . I'm bringing my mistress a midwife from the hospital. . . . I suppose she's tired of waiting; she must be all wet by now, poor dear. . . . (*Runs out.*)

TIHON (*after a pause*). Hey, you! What's your name! Come and have a drink, poor fellow! (*Pours.*)

BORTSOV (*comes up to the counter hesitatingly and drinks*). That means I owe you now for two glasses.

TIHON. What do you mean, owe? Drink—and forget it. Drown your sorrows, poor fellow!

FEDYA. Drink mine too, sir! Ach! (*Throws down a five-kopeck piece on the counter.*) Drink—and you die—you die even if you don't drink. It's good not to drink vodka, but with vodka, by God, what freedom! Grief isn't grief when you've had a drink. . . . It's hot!

BORTSOV. Fool! It's hot!

MERIK. Give it here! (*Takes the locket from* TIHON *and examines the portrait.*) Hm. . . . Ran away after the wedding. . . . What kind of woman is that!

VOICE FROM THE CORNER. Pour him another glass, Tisha. Let him have a drink on me!

MERIK (*flings the locket on the ground with force*). Damn her! (*Goes quickly to his place and lies down, face to the wall.*)

(*General excitement.*)

BORTSOV. What's this? What's the meaning of this? (*Picks up locket.*) How dare you, you beast? What right have you? (*Tearfully.*) Do you want me to kill you? Yes? Muzhik! Boor!

TIHON. Don't be angry, sir . . . it's not made of glass, it's not broken. . . . Have another drink and go to sleep. . . . (*Pours.*) I've been listening to you all and I should have closed up long ago. (*Goes and shuts outer door.*)

BORTSOV (*drinks*). How dare he? The fool! (*To* MERIK.) Do you understand? You're a fool, an ass!

SAVVA. Children! A little respect! You're not supposed to talk so much. What's the good of so much noise? Let people sleep!

TIHON. Lie down, lie down . . . that's enough! (*Goes behind counter and locks the till with the receipts.*) It's bedtime!

FEDYA. It's time! (*Lies down.*) Pleasant dreams, brothers!

MERIK (*gets up and spreads his sheepskin coat on the bench. To* BORTSOV). Come and lie down, sir.

TIHON. Where are you going to lie down?

MERIK. Anywhere . . . on the floor, if you like. . . . (*Spreads heavy coat on the floor.*) It's all the same to me. (*Places the ax beside him.*) It would be torture for him to sleep on the floor . . . he's accustomed to silks and down. . . .

TIHON (*to* BORTSOV). Lie down, Your Honor! You've looked at the portrait long enough. (*Puts out candle.*) Give her up!

BORTSOV (*reeling*). Where can I lie down?

TIHON. In the tramp's place! Didn't you hear him giving it up to you?

BORTSOV (*goes to the vacant place*). I'm a little . . . drunk . . . this . . . where . . . is this where I'm to lie down? Hm?

TIHON. Yes, yes, here, don't be afraid . . . lie down. . . . (*Stretches out on the counter.*)

BORTSOV (*lying down*). I . . .'m drunk . . . everything's

going round. (*Opens the locket.*) Do you have a little candle?
(*Pause.*) You, Masha, funny little woman! . . . looking at me
from out of that frame and laughing. . . . (*Laughs.*)
Drunk! Is it possible to laugh at a man because he's drunk?
You let go, as Schastlivtsev says, and . . . love the drunkard.

FEDYA. How the wind howls! It's terrifying!

BORTSOV. What a woman . . . how can you keep on turning round like that? I can't catch you!

MERIK. He's wandering. He just keeps staring at the portrait. (*Laughs.*) That's a case! These educated gentry have
invented all kinds of machines and medicines but there
hasn't been a man clever enough to find a cure for the female sex . . . they try and find a cure for every disease but
the idea never occurs to them that more people die of women
than of disease . . . they're cunning, greedy, severe, senseless. . . . The mother-in-law torments her daughter-in-law, the
daughter-in-law tries to deceive the husband . . . and there's
no end to it. . . .

TIHON. The women have pulled his hair, and he's bris-
tling. . . .

MERIK. I'm not the only one. From time immemorial, since
the world has been in existence, men have been weeping. It's
not for nothing and to no purpose that in songs and stories
the devil and woman are put side by side. . . . Not for
nothing! It's more than half true, you know. . . . (*Pause.*) This
gentleman here is playing the fool, but did I have more wisdom when I became a tramp and left my father and mother?

FEDYA. Was it because of a woman?

MERIK. Just like the gentleman here. I went about like
one of the damned, bewitched . . . boasted of my happiness. . . . Day and night, as though on fire, until the time
came for my eyes to be opened. . . . It wasn't love, but only
a fraud. . . .

FEDYA. What did you do to her?

MERIK. That's none of your business. . . . (*Pause.*) Killed

her, do you think? I couldn't. . . . You don't kill them for
that, you even feel sorry for them. . . . Live and . . . be . . .
happy! If only I hadn't set eyes on you, then I could forget
you, snake in the grass!

(*Knock at the door.*)

TIHON. Who the devil's there? Who's that? (*A knock.*)
Who's knocking? (*Gets up and goes to the door.*) Who's
knocking? Go away, we're locked up!

VOICE FROM THE DOOR. Let me in, Tihon, for goodness'
sake. The carriage spring is broken! Help me, be a father to
me! If only we had a little piece of rope to tie around it,
then we'd get there somehow. . . .

TIHON. Who is it?

VOICE FROM THE DOOR. My mistress is driving from town
to Varsonofyevo . . . only four miles more. . . . Help me,
for goodness' sake!

TIHON. Go and tell your mistress that if she gives us ten
rubles, there'll be a cord and we'll mend the spring. . . .

VOICE FROM THE DOOR. Have you gone mad, or something? Ten rubles! You mad dog! You're glad for other people's troubles!

TIHON. You know best. . . . There's no need . . . if you
don't want to!

VOICE FROM THE DOOR. Well, all right, wait a moment.
(*Pause.*) The mistress said: all right.

TIHON. Welcome then! (*Opens door and* COACHMAN
enters.)

COACHMAN. Good evening, Christians! Well, give me the
rope! Quickly! Children, who will come out and help?
There'll be some left over for your trouble!

TIHON. There won't be any left over . . . let them sleep.
We can manage the job together.

COACHMAN. Phew, I'm all exhausted! It's cold, muddy, not a dry spot on me. . . . And another thing, my good fellow. . . . Haven't you a little room in here for my mistress to warm herself? The carriage is pushed to one side and it isn't possible to sit in it. . . .

TIHON. She wants a room, then, too? Let her get warm here, if she's cold. . . . We'll find a place. (*Goes to* BORTSOV *and clears a place next to him.*) Get up, get up! Just lie on the floor for an hour, while the lady gets warm. (*To* BORTSOV.) Get up, Your Honor! Sit up! (BORTSOV *sits up.*) Here's a place for you. (COACHMAN *goes out.*)

FEDYA. Here's our visitor now, devil take her! Now there'll be no sleep before daylight.

TIHON. It's a pity I didn't ask for fifteen. . . . She'd have given it. . . (*Stands before the door in expectant pose.*) You people must be on your best behavior. . . . No crude words now. . . .

(*Enter* MARYA YEGOROVNA, *followed by* COACHMAN.)

(*Bows.*) Welcome, Your Excellency! To our poor abode, fit for peasants and cockroaches. Don't be squeamish!

MARYA YEGOROVNA. I can't see anything. . . . Which way do I go?

TIHON. Here, Your Excellency! (*Leads her to the seat beside* BORTSOV.) This way, please. (*Blows on the seat.*) I have no separate rooms, excuse me, but don't be afraid, madam; they are good, quiet people . . .

MARYA YEGOROVNA (*sits down next to* BORTSOV). How terribly stuffy! Open the door, at least!

TIHON. Yes, madam. (*Runs and opens the door wide.*)

MERIK. People are cold and they open the doors wide! (*Gets up and slams the door.*) Who is she to give orders? (*Lies down.*)

TIHON. Excuse me, Your Excellency. He's our village idiot

. . . a little cracked . . . don't be frightened, he won't hurt you. Only, excuse me, madam, I didn't agree to do it for ten rubles . . . for fifteen, if you like.

MARYA YEGOROVNA. Very well, only hurry.

TIHON. This minute . . . this very minute . . . (*Pulls out a rope from under the counter.*) This minute . . . (*Pause.*)

BORTSOV (*looks intently at* MARYA YEGOROVN). Masha . . . Masha . . .

MARYA YEGOROVNA (*looks at* BORTSOV). Now what?

BORTSOV. Marie . . . is it you? Where did you come from?

(MARYA YEGOROVNA, *recognizing* BORTSOV, *screams and jumps away to the center of the inn.*)

(*He follows her.*) Marya, it's me . . . me . . . (*Laughs.*) My wife! Marie! Where am I? People, a candle!

MARYA YEGOROVNA. Get away! You're lying! It's not you! It's not possible! (*Buries her face in her hands.*) It's a lie! It's idiotic!

BORTSOV. Her voice, her movements . . . Marie, it's me! I'll stop soon . . . being drunk . . . my head's going round. . . . My God! Wait, wait . . . I don't understand anything. (*Yells.*) My wife! (*Falls at her feet and sobs.*)

(*A group gathers round husband and wife.*)

MARYA YEGOROVNA. Get away! (*To the* COACHMAN.) Denis, let's go! I can't stay here any longer!

MERIK (*leaps up and looks at her face intently*). The portrait! (*Clutches her arm.*) It's her! Eh, people! She's the gentleman's wife!

MARYA YEGOROVNA. Get away, muzhik! (*Tries to pull her hand away from him.*) Denis, what are you waiting for? (COACHMAN *and* TIHON *run up to her and seize* MERIK *by the arm.*) This is a den of thieves! Let go of my arm! I'm not afraid! Get away!

MERIK. Wait, I'll let you go. . . . Let me say only one thing to you. . . . One word, so you may understand. . . . Wait . . . (*Turns to* TIHON *and* DENIS.) Get away, you boors, don't hold on to me! I won't let her go till I've said my word . . . wait . . . in a moment. (*Strikes his forehead with his fist.*) No, God has given me no sense! I can't think of what I want to say to you!

MARYA YEGOROVNA (*pulls away her hand*). Go away! They're drunk. . . . Let's go, Denis! (*Tries to go toward door.*)

MERIK (*blocks the way*). Come, give him just one look! Caress him, just a little kind word, for God's sake.

MARYA YEGOROVNA. Take him away from me . . . this crazy fool.

MERIK. Then go to the devil, be damned! (*Swings the ax.*)

(*Terrible commotion. They all leap up with noise and cries of horror.* SAVVA *stands between* MERIK *and* MARYA YEGOROVNA. . . . DENIS *pushes* MERIK *forcibly to one side and carries his lady out. After that, all stand rooted to the spot. Prolonged pause.*)

BORTSOV (*grasping at the air with his hands*). Marie. . . . Where are you, Marie?

NAZAROVNA. My God, oh my God. . . . You've wrung my heart, you murderers! What a cursed night!

MERIK (*lowering the hand which holds the ax*). Did I kill her or not? . . .

TIHON. Thank God, your head is safe. . . .

MERIK. So I haven't killed her. . . . (*Staggering, goes to his place.*) Not my luck to die for a stolen ax. (*Sinks down on his coat and sobs.*) Misery! Cruel misery! Have pity on me, good Christians!

CURTAIN

ON THE HARMFULNESS
OF TOBACCO

A Dramatic Monologue

CHARACTER

IVAN IVANOVICH NYUHIN, *a henpecked husband, landlord of his wife's music school and girls' boarding school*

The scene takes place on the rostrum of one of the provincial clubhouses.

NYUHIN (*has long sidewhiskers without mustache, wears an old frayed frock coat. Makes a majestic entrance, bows to the audience, and adjusts his waistcoat*). Ladies and, so to speak, gentlemen!

(*Smoothing his whiskers.*) It was suggested to my wife that I deliver a popular lecture here for charity. Why not? So, I'll deliver a lecture. It's all the same to me. I, of course, am not a professor and I never got a degree, but nevertheless, in the last thirty years, it could be said that I've been ruining my health working, et cetera, on matters which are strictly scientific, pondering and sometimes even writing, as you can imagine, scientific articles, that is to say, not exactly scientific, but, if you will pardon the expression, approximately scientific. By the way, the other day I wrote a huge article with the title: "On the Harmfulness of Certain Insects." My daughters liked it very much, particularly the part about bedbugs, but I just read it over and tore it up. You see, it makes no difference whether it was written or not, because without insect powder you can't get along. In our house, we even have bedbugs in the grand piano. . . . The subject of today's lecture I have chosen to be, so to speak, the harmfulness that the consumption of tobacco brings on mankind. I myself smoke, but my wife told me to lecture today about the harmfulness of tobacco, and so what else is there to say? If it's about tobacco, well then, it's about tobacco, it's all the same to me. As for you, ladies and gentlemen, I appeal to you to take my lecture with the proper seriousness, otherwise I won't answer for the consequences. Anybody who is afraid of a dry, scientific lecture, who doesn't like it, doesn't need to listen and can go home. (*Adjusts his waistcoat.*)

I particularly wish to ask for the attention of any doctor who might be present, and who will get from my lecture much helpful information, since tobacco, besides its harmful effects, is used in medicine as well. For example, if you put a fly in a snuffbox, then it dies, probably from a nervous breakdown. Tobacco is, for the most part, a plant. . . . When I deliver a lecture, I've gotten into the habit of blinking with my right eye, but don't pay any attention: it's just nervousness. I'm a very nervous man, generally speaking, and my eyes began to blink in 1889, on the thirteenth of September, on the very day when my wife gave birth, as it were, to our fourth daughter, Varvara. All of my daughters were born on the thirteenth. However (*Looks at his watch.*), there is much time for digressing from the subject of the lecture. I must mention to you that my wife runs a music school and a private boarding school, well not really a boarding school, but, in its way, a boarding school. Let it be said between us, my wife likes to complain of the shortage of money, but she's put aside a little something, about forty or fifty thousand; I myself haven't a kopeck to my name, not even one—but what's the use of talking about that!

In the boarding school I'm in charge of the housekeeping. I buy the provisions, check up on the servants, keep the accounts, stitch the exercise books together, exterminate the bedbugs, take my wife's little dog for walks, catch mice. . . . Last night one of my duties was to issue flour and butter to the cook for the making of pancakes. Well, to make a long story short, today, when the pancakes were already fried, my wife came into the kitchen to say that three of the girls would not be able to eat the pancakes because they had swollen glands. So it looked as if we'd made too many pancakes. What would we do with them? First my wife said to take them to the cellar but then, after thinking it over, she said: "Eat these pancakes yourself, you dumbbell." When she happens not to be in a good mood, that's what she calls me: dumbbell, you snake, or you devil. What kind of devil am I? She's always not in a good mood. I didn't eat them. I gulped them down without chewing, because, as it happens, I'm always starving. Yesterday, for example, she didn't give me any supper. "You," she said, "you dumbbell, why should I feed you?" But anyway . . . (*Looks at his watch.*) I've strayed somewhat from the subject. To continue. Though, of course. you'd rather listen to a love song, or some symphony or other, or an aria. (*He starts singing and conducting.*) "We do not blink our eyes in the heat of battle. . . ." I don't remember now where that comes from. . . .

By the way, I forgot to tell you what my life at the music school is like; besides managing the housekeeping, it also falls to me to teach mathematics, literature, chemistry, geography, history, solfeggio, literature, and all that sort of thing. For dancing, singing, and drawing my wife charges extra, although the dancing and singing teacher is also myself. Our music school is located at 5 Dog Alley, number thirteen. That's probably why my life is so unlucky, because the number of the house we live in is thirteen. And my daughters were born on the thirteenth, and our house has thirteen windows. . . . So, why go on talking? Appointments with my wife can be set up at home at any time, and the prospectus of the school, if you want one, you can get from the janitor for thirty kopecks each. (*Takes some brochures from his pocket.*) And if you like, I can let you have some now. Thirty kopecks a copy. Who would like one?

(*Pause.*) Nobody wants one? Well, how about twenty kopecks.

(*Pause.*) What a pity! Yes, house number thirteen. Nothing works for me. I'm growing old and stupid. . . . Here I am delivering a lecture, to all appearances I'm enjoying myself, but at the same time I'd like to shout at the top of my voice or fly away somewhere to the other end of the earth. And there's nobody to complain to; I even feel like crying. . . . You'll say: your daughters. What about my daughters? I tell them, but they only laugh. . . . From my wife, I have seven daughters. . . . No, sorry, it seems there are six. (*Quickly.*) Seven! The eldest, Anna, is twenty-seven, the youngest is seventeen.

Ladies and gentlemen! (*Looks around.*) I'm unhappy. I've turned into a fool, a nobody; but as a matter of fact, you see before you the happiest of fathers. As a matter of fact, that's how it should be, and who am I to say different. If you only knew! I've been living with my wife for thirty-three years and I can say they were the best years of my life, well not the best, but generally speaking. . . . They've flown by, in a word, like one happy moment, and strictly speaking, the hell with them!

(*Looks around.*) It seems she hasn't gotten here yet. She isn't here: I can say what I please. . . . I get terribly frightened . . . frightened when she looks at me. Yes, as I was saying: my daughters won't be getting married for some time, most likely because they're bashful, and because men can't get a look at them. My wife doesn't like to have evening parties; she never invites anybody to dinner; she's a very stingy, nasty, shrewish woman and that's why nobody ever visits us, also . . . I can tell you confidentially . . . (*Comes down close to the footlights.*) My wife's daughters can be seen on the high holidays at the house of their aunt Natalya Semyonova's, the woman that suffers from rheumatism and walks around in that yellow dress with black spots, like she has cockroaches all over her. Refreshments are served. And when you don't see my wife, then you can . . .

(*His fist to his lips, in a gesture of defiance.*) You will notice that I get drunk on one glass from which I feel marvelous, and at the same time so sad that I can't express it; for some reason, I remember my younger days, and for some reason I feel like running away; oh if you only knew how I long to run. . . . (*Passionately.*) To run away, to throw everything over and run for my life. . . . But where? It doesn't matter where . . . if only to run away from this rotten, vulgar, cheap life which is turning me into an old idiot, foolish, old, pitiful, idiotic, running away from that silly, petty, vicious, vicious, vicious miser, my wife, who has been tormenting me for thirty-three years; to run away from the music, the kitchen, her money, from all the triviality and vulgarity . . . and stop somewhere far away in a field, and stand there like a tree, a post, a kitchen-garden scarecrow, under the wide sky, and watch the bright moon all night as it looks down quietly, and forget, forget. . . . Oh, how it would be not to remember anything! How I'd like to tear off this miserable old frock coat that I wore thirty years ago at my wedding . . . (*Tears off the frock coat.*) and which I am still constantly wearing when I give lectures for charity. (*Tramples on the frock coat.*) Take that! I'm old, poor, pitiful, like this shabby old vest, all worn out in the back. . . . (*Shows his back.*) I don't want anything! I'm above all this, I'm better; I was once young, clever, intelligent; I studied at the university, I had dreams, I thought of myself as a human being. . . . Now I don't want anything! Nothing but peace . . . peace!

(*Looks around, quickly puts on the frock coat.*) My wife is standing in the wings. . . . She's arrived and is waiting for me there. (*Looks at his watch.*) My time is up. . . . If she asks you, then, please, I beg of you, tell her that there was a lecture . . . that her idiot of a husband, I mean myself, behaved himself with dignity. (*Looks to wings, clears his throat.*) She's looking at me.

(*Raises his voice.*) In view of the situation that tobacco contains a terrible poison, which I have just talked about, you should on no account smoke and I allow myself to hope, in any case, that my lecture on the harmfulness of tobacco will benefit the public. *Dixi et animam levavi.**

(*Bows; majestic exit.*)

* I have spoken and relieved my mind.

SWAN SONG

❧

A Dramatic Study in One Act

CHARACTERS

VASSILI VASSILIEVICH SVETLOVIDOV, *an old actor, in his sixty-eighth year*

NIKITA IVANICH, *a prompter, an old man*

The scene is set on the stage of a provincial theater at night, after the play. The empty stage at center. Stage right, a row of unpainted, crude, makeshift doors, leading to the dressing rooms. Stage left and to the back is overloaded with trash, remains of the evening's scenery. An overturned stool at center stage. It is night and the stage is dark.

SVETLOVIDOV (*in the costume of Calchas, candle in hand. Comes out of a dressing room roaring with laughter*). Well, how do you like that? That's a fine state of affairs! I fell asleep in the dressing room! The show was over hours ago, everybody's out of the theater and there I am, quietly snoring my head off. Oh, I am an old clown. An old fool! An old dog! Well, I drank so much I fell asleep sitting up! That was clever of me! Good for me!

(*Shouts.*) Yegorka! Yegorka! Where are you, you devil! Petrushka! They're asleep, the devils, a pox on them! Yegorka!

(*Picks up stool, sits on it, and puts the candle on the floor.*) Not a sound. Only the echo replies. . . . Only today I gave both Yegorka and Petrushka a tip for their services—three rubles—and now bloodhounds couldn't trace them. . . . They've disappeared and the rascals have probably locked up the theater. . . . (*Shakes his head.*) I'm drunk! Oof! It was a benefit performance in my honor, and my God, how I poured wine and beer into myself! I'm shaky all over and it feels like twenty tongues had spent the night in my mouth . . . disgusting . . .

(*Pause.*) It's stupid! When an old booby drinks, he doesn't know his own joy. . . . Oh, my God! I have a splitting headache, I'm shivering, my soul is as dark and cold as a cellar. If you care about your health, then at least show some mercy for your old age, you old buffoon! . . . (*Pause.*) Old age . . . I can play the fool, pretend, act big, put up a big front, but my life has been lived . . . sixty-eight years of age, my compliments! They'll never return. . . . They've gone down the drain. Nothing left at the bottom but the dregs . . . that's how it is, Vasiusha, my boy . . . whether you like it or not, you're ready to rehearse the role of a corpse. Death is ahead, my boy, waiting in the wings. . . .

(*Looks straight ahead of him.*) But, listen! I've been on the stage for forty-five years, and it seems this is the first time I've stayed in the theater late at night. . . . Yes, the first time. . . . You know, it's strange . . . spooky . . . (*Goes up to the footlights.*) I can't see anything. . . . I can just make out the prompter's box . . . and there's the conductor's podium, his rostrum . . . and the rest is . . . darkness! A black, bottomless pit, like a grave, in which death itself is concealed. . . . Brr! . . . It's cold! The wind blows in and out of the house as it does down a fireplace chimney. . . . It's terrifying, the place is filled with ghosts, I have goose pimples running up and down my back. . . .

(*Shouts.*) Yegorka! Petrushka! Where are you, you devils? Good heavens, why do I think of such terrible things? Oh, my God, stop saying these thoughts, stop drinking, you're old, ready to die. . . . In their sixty-eighth year, people go to church in the morning, ready themselves for death, and you— Oh, God! cursing my head off, an ugly, drunken mug, dressed as a Greek buffoon! . . . A sickening sight, I should go and change right away. . . . It's terrifying! If I spent the whole night here, I'd die of fright. . . .

(*Goes toward his dressing room; at the same time,* NIKITA IVANICH *comes out of the farthest dressing room backstage, appears to* SVETLOVIDOV *in a white bathrobe.*)

(*Seeing* NIKITA IVANICH, SVETLOVIDOV *shrieks with terror and steps back.*) Who are you? What do you want? Who are you? (*Stamps his foot.*) Who are you?

NIKITA IVANICH. It's only me.

SVETLOVIDOV. Who?

NIKITA IVANICH (*slowly approaches him*). It's me, the

prompter, Nikita Ivanich. . . . Vassili Vassilich, it's me! . . .

SVETLOVIDOV (*sinks down exhausted onto the stool, breathing heavily, trembling all over*). My God! Who is it? Is it you, really you, Nikitushka? What . . . what are you doing here?

NIKITA IVANICH. I spend my nights here in the dressing room. Please don't tell Alexey Fomich . . . I have nowhere else to go at night; so help me God. . . .

SVETLOVIDOV. You, Nikitushka. . . . My God! My God! They gave me sixteen curtain calls tonight, I received three wreaths and lots of other little things . . . they were all in raptures over me, but not a single solitary soul came back to wake up the old drunkard and take him home. . . . I'm an old man, Nikitushka . . . I'm sixty-eight years old . . . I'm sick! My soul is tormented by weakness. . . . (*Leans on* PROMPTER's *arms and weeps.*) Don't leave me, Nikitushka, I'm old and feeble, ready to die. . . . It's terrible, terrible!

NIKITA IVANICH (*tenderly and respectfully*). Vassili Vassilich, it's time for you to go home!

SVETLOVIDOV. I won't go! I have no home—none, none, none!

NIKITA IVANICH. Good heavens! Have you forgotten where you live?

SVETLOVIDOV. I don't want to go there; I don't want to! I'm alone there . . . I have nobody, Nikitushka, no relatives, no wife, no children. . . . I'm alone, like the wind in the fields. When I die, nobody will pray for me . . . it's terrible to be alone . . . nobody to warm me, to be kind to me, to put me to bed when I'm drunk. . . . Who do I belong to? Who needs me? Who loves me? Nobody loves me, Nikitushka!

NIKITA IVANICH (*through his tears*). The public loves you, Vassili Vassilich!

SVETLOVIDOV. The public has gone home, they're asleep and have forgotten their jester! No, nobody needs me, nobody loves me. . . . I have no wife, no children.

NIKITA IVANICH. Then why do you feel so bad about it?

SVETLOVIDOV. I'm a human being, you know. I'm alive, you know. Blood flows through my veins, not water. I'm a nobleman, Nikitushka, from an excellent family . . . before I fell into this pit, I served in the army, in the artillery. . . . What a fine fellow I was then! Handsome, honest, courageous, passionate! My God, where has it all gone to? I was quite an actor, wasn't I, Nikitushka? (*Rising, leans on the* PROMPTER.) What has become of it, where has it gone, that time? My God! I looked into this pit a while ago—and I remembered it all, all! That pit has swallowed up forty-five years of my life, and what a life, Nikitushka! I look into the pit now and I see every last detail, as clearly as I see your face. The joy of youth, faith, passion, the love of women! Women, Nikitushka!

NIKITA IVANICH. It's your bedtime, Vassili Vassilich.

SVETLOVIDOV. When I was a young actor, when I first began to know the meaning of passion, one woman fell in love with me only for my acting . . . she was graceful, slim as a poplar, young, innocent, pure, radiant as a summer dawn! No night could withstand a glance from those light blue eyes, that beautiful smile. As a wave in the sea breaks upon the rocks, so the waves of her hair shattered blocks of ice and snow! I remember, I stood before her as I stand before you now . . . she was lovelier that day than ever before, and she looked at me so, I'll never forget that look till the day I die . . . caressing, velvety, deep, the brilliance of youth! Intoxicated, happy, I fell on my knees before her, begging for happiness. . . . (*Continues in a disappointed voice.*) And she . . . she said: Give up the stage! Give-up-the-stage! . . . Do you understand? She could love an actor, but to be his wife—never! I remember on that day I had been acting . . . I had a stupid role, I played a buffoon and I felt my eyes beginning to open . . . I understood then that acting is no sacred art, that it is all gibberish and a fraud, that I . . . was a slave, a plaything of a stranger's idleness, a jester, a buffoon! I understood that public! Since that time I have not believed in their applause, wreathes, or raves. . . . Yes,

Nikitushka! They applaud me, they buy my photograph for one ruble, but I'm a stranger to them; for them I'm . . . dirt, almost a courtesan! . . . To please their vanity, they arrange an introduction but they wouldn't stoop to giving me their sisters or daughters for a wife. . . . I don't believe in them! (*Drops on the stool.*) I don't believe!

NIKITA IVANICH. You don't look like your old self, Vassili Vassilich! You're frightening me! Go home, be so kind!

SVETLOVIDOV. My eyes were opened that day . . . and that enlightenment cost me a great deal, Nikitushka! I was put in my place by that turn of events . . . after that girl. . . . I staggered about . . . I lived without any purpose, not looking ahead . . . I took the parts of buffoons, banterers, clowns; I let my mind be corrupted. And you know, I was such an artist, such a talent! I wasted my talent, I became vulgar, my speech became affected, I lost my looks and my identity. I guzzled and this black pit engulfed me! I never felt it before, but tonight . . . when I woke up . . . I looked back at those sixty-eight years. Only now did I realize I was an old man! Swan song! (*Sobs.*) Swan song!

NIKITA IVANICH. Vassili Vassilich! Good gracious! My dear . . . calm yourself! . . . My God! (*Shouts.*) Petrushka! Yegorka!

SVETLOVIDOV. You know what a talent I had, what power! But you can't imagine what eloquence, such feeling and grace, what a touch, the strings . . . (*Beats his breast.*) in this breast! To think of it, I could choke! . . . Listen, old man. . . . Wait, let me catch my breath. . . . Here, from Godunov: (*Proudly.*)

> The phantom of the Terrible adopted
> Me as his son; from out the grave hath named me
> Dimitry, hath stirred up the nations round me,
> And hath consigned Boris to be my victim.
> I am Czarevitch. Enough! 'Twere shame for me
> To stoop before a haughty Polish woman.
> Farewell forever; the bloody game of war,
> The vast cares of my destiny, will stifle,
> I hope, the pangs of love.

That wasn't bad, was it? Wait, here's something from *King*

Lear. . . . Remember, the sky is black, it's raining, there's thunder . . . *rrrr!*—lightning . . . *zhzhzhzhzhzh* . . . slashes the sky, and then:

> Blow, winds, and crack your cheeks! rage! blow!
> You cataracts and hurricanoes, spout
> Till you have drench'd our steeples, drown'd the cocks!
> You sulphurous and thought–executing fires,
> Vaunt-couriers to oak-cleaving thunderbolts,
> Singe my white head! And thou, all-shaking thunder,
> Strike flat the thick rotundity o' the world!
> Crack nature's moulds, all germens spill at once,
> That make ingrateful man!

(*Impatiently.*) Now the words of the Fool! (*Stamps his foot.*) Give me the Fool's cue! Don't keep me waiting!

NIKITA IVANICH (*plays the Fool*). "O nuncle, court holy water in a dry house is better than this rain water out o' door. Good nuncle, in, and ask thy daughters' blessing; here's a night pities neither wise man nor fool."

SVETLOVIDOV.

> Rumble thy belly-full! Spit, fire! spout, rain!
> Nor rain, wind, thunder, fire, are my daughters:
> I tax not you, you elements, with unkindness:
> I never gave you kingdom, call'd you children . . .

Ah, what power! What genius! I'm an artist! Some more . . . something from the same . . . to recall the old days. . . . Let's have a go at it. . . . (*Breaks into joyous laughter.*) From *Hamlet!* So, I'll begin. . . . What will it be? Ah, yes. . . . Let me see, how does it go? (*Playing Hamlet.*) "O! the recorders: let me see one." (*To* NIKITA IVANICH.) "To withdraw with you: why do you go about to recover the wind of me, as if you would drive me into a toil?"

NIKITA IVANICH. "O! my lord, if my duty be too bold, my love is too unmannerly."

SVETLOVIDOV. "I do not well understand that. Will you play upon this pipe?"

NIKITA IVANICH. "My lord, I cannot."

SVETLOVIDOV. "I pray you."

NIKITA IVANICH. "Believe me, I cannot."

SVETLOVIDOV. "I do beseech you."

NIKITA IVANICH. "I know no touch of it, my lord."

SVETLOVIDOV. " 'Tis as easy as lying; govern these vent-ages with your finger and thumb, give it breath with your mouth, and it will discourse most eloquent music."

NIKITA IVANICH. "I have not the skill."

SVETLOVIDOV. "Why, look you now, how unworthy a thing you make of me. You would play upon me; you would seem to know my stops; you would pluck out the heart of my mystery . . . Do you think I am easier to be played on than a pipe? Call me what instrument you will, though you can fret me, you cannot play upon me." (*Laughs and applauds.*) Bravo! Encore! Where the devil is there any old age in that? I'm not old at all; I'm healthy; it's all nonsense! Power gushes forth from all my veins—youth, freshness, life! Where there is talent, Nikitushka, there is no old age! So you think I'm crazy, Nikitushka? Have I gone mad? Wait a moment, give me a moment and let me come back to my senses. . . . Oh, my God! Now listen, what delicacy and subtlety, what music! Hush! . . .

> Quiet Ukrainian night.
> Limpid sky, falling stars flashing brilliantly.
> Overcome by drowsiness, he wishes no air.
> The silvery poplar leaves quiver ever so slightly.

(*The sound of opening doors is heard.*)

What's that?

NIKITA IVANICH. It must be Yegorka and Petrushka coming. . . . That was genius, Vassili Vassilich! Genius!

SVETLOVIDOV (*shouts, turning toward the direction of the noise*). This way, children! (*To* NIKITA IVANICH.) Let's go get dressed. . . . I'm not old, all this is nonsense, sheer nonsense. . . . (*Laughs gaily.*) What are you crying for? My poor old sweet fool. Why are you sniveling? That's not nice! That's not nice at all! Well, well, old man, stop looking at me like that! What are you looking at me that way for? Well, well . . . (*Embraces him through tears.*) Don't cry! Where there is art, where there is talent, there is no old age, there is no solitude or sickness and even death is not half so frightening. . . . (*Weeps.*) No, Nikitushka, our song is sung. . . . What kind of genius am I? The lemon has been squeezed dry, the bottle is cracked, the nail is rusted . . . and you . . . you're an old theater rat, a prompter. . . . Let's go! (*They go.*) What kind of genius am I? In serious plays, I'm only fit to play in the retinue of Fortinbras. . . . Yes, and I'm even too old for that. . . . Yes. . . . Do you remember the lines from *Othello*, Nikitushka?

> Farewell the tranquil mind! farewell content!
> Farewell the plumed troop and the big wars
> That make ambition virtue! O, farewell!
> Farewell the neighing steed, and the shrill trump,
> The spirit-stirring drum, th' ear-piercing fife,
> The royal banner, and all quality,
> Pride, pomp, and circumstance of glorious war!

NIKITA IVANICH. Genius! Genius!

SVETLOVIDOV. And this:

> Out of Moscow! I'll go there no more,
> I run and look not back, but go searching through
>   the world,
> Outraged feelings at every turn!
> My coach, my coach!

(*He goes out with* NIKITA IVANICH.)

CURTAIN FALLS SLOWLY

THE BEAR

A Joke in One Act
Dedicated to H. H. Solovitsov

CHARACTERS

ELENA IVANOVNA POPOVA, *a young widow with dimpled cheeks, landowner*
GRIGORY STEPANOVICH SMIRNOV, *a middle-aged landowner*
LUKA, *Popova's old servant*

The drawing room of POPOVA's *country home.*

(POPOVA, *in deep mourning, does not remove her eyes from a photograph.*)

LUKA. It isn't right, madam . . . you're only destroying yourself . . . the chambermaid and the cook have gone off berry picking, every living being is rejoicing; even the cat knows how to be content, walking around the yard catching birdies, and you sit in your room all day as if it were a convent, and you don't take pleasure in anything. Yes, really! Almost a year has passed since you've gone out of the house!

POPOVA. And I shall never go out. . . . What for? My life is already ended. He lies in his grave; I have buried myself in these four walls . . . we are both dead.

LUKA. There you go again! Nikolai Mikhailovich is dead, that's as it was meant to be, it's the will of God, may he rest in peace. . . . You've done your mourning and that will do. You can't go on weeping and mourning forever. My wife died when her time came, too. . . . Well? I grieved, I wept for a month, and that was enough for her; and if I had to weep like Lazarus, for four days, well, the old lady just wasn't worth it. (*Sighs.*) You've forgotten all your neighbors. You don't go anywhere or accept any calls. We live, so to speak, like spiders. We never see the light. The mice have eaten my livery. It isn't as if there weren't any nice neighbors—the district is full of them . . . there's a regiment stationed at Riblov, such officers—they're like bonbons—you'll never get your fill of them! And in the barracks, never a Friday goes by without a ball; and, if you please, the military band plays music every day. . . . Yes, madam, my dear

227

lady: you're young, beautiful, in the full bloom of youth—
if only you took a little pleasure in life . . . beauty doesn't
last forever, you know! In ten years' time, you'll be wanting
to spread your tail like a peahen in front of the officers—
and it will be too late.

POPOVA (*determined*). I must ask you never to talk to
me like that! You know that when Nikolai Mikhailovich
died, life lost all its salt for me. It may seem to you that I
am alive, but that's only conjecture! I vowed to wear mourning to my grave and not to see the light of day. . . . Do
you hear me? May his departed spirit see how much I love
him. . . . Yes, I know, it's no mystery to you that he was
often mean to me, cruel . . . and even unfaithful, but I
shall remain true to the grave and show him I know how to
love. There, beyond the grave, he will see me as I was before his death. . . .

LUKA. Instead of talking like that, you should be taking a
walk in the garden or have Toby or Giant harnessed and go
visit some of the neighbors . . .

POPOVA. Ai! (*She weeps.*)

LUKA. Madam! Dear lady! What's the matter with you!
Christ be with you!

POPOVA. Oh, how he loved Toby! He always used to ride
on him to visit the Korchagins or the Vlasovs. How wonder-
fully he rode! How graceful he was when he pulled at the
reins with all his strength! Do you remember? Toby, Toby!
Tell them to give him an extra bag of oats today.

LUKA. Yes, madam.

(*Sound of loud ringing.*)

POPOVA (*shudders*). Who's that? Tell them I'm not at
home!

LUKA. Of course, madam. (*He exits.*)

POPOVA (*alone. Looks at the photograph*). You will see,
Nicholas, how much I can love and forgive . . . my love will

die only when I do, when my poor heart stops beating. (*Laughing through her tears.*) Have you no shame? I'm a good girl, a virtuous little wife. I've locked myself in and I'll be true to you to the grave, and you . . . aren't you ashamed, you chubby cheeks? You deceived me, you made scenes, for weeks on end you left me alone. . . .

LUKA (*enters, alarmed*). Madam, somebody is asking for you. He wants to see you. . . .

POPOVA. But didn't you tell them that since the death of my husband, I don't see anybody?

LUKA. I did, but he didn't want to listen; he spoke about some very important business.

POPOVA. I am *not at home!*

LUKA. That's what I told him . . . but . . . the devil . . . he cursed and pushed past me right into the room . . . he's in the dining room right now.

POPOVA (*losing her temper*). Very well, let him come in . . . such manners! (LUKA *goes out.*) How difficult these people are! What does he want from me? Why should he disturb my peace? (*Sighs.*) But it's obvious I'll have to go live in a convent. . . . (*Thoughtfully.*) Yes, a convent. . . .

SMIRNOV (*to* LUKA). You idiot, you talk too much. . . . Ass! (*Sees* POPOVA *and changes to dignified speech.*) Madam, may I introduce myself: retired lieutenant of the artillery and landowner, Grigory Stepanovich Smirnov! I feel the necessity of troubling you about a highly important matter. . . .

POPOVA (*refusing her hand*). What do you want?

SMIRNOV. Your late husband, whom I had the pleasure of knowing, has remained in my debt for two twelve-hundred-ruble notes. Since I must pay the interest at the agricultural bank tomorrow, I have come to ask you, madam, to pay me the money today.

POPOVA. One thousand two hundred. . . . And why was my husband in debt to you?

SMIRNOV. He used to buy oats from me.

POPOVA (*sighing, to* LUKA). So, Luka, don't you forget to tell them to give Toby an extra bag of oats.

(LUKA *goes out.*)

(*To* SMIRNOV.) If Nikolai Mikhailovich was in debt to you, then it goes without saying that I'll pay; but please excuse me today. I haven't any spare cash. The day after tomorrow, my steward will be back from town and I will give him instructions to pay you what is owed; until then I cannot comply with your wishes. . . . Besides, today is the anniversary—exactly seven months ago my husband died, and I'm in such a mood that I'm not quite disposed to occupy myself with money matters.

SMIRNOV. And I'm in such a mood that if I don't pay the interest tomorrow, I'll be owing so much that my troubles will drown me. They'll take away my estate!

POPOVA. You'll receive your money the day after tomorrow.

SMIRNOV. I don't want the money the day after tomorrow. I want it today.

POPOVA. You must excuse me. I can't pay you today.

SMIRNOV. And I can't wait until after tomorrow.

POPOVA. What can I do, if I don't have it now?

SMIRNOV. You mean to say you can't pay?

POPOVA. I can't pay. . . .

SMIRNOV. Hm! Is that your last word?

POPOVA. That is my last word.

SMIRNOV. Positively the last?

POPOVA. Positively.

SMIRNOV. Thank you very much. We'll make a note of that. (*Shrugs his shoulders.*) And people want me to be calm and collected! Just now, on the way here, I met a tax officer and he asked me: why are you always so angry, Grigory Stepanovich? Goodness' sake, how can I be anything but angry? I need money desperately . . . I rode out yesterday early in the morning, at daybreak, and went to see all my debtors; and if only one of them had paid his debt. . . . I was dog-tired, spent the night God knows where—a Jewish tavern beside a barrel of vodka. . . . Finally I got here, fifty miles from home, hoping to be paid, and you treat me to a "mood." How can I help being angry?

POPOVA. It seems to me that I clearly said: My steward will return from the country and then you will be paid.

SMIRNOV. I didn't come to your steward, but to you! What the hell, if you'll pardon the expression, would I do with your steward?

POPOVA. Excuse me, my dear sir, I am not accustomed to such unusual expressions nor to such a tone. I'm not listening to you any more. (*Goes out quickly.*)

SMIRNOV (*alone*). Well, how do you like that? "A mood." . . . "Husband died seven months ago"! Must I pay the interest or mustn't I? I ask you: Must I pay, or must I not? So, your husband's dead, and you're in a mood and all that finicky stuff . . . and your steward's away somewhere, may he drop dead. What do you want me to do? Do you think I can fly away from my creditors in a balloon or something? Or should I run and bash my head against the wall? I go to Gruzdev—and he's not at home; Yaroshevich is hiding, with Kuritsin it's a quarrel to the death and I almost throw him out the window; Mazutov has diarrhea, and this one is in a "mood." Not one of these swine wants to pay me! And all because I'm too nice to them. I'm a sniveling idiot, I'm spineless, I'm an old lady! I'm too delicate with them! So, just you wait! You'll find out what I'm like! I won't let you play around with me, you devils! I'll stay and stick it out until she pays. Brr! . . . How furious I am today, how furious! I'm shaking inside from rage and I can hardly catch my breath. . . . Damn it! My God, I even feel sick! (*He shouts.*) Hey, you!

LUKA (*enters*). What do you want?

SMIRNOV. Give me some kvass or some water! (LUKA *exits.*) What logic is there in this! A man needs money desperately, it's like a noose around his neck—and she won't pay because, you see, she's not disposed to occupy herself with money matters! . . . That's the logic of a woman! That's why I never did like and do not like to talk to women. I'd rather sit on a keg of gunpowder than talk to a woman. Brr! . . . I even have goose pimples, this skirt has put me in such a rage! All I have to do is see one of those poetical creatures from a distance, and I get so angry it gives me a cramp in the leg. I just want to shout for help.

LUKA (*entering with water*). Madam is sick and won't see anyone.

SMIRNOV. Get out! (LUKA *goes.*) Sick and won't see anyone! No need to see me . . . I'll stay and sit here until you give me the money. You can stay sick for a week, and I'll stay for a week . . . if you're sick for a year, I'll stay a year. . . . I'll get my own back, dear lady! You can't impress me with your widow's weeds and your dimpled cheeks . . . we know all about those dimples! (*Shouts through the window.*) Semyon, unharness the horses! We're not going away quite yet! I'm staying here! Tell them in the stable to give the horses some oats! You brute, you let the horse on the left side get all tangled up in the reins again! (*Teasing.*) "Never mind" . . . I'll give you a never mind! (*Goes away from the window.*) Shit! The heat is unbearable and nobody pays up. I slept badly last night and on top of everything else this skirt in mourning is "in a mood" . . . my head aches . . . should I have some vodka? I wonder, should I? (*Shouts.*) Hey, you!

LUKA (*enters*). What is it?

SMIRNOV. Give me a glass of vodka. (LUKA *goes out.*) Oof! (*Sits down and examines himself.*) Nobody would say

I was looking well! Dusty all over, boots dirty, unwashed, unkempt, straw on my waistcoat. . . . The dear lady probably took me for a robber. (*Yawns.*) It's not very polite to present myself in a drawing room looking like this; oh well, who cares? . . . I'm not here as a visitor but as a creditor, and there's no official costume for creditors. . . .

LUKA (*enters with vodka*). You're taking liberties, my good man. . . .

SMIRNOV (*angrily*). What?

LUKA. I . . . nothing . . . I only . . .

SMIRNOV. Who are you talking to? Shut up!

LUKA (*aside*). The devil sent this leech. An ill wind brought him. . . . (LUKA *goes out.*)

SMIRNOV. Oh how furious I am! I'm so mad I could crush the whole world into a powder! I even feel faint! (*Shouts.*) Hey, you!

POPOVA (*enters, eyes downcast*). My dear sir, in my solitude, I have long ago grown unaccustomed to the masculine voice and I cannot bear shouting. I must request you not to disturb my peace and quiet!

SMIRNOV. Pay me my money and I'll go.

POPOVA. I told you in plain language: I haven't any spare cash now; wait until the day after tomorrow.

SMIRNOV. And I also told you respectfully, in plain language: I don't need the money the day after tomorrow, but today. If you don't pay me today, then tomorrow I'll have to hang myself.

POPOVA. But what can I do if I don't have the money? You're so strange!

SMIRNOV. Then you won't pay me now? No?

POPOVA. I can't. . . .

SMIRNOV. In that case, I can stay here and wait until you pay. . . . (*Sits down.*) You'll pay the day after tomorrow? Excellent! In that case I'll stay here until the day after tomorrow. I'll sit here all that time . . . (*Jumps up.*) I ask you: Have I got to pay the interest tomorrow, or not? Or do you think I'm joking?

POPOVA. My dear sir, I ask you not to shout! This isn't a stable!

SMIRNOV. I wasn't asking you about a stable but about this: do I have to pay the interest tomorrow or not?

POPOVA. You don't know how to behave in the company of a lady!

SMIRNOV. No, I don't know how to behave in the company of a lady!

POPOVA. No, you don't! You are an ill-bred, rude man! Respectable people don't talk to a woman like that!

SMIRNOV. Ach, it's astonishing! How would you like me to talk to you? In French, perhaps? (*Lisps in anger.*) *Madame, je vous prie* . . . how happy I am that you're not paying me the money. . . . Ah, pardon, I've made you uneasy! Such lovely weather we're having today! And you look so becoming in your mourning dress. (*Bows and scrapes.*)

POPOVA. That's rude and not very clever!

SMIRNOV (*teasing*). Rude and not very clever! I don't know how to behave in the company of ladies. Madam, in my time I've seen far more women than you've seen sparrows. Three times I've fought duels over women; I've jilted twelve women, nine have jilted me! Yes! There was a time when I played the fool; I became sentimental over women, used honeyed words, fawned on them, bowed and scraped. . . . I loved, suffered, sighed at the moon; I became limp, melted, shivered . . . I loved passionately, madly, every which way, devil take me, I chattered away like a magpie about the emancipation of women, ran through half my fortune as a result of my tender feelings; but now, if you will excuse me, I'm on to your ways! I've had enough!

Dark eyes, passionate eyes, ruby lips, dimpled cheeks; the moon, whispers, bated breath—for all that I wouldn't give a good goddamn. Present company excepted, of course, but all women, young and old alike, are affected clowns, gossips, hateful, consummate liars to the marrow of their bones, vain, trivial, ruthless, outrageously illogical, and as far as this is concerned (*Taps on his forehead.*), well, excuse my frankness, any sparrow could give pointers to a philosopher in petticoats! Look at one of those poetical creatures: muslin, ethereal demigoddess, a thousand raptures, and you look into her soul—a common crocodile! (*Grips the back of a chair; the chair cracks and breaks.*) But the most revolting part of it all is that this crocodile imagines that she has a chef d'oeuvre, her own privilege, a monopoly on tender feelings. The hell with it—you can hang me upside down by that nail if a woman is capable of loving anything besides a lapdog. All she can do when she's in love is slobber! While the man suffers and sacrifices, all her love is expressed in playing with her skirt and trying to lead him around firmly by the nose. You have the misfortune of being a woman, you know yourself what the nature of a woman is like. Tell me honestly: have you ever in your life seen a woman who is sincere, faithful, and constant? You never have! Only old and ugly ladies are faithful and constant! You're more liable to meet a horned cat or a white woodcock than a faithful woman!

POPOVA. Pardon me, but in your opinion, who is faithful and constant in love? The man?

SMIRNOV. Yes, the man!

POPOVA. The man! (*Malicious laugh.*) Men are faithful and constant in love! That's news! (*Heatedly.*) What right have you to say that? Men are faithful and constant! For that matter, as far as I know, of all the men I have known and now know, my late husband was the best. . . . I loved him passionately, with all my being, as only a young intellectual woman can love; I gave him my youth, my happiness, my life, my fortune; he was my life's breath; I worshiped him as if I were a heathen, and . . . and, what good did it do—this best of men himself deceived me shamelessly at every step of the way. After his death, I found his desk full of love letters; and when he was alive—it's terrible to remember—he used to leave me alone for weeks at a time, and before my very eyes he paid court to other women and deceived me. He squandered my money, made a mockery of my feelings . . . and, in spite of all that, I loved him and was true to him . . . and besides, now that he is dead, I am still faithful and constant. I have shut myself up in these four walls forever and I won't remove these widow's weeds until my dying day. . . .

SMIRNOV (*laughs contemptuously*). Widow's weeds! . . . I don't know what you take me for! As if I didn't know why you wear that black domino and bury yourself in these four walls! Well, well! It's so secret, so poetic! When a Junker or some fool of a poet passes by this country house, he'll look up at your window and think: "Here lives the mysterious Tamara, who, for the love of her husband, buried herself in these four walls." We know these tricks!

POPOVA (*flaring*). What? How dare you say that to me?

SMIRNOV. You may have buried yourself alive, but you haven't forgotten to powder yourself!

POPOVA. How dare you use such expressions with me?

SMIRNOV. Please don't shout. I'm not your steward! You must allow me to call a spade a spade. I'm not a woman and I'm used to saying what's on my mind! Don't you shout at me!

POPOVA. I'm not shouting, you are! Please leave me in peace!

SMIRNOV. Pay me my money and I'll go.

POPOVA. I won't give you any money!

SMIRNOV. Yes, you will!

POPOVA. To spite you, I won't pay you anything. You can leave me in peace!

SMIRNOV. I don't have the pleasure of being either your

husband or your fiancé, so please don't make scenes! (*Sits down.*) I don't like it.

POPOVA (*choking with rage*). You're sitting down?

SMIRNOV. Yes, I am.

POPOVA. I ask you to get out!

SMIRNOV. Give me my money . . . (*Aside.*) Oh, I'm so furious! Furious!

POPOVA. I don't want to talk to impudent people! Get out of here! (*Pause.*) You're not going? No?

SMIRNOV. No.

POPOVA. No?

SMIRNOV. No!

POPOVA. Good for you! (*Rings.*)

(LUKA *enters.*)

Luka, show the gentleman out!

LUKA (*goes up to* SMIRNOV). Sir, will you please leave, as you have been asked. You mustn't . . .

SMIRNOV (*jumping up*). Shut up! Who do you think you're talking to? I'll make mincemeat out of you!

LUKA (*his hand to his heart*). Oh my God! Saints above! (*Falls into chair.*) Oh, I feel ill! I feel ill! I can't catch my breath!

POPOVA. Where's Dasha? Dasha! (*She shouts.*) Dasha! Pelagea! Dasha! (*She rings.*)

LUKA. Oh! They've all gone berry picking . . . there's nobody at home . . . I'm ill! Water!

POPOVA. Will you please get out!

SMIRNOV. Will you please be more polite?

POPOVA (*clenches her fist and stamps her feet*). You're a muzhik! You're a crude bear! A brute! A monster!

SMIRNOV. What? What did you say?

POPOVA. I said that you were a bear, a monster!

SMIRNOV (*advancing toward her*). Excuse me, but what right do you have to insult me?

POPOVA. Yes, I am insulting you . . . so what? Do you think I'm afraid of you?

SMIRNOV. And do you think just because you're one of those poetical creatures, that you have the right to insult me with impunity? Yes? I challenge you!

LUKA. Lord in Heaven! Saints above! . . . Water!

SMIRNOV. Pistols!

POPOVA. Do you think just because you have big fists and you can bellow like a bull, that I'm afraid of you? You're such a bully!

SMIRNOV. I challenge you! I'm not going to let anybody insult me, and I don't care if you are a woman, a fragile creature!

POPOVA (*trying to get a word in edgewise*). Bear! Bear! Bear!

SMIRNOV. It's about time we got rid of the prejudice that only men must pay for their insults! Devil take it, if women want to be equal, they should behave as equals! Let's fight!

POPOVA. You want to fight! By all means!

SMIRNOV. This minute!

POPOVA. This minute! My husband had some pistols . . . I'll go and get them right away. (*Goes out hurriedly and then returns.*) What pleasure I'll have putting a bullet through that thick head of yours! The hell with you! (*She goes out.*)

SMIRNOV. I'll shoot her down like a chicken! I'm not a little boy or a sentimental puppy. Fragile creatures don't exist for me.

LUKA. Kind sir! Holy father! (*Kneels.*) Have pity on a poor old man and go away from here! You've frightened her to death and now you're going to shoot her?

SMIRNOV (*not listening to him*). If she fights, then it means she believes in equality of rights and the emancipation of women. Here the sexes are equal! I'll shoot her like a chicken! But what a woman! (*Imitates her.*) "The hell with you! . . . I'll put a bullet through that thick head of yours! . . ." What a woman! How she blushed, her eyes shone . . . she accepted my challenge! To tell the truth, it was the first time in my life I've seen a woman like that. . . .

LUKA. Dear sir, please go away! I'll pray to God on your behalf as long as I live!

SMIRNOV. That's a woman for you! A woman like that I can understand! A real woman! Not a sour-faced nincompoop but fiery, gunpowder! Fireworks! I'm even sorry to have to kill her!

LUKA (*weeps*). Dear sir . . . go away!

SMIRNOV. I positively like her! Positively! Even though she has dimpled cheeks, I like her! I'm almost ready to forget about the debt. . . . My fury has diminished. Wonderful woman!

POPOVA (*enters with pistols*). Here they are, the pistols. Before we fight, you must show me how to fire. . . . I've never had a pistol in my hands before . . .

LUKA. Oh dear Lord, for pity's sake. . . . I'll go and find the gardener and the coachman. . . . What did we do to deserve such trouble? (*Exits.*)

SMIRNOV (*examining the pistols*). You see, there are several sorts of pistols . . . there are special dueling pistols, the Mortimer with primers. Then there are Smith and Wesson revolvers, triple action with extractors . . . excellent pistols! . . . they cost a minimum of ninety rubles a pair. . . . You must hold the revolver like this . . . (*Aside.*) What eyes, what eyes! A woman to set you on fire!

POPOVA. Like this?

SMIRNOV. Yes, like this . . . then you cock the pistol . . . take aim . . . put your head back a little . . . stretch your arm out all the way . . . that's right . . . then with this finger press on this little piece of goods . . . and that's all there is to do . . . but the most important thing is not to get excited and aim without hurrying . . . try to keep your arm from shaking.

POPOVA. Good . . . it's not comfortable to shoot indoors. Let's go into the garden.

SMIRNOV. Let's go. But I'm giving you advance notice that I'm going to fire into the air.

POPOVA. That's the last straw! Why?

SMIRNOV. Why? . . . Why . . . because it's my business, that's why.

POPOVA. Are you afraid? Yes? Aahhh! No, sir. You're not going to get out of it that easily! Be so good as to follow me! I will not rest until I've put a hole through your forehead . . . that forehead I hate so much! Are you afraid?

SMIRNOV. Yes, I'm afraid.

POPOVA. You're lying! Why don't you want to fight?

SMIRNOV. Because . . . because you . . . because I like you.

POPOVA (*laughs angrily*). He likes me! He dares say that he likes me! (*Points to the door.*) Out!

Smirnov (*loads the revolver in silence, takes cap and goes; at the door, stops for half a minute while they look at each other in silence; then he approaches* Popova *hesitantly*). Listen. . . . Are you still angry? I'm extremely irritated, but, do you understand me, how can I express it . . . the fact is, that, you see, strictly speaking . . . (*He shouts.*) Is it my fault, really, for liking you? (*Grabs the back of a chair; chair cracks and breaks.*) Why the hell do you have such fragile furniture! I like you! Do you understand? I . . . I'm almost in love with you!

Popova. Get away from me—I hate you!

Smirnov. God, what a woman! I've never in my life seen anything like her! I'm lost! I'm done for! I'm caught like a mouse in a trap!

Popova. Stand back or I'll shoot!

Smirnov. Shoot! You could never understand what happiness it would be to die under the gaze of those wonderful eyes, to be shot by a revolver which was held by those little velvet hands. . . . I've gone out of my mind! Think about it and decide right away, because if I leave here, then we'll never see each other again! Decide . . . I'm a nobleman, a respectable gentleman, of good family. I have an income of ten thousand a year. . . . I can put a bullet through a coin tossed in the air . . . I have some fine horses. . . . Will you be my wife?

Popova (*indignantly brandishes her revolver*). Let's fight! I challenge you!

Smirnov. I'm out of my mind . . . I don't understand anything . . . (*Shouts.*) Hey, you, water!

Popova (*shouts*). Let's fight!

Smirnov. I've gone out of my mind. I'm in love like a boy, like an idiot! (*He grabs her hand, she screams with pain.*) I love you! (*Kneels.*) I love you as I've never loved before! I've jilted twelve women, nine women have jilted me, but I've never loved one of them as I love you. . . . I'm weak, I'm a limp rag . . . I'm on my knees like a fool, offering you my hand. . . . Shame, shame! I haven't been in love for five years, I vowed I wouldn't; and suddenly I'm in love, like a fish out of water. I'm offering my hand in marriage. Yes or no? You don't want to? You don't need to! (*Gets up and quickly goes to the door.*)

POPOVA. Wait!

SMIRNOV (*stops*). Well?

POPOVA. Nothing . . . you can go . . . go away . . . wait. . . . No, get out, get out! I hate you! But— Don't go! Oh, if you only knew how furious I am, how angry! (*Throws revolver on table.*) My fingers are swollen from that nasty thing. . . . (*Tears her handkerchief furiously.*) What are you waiting for? Get out!

SMIRNOV. Farewell!

POPOVA. Yes, yes, go away! (*Shouts.*) Where are you going? Stop. . . . Oh, go away! Oh, how furious I am! Don't come near me! Don't come near me!

SMIRNOV (*approaching her*). How angry I am with myself! I'm in love like a student, I've been on my knees. . . . It gives me the shivers. (*Rudely.*) I love you! A lot good it will do me to fall in love with you! Tomorrow I've got to pay the interest, begin the mowing of the hay. (*Puts his arm around her waist.*) I'll never forgive myself for this. . . .

POPOVA. Get away from me! Get your hands away! I . . . hate you! I . . . challenge you!

(*Prolonged kiss. LUKA enters with an ax, the GAR-DENER with a rake, the COACHMAN with a pitchfork, and WORKMEN with cudgels.*)

LUKA (*catches sight of the pair kissing*). Lord in heaven! (*Pause.*)

POPOVA (*lowering her eyes*). Luka, tell them in the stable not to give Toby any oats today.

CURTAIN

THE PROPOSAL

❦

A Joke in One Act

CHARACTERS

STEPAN STEPANOVICH CHUBUKOV, *landowner*

NATALYA STEPANOVNA, *his daughter, aged twenty-five*

IVAN VASSILIEVICH LOMOV, *a neighbor of the Chubukov's, hale and hearty, but overanxious about his health*

(*The curtain rises on* CHUBUKOV *and* LOMOV, *the latter in evening dress and white gloves.*)

CHUBUKOV (*rising to meet* LOMOV). My dear friend, is it really you? Ivan Vassilievich! I'm so happy! (*Squeezes his hand.*) Well, this is a surprise, my boy. . . . How are you?

LOMOV. Thank you. And how are you?

CHUBUKOV. Making do, my dear, thanks to your prayers and things. Please sit down. . . . Now you know it's not nice to forget your neighbors, my dear. But, dear friend, why such formality? Evening dress, with gloves and things. Are you going visiting or something, my boy?

LOMOV. No, only visiting you, my dear Stepan Stepanovich.

CHUBUKOV. Then why are you wearing tails, dear boy? As though you were making a formal New Year's visit?

LOMOV. You see, it's like this. (*Takes his arm.*) I've come to see you, dear Stepan Stepanovich, to trouble you with a request. I've come, honorably, to ask for your help more than once, and always you have, so to speak— But forgive me, I'm so excited . . . I'll drink some water, dear Stepan Stepanovich. (*Goes for water.*)

CHUBUKOV (*aside*). He's come to ask for money! I won't give him any! (*To* LOMOV.) What is it, you handsome fellow?

LOMOV. You see, my dear Stepanich. . . . Forgive me, Stepan, I mean ovich. . . . You see, I'm so terribly unnerved, as you will please notice. . . . In short, you're the only one who can help me, though, of course, I don't deserve it . . . and I have no right to count on your help. . . .

CHUBUKOV. Don't drag it out, my dear! Spit it out! Well?

LOMOV. Right away . . . this minute. . . . The fact is, I've come to ask for the hand of your daughter, Natalya Stepanovna.

CHUBUKOV (*joyfully*). You darling! Ivan Vassilievich! Say it again—I didn't quite hear you!

LOMOV. I have the honor to ask you . . .

CHUBUKOV. My own boy . . . I'm so glad and things. . . . Yes, indeed, and all that sort of thing. (*Embraces and kisses him.*) For a long time I've been hoping. It was what I always hoped for. (*Sheds a tear.*) I've always loved you, my precious boy, as if you were my very own son. May God give you both His love and council and things, and I always hoped— Why am I standing here like an idiot? I'm taken aback with joy, completely taken aback! Oh, with all my soul . . . I'll go and call Natasha and things.

LOMOV (*touched*). Dear Stepan Stepanovich, what do you think? Can I count on her consent?

CHUBUKOV. Well, of course, my handsome boy . . . and . . . as if she wouldn't consent! She's like a lovesick cat in heat . . . *you know.* . . . I'll be right back! (*He goes out.*)

LOMOV (*alone*). I'm cold . . . I'm trembling all over as if I were about to take an examination. The main thing is to make up my mind. If I think too much, and hesitate, talk too much, searching for ideal woman love, I'll never get married. . . . Brr! It's cold! Natalya Stepanovna is an excellent housekeeper, she's not bad looking, she's educated. . . . What more do I want? But I'm so nervous, I hear noises in my ear. (*Drinks water.*) It's impossible for me not to get married. . . . In the first place, I'm already thirty-five years old —a critical age, so to speak. In the second place, I need an orderly, regular existence. . . . I have heart disease . . . constant palpitations of the heart . . . I'm forever flaring up and always so excitable. . . . At this very moment my lips are trembling and there's a twitch in my right eyelid. . . . But the most terrible thing of all is the way I sleep. As soon as I get to bed and begin to fall asleep, something in my left side gives . . . a twinge! And then it happens twenty times . . .

NATALYA STEPANOVNA (*entering*). Well, well! So it's you, and Papa said: "Go inside. There's a merchant who's come for his goods." Hello, Ivan Vassilievich!

LOMOV. How do you do, dear Natalya Stepanovna!

NATALYA STEPANOVNA. You must excuse my apron and my negligee. . . . We're shelling peas for drying. Why haven't you been to see us for such a long time? Have a seat. . . . (*They sit down.*) Would you like to have some lunch?

LOMOV. No, thank you, I've already eaten.

NATALYA STEPANOVNA. Then smoke . . . here are some matches. . . . We're having wonderful weather, but yesterday it rained so hard that the workmen did nothing all day long. How much hay have you stacked? Can you imagine, I was so greedy, I had them cut a whole field of hay and now I'm not at all happy about it; I'm afraid my hay may just rot. It might have been better to wait. But what's this? You in evening dress? Well, that's a surprise! Are you going to a ball or something? I think it's improved you, by the way. . . . Tell me truly, why are you playing the dandy?

LOMOV (*excited*). You see, my dear Natalya Stepanovna . . . the fact is, I've made up my mind to ask you to listen to me. . . . Of course, you'll be surprised and even angry, but I . . . (*Aside.*) It's terribly cold!

NATALYA STEPANOVNA. Well, what is it? (*Pause.*) Well?

LOMOV. I'll try to be brief. You must know, Natalya Stepanovna, that for a long time now, ever since my childhood, I have had the privilege of knowing your family. My late aunt and her husband, from whom, as you must know, I inherited, always had the greatest respect for your father and your late mother. The Lomov family and the Chubukov family have always been on the most friendly, and, it may even be said, intimate terms. And, as you must know, my land is in close proximity to yours. If you recollect, my Volovy Meadows are right next to your birchwoods.

NATALYA STEPANOVNA. Excuse my interrupting you. You said, "My Volovy Meadows." . . . But are they really yours?

LOMOV. Yes, they're mine. . . .

NATALYA STEPANOVNA. Well, what can we expect next? The Volovy Meadows are ours, not yours!

LOMOV. No, they're mine, dear Natalya Stepanovna.

NATALYA STEPANOVNA. That's news to me. How did they come to be yours?

LOMOV. How do you mean, how? I'm speaking about the Volovy Meadows which are wedged in between your birches and the Burnt Swamp.

NATALYA STEPANOVNA. Yes, yes, well . . . they're ours. . . .

LOMOV. No, you're mistaken, dear Natalya Stepanovna— they're mine.

NATALYA STEPANOVNA. Collect yourself, Ivan Vassilievich! How long have they been yours?

LOMOV. What do you mean, how long? As long as I can remember, they have been ours!

NATALYA STEPANOVNA. Well, I'm sorry, but I can't accept that!

LOMOV. But you can see from the documents, dear Natalya Stepanovna. Volovy Meadows were once in dispute, that's true; but now everybody knows they're mine! There's really nothing to argue about. You see, my aunt's grandmother gave those meadows on permanent loan, rent-free, to your father's grandfather's peasants, in return for which they fired her bricks. Your great-grandfather's peasants used the

Lomov. Mine!

Chubukov (*entering*). What's the matter? What are you shouting about?

Natalya Stepanovna. Papa, please explain to this gentleman to whom the Volovy Meadows belong, to us or to him?

Chubukov (*to him*). The meadows are ours, darling!

Lomov. But forgive me, Stepan Stepanich, how could they be yours? Be reasonable! My aunt's grandmother gave the meadows to your peasants temporarily, free of charge. The peasants had the use of the land for forty years and got accustomed to thinking of it as their own, when the situation occurred ...

Chubukov. Excuse me, my dear friend ... you forget that the peasants didn't pay your grandmother just because the meadows were in dispute and things. Every dog knows they're ours, after all. You can't have seen the plans!

Lomov. And I'll prove to you that they're mine!

Chubukov. You won't prove it, my dear boy!

Lomov. Yes, I will!

Chubukov. Why shout like that, my dear fellow? Shouting like that doesn't prove anything at all! I don't want anything of yours and I have no intention of letting anything of my own get away from me. Why should I? As far as that goes, my dear boy, if you have the intention of disputing the meadows, and things, I'd rather give them to the peasants than to you. There!

Lomov. I don't understand! What right have you to give away somebody else's property?

Chubukov. Please let me know whether I have the right or not. Young man, I am not accustomed to being spoken to in that tone of voice, and things. I'm twice your age, young man, and I ask you to speak to me without exciting yourself, and things.

LOMOV. No, no! You take me for a fool, and you're laughing at me! You call my land yours, and then you want me to keep calm and speak to you as a gentleman! Good neighbors don't behave this way, Stepan Stepanich! You're not a neighbor, you're a usurper!

CHUBUKOV. What's that? What did you say?

NATALYA STEPANOVNA. Papa, send the mowers to the meadows at once!

CHUBUKOV (to LOMOV). What did you say, sir?

NATALYA STEPANOVNA. Volovy Meadows are ours, and I won't give them up, I won't, I won't!

LOMOV. We'll see about that! I'll prove to you in court they're mine!

CHUBUKOV. In court? You can take it to court, my dear sir, and things! Go ahead! I know you—you're just waiting for the opportunity to go to court, and things . . . you have a niggling nature! Your whole family is litigation-minded! All of them!

LOMOV. Please don't insult my family! The Lomovs have all been honest people and not one of them has been on trial for embezzling, like your dear uncle!

CHUBUKOV. And you Lomovs—your whole family's full of lunatics!

NATALYA STEPANOVNA. All of them! All of them!

CHUBUKOV. Your grandfather was a dipsomaniac and your youngest aunt, Nastasya Mikhailovna, ran away with an architect, and things . . .

LOMOV. And your mother was a hunchback. (Clutches his heart.) I have a twinge in my side . . . now it's in my head! Dear Lord! Water!

CHUBUKOV. And your father was a gambler and a glutton!

NATALYA STEPANOVNA. And your aunt was a scandal-monger—hard to find her equal!

LOMOV. My left foot is asleep . . . and you're an in-triguer . . . oh, my heart! And it's no secret that before the last elections . . . there are stars in front of my eyes . . . where's my hat?

NATALYA STEPANOVNA. It's low! Dishonest! Despicable!

CHUBUKOV. And you're just a venomous, two-faced poseur! That's what you are!

LOMOV. Here's my hat . . . my heart— Which way do I go? Where's the door? Oh! . . . I think I'm dying! . . . My foot's asleep. (*He goes to the door.*)

CHUBUKOV (*calls after him*). And never set foot in my house again!

NATALYA STEPANOVNA. Take it to court! We'll see about that!

(LOMOV *goes out, reeling.*)

CHUBUKOV. The villain! The scarecrow!

NATALYA STEPANOVNA. The monster! Grabbing other peo-ple's land, and then daring to insult us besides!

CHUBUKOV. That ridiculous boy, that dolt, dared to come here and make a proposal, and things! Would you believe it, a proposal!

NATALYA STEPANOVNA. What proposal?

CHUBUKOV. Imagine! He came here in order to propose to you.

NATALYA STEPANOVNA. Propose? To me? Why didn't you tell me that before?

CHUBUKOV. That's why he got all dressed up in evening clothes! The sausage! The shrimp!

NATALYA STEPANOVNA. To me? Propose? (*Falls into easy chair and moans.*) Bring him back! Bring him back! Oh! Bring him back! Make him come back!

CHUBUKOV. Bring whom back?

NATALYA STEPANOVNA. Quickly! Quickly! I feel faint! Bring him back! Oh! (*She is in hysterics.*)

CHUBUKOV. What do you mean? What's the matter with you? (*Clutches at his head.*) What an unfortunate man I am! I'll shoot myself! I'll hang myself! They're torturing me!

NATALYA STEPANOVNA. I'm dying! Bring him back!

CHUBUKOV. Fool! In a moment. Don't howl! (*Runs out.*)

NATALYA STEPANOVNA (*alone, moans*). What have we done? Bring him back! Bring him back!

CHUBUKOV (*runs in*). He's coming, and things. Damn him! Oof! Talk to him yourself, I just don't want to . . .

NATALYA STEPANOVNA (*moans*). Bring him back!

CHUBUKOV (*shouts*). He's coming! I told you. Oh, what a burden, dear Lord, to be the father of a grownup daughter! I'll cut my throat! I will, I'll cut my throat! We've insulted the boy, shamed him, driven him out, and it was all your doing! . . . Yours!

NATALYA STEPANOVNA. No, it was yours!

CHUBUKOV. So now it's my fault, what can you expect? (*Lomov appears at the door.*) Well, you talk to him yourself! (*Goes out.*)

LOMOV (*enters, exhausted*). Those awful palpitations . . . my foot's gone to sleep . . . there's a twinge in my side. . . .

NATALYA STEPANOVNA. Forgive us, we were rather hasty, Ivan Vassilievich. . . . Now I remember: Volovy Meadows are really yours.

LOMOV. My heart is beating so fast . . . my meadows . . . both my eyelids are twitching . . .

NATALYA STEPANOVNA. Yes, they're yours, the meadows are yours. . . . Sit down. . . . (*They sit.*) We were wrong.

LOMOV. For me, it was a matter of principle. The land is not what I care about, it was the principle.

NATALYA STEPANOVNA. Just the principle. . . . Let's talk about something else.

LOMOV. Especially since I have proof. My aunt's grandmother gave your father's grandfather's peasants . . .

NATALYA STEPANOVNA. That's enough; enough of all of that. . . . (*Aside.*) I don't know how to get him started. . . . (*To him.*) Are you going hunting soon?

LOMOV. I expect to go after some black grouse when the harvest is over, dear Natalya Stepanovna. But have you heard? You can't imagine what trouble I've been having! My dog Humper—you know him—has begun to limp.

NATALYA STEPANOVNA. What a pity! Why?

LOMOV. I don't know . . . he dislocated his paw and another dog bit him. (*Sighs.*) My very best dog, to say nothing of the money. I paid Mironov a hundred and twenty-five rubles for him.

NATALYA STEPANOVNA. You paid too much, Ivan Vassilievich!

LOMOV. Well, in my opinion, that was very cheap. He was a wonderful dog.

NATALYA STEPANOVNA. Papa spent eighty-five rubles for his Pumper and Pumper is so much better than Humper!

LOMOV. Pumper better than Humper? You're joking! (*Laughs.*) Pumper better than Humper!

NATALYA STEPANOVNA. Of course he's better! Of course,

Pumper *is* young, he's not full-grown yet, but in points and pedigree he's better than any of Volchanyetski's dogs.

LOMOV. Excuse me, Natalya Stepanovna, but you've forgotten that he's overshot and an overshot dog can never grip properly.

NATALYA STEPANOVNA. Overshot? That's the first time I've heard that!

LOMOV. I assure you his lower jaw is shorter than his upper.

NATALYA STEPANOVNA. Did you measure it?

LOMOV. Yes, I did. He's all right for driving, of course, but when it comes to gripping, then he's hardly . . .

NATALYA STEPANOVNA. In the first place, our Pumper is a thoroughbred. He's the son of Harness and Chisels, and nobody could ever tell what species your dog was. . . . He's as old and ugly as a hack.

LOMOV. He's old, but I wouldn't give five of your Pumpers for him. Really, how can you? Humper is a dog, but Pumper . . . it's laughable to argue about it. . . . Every sportsman has a Pumper. They're cheap and easy to come by. Twenty-five rubles is too much to pay for them.

NATALYA STEPANOVNA. Ivan Vassilievich, there's a demon of contradiction in you, today. First you invent a story to say that Volovy Meadows are yours, then you say that Humper is better than Pumper. I don't like it when people don't say what they mean. You see, you know perfectly well that Pumper is a hundred times better than . . . your silly Humper. Then why do you want to say the contrary?

LOMOV. I see, Natalya Stepanovna, that you think I am either blind or a fool. Don't you want to understand that Pumper is overshot!

NATALYA STEPANOVNA. That's not true.

LOMOV. He is!

NATALYA STEPANOVNA (*shouts*). He isn't!

LOMOV. Why are you shouting, Mademoiselle?

NATALYA STEPANOVNA. Why talk nonsense? This is outrageous. It's time your Humper was shot, and you compare him with Pumper!

LOMOV. Excuse me, I cannot continue this argument. My heart is palpitating.

NATALYA STEPANOVNA. I've noticed that the hunters who argue the most know the least.

LOMOV. Mademoiselle, please, I ask you; keep quiet. . . . My heart is bursting. . . . (*Shouts.*) Shut up!

NATALYA STEPANOVNA. I will not shut up until you acknowledge that Pumper is a hundred times better than Humper!

LOMOV. A hundred times worse! I hope your Pumper drops dead! Oh, my temples, my eyes, my shoulders . . .

NATALYA STEPANOVNA. And your stupid idiotic Humper —there's no need to kill him because he's already half dead!

LOMOV (*cries*). Shut up! My heart is bursting!

NATALYA STEPANOVNA. I will not!

CHUBUKOV (*enters*). Now what?

NATALYA STEPANOVNA. Papa, tell us truly, with a clear conscience. Which dog is better—our Pumper or his Humper?

LOMOV. Stepan Stepanovich, I implore you, tell me only one thing: is your Pumper overshot or is he not? Yes or no?

CHUBUKOV. Well, suppose he is. It doesn't make any difference! There isn't a better dog in the whole district, and things.

LOMOV. But isn't my Humper better? Tell the truth!

CHUBUKOV. Don't get so excited, my boy. . . . Permit me.
. . . Your Humper, of course, has his good points, he's a
thoroughbred, firm on his feet, well built, and things, but,
my dear boy, if you really want to know the truth about
that dog, he has two important deficiencies: he's old and he's
snubnosed.

LOMOV. Excuse me, I have heart palpitations. . . . Let's
look at the facts. . . . You will remember that on the
Maruskin fields my Humper kept up with the Count's
Avenger neck and neck, while your Pumper remained a half
a mile behind.

CHUBUKOV. He fell behind because the Count's hunter
whipped him with his riding crop.

LOMOV. He deserved it. The dogs were all chasing the fox
and Pumper started to annoy the sheep.

CHUBUKOV. That's not true! . . . My dear boy, I have a
violent temper so I am asking you to stop this argument. He
was hit because everybody is jealous of everybody else's
dogs. . . . Yes! They all hate! And you, sir, are just as
much to blame! No sooner do you notice that some dog is
superior to Humper than you start something . . . and
things. . . . You see, I remember everything!

LOMOV. And so do I!

CHUBUKOV (mimics him). So do I! And what do you
remember?

LOMOV. Palpitations . . . my foot's paralyzed . . . I
can't . . .

NATALYA STEPANOVNA (mimics him). Palpitations! . . .
What sort of a hunter are you? You should lie on the kitchen
stove crushing cockroaches . . . and not go out hunting
foxes! Palpitations!

CHUBUKOV. Really, what kind of hunter are you? You

should sit at home with your palpitations rather than hanging off a saddle. It would be fine if you went to hunt, but you only go so that you can argue or disturb other people's dogs, or things. . . . I lose my temper easily, so let's stop this conversation! You're just not a sportsman, that's all there is to it!

LOMOV. Are you a sportsman? You only go hunting to butter up the Count and to intrigue. . . . Palpitations! You're a troublemaker!

CHUBUKOV. What? I, a troublemaker? (*Shouts.*) Shut up!

LOMOV. Troublemaker!

CHUBUKOV. Guttersnipe! Puppy!

LOMOV. You old rat! Jesuit!

CHUBUKOV. Shut up, or I'll shoot you with a rusty shotgun like a partridge! Windbag!

LOMOV. Everybody knows that—oh, my heart!—your poor late wife used to beat you . . . my leg . . . my forehead . . . sparks in front of my eyes. . . . I'm falling! I'm falling!

CHUBUKOV. And your housekeeper has you under her thumb!

LOMOV. Oh! oh! oh! My heart has burst! My shoulders have come off. . . . Where is my shoulder? I'm dying! (*Falls into armchair.*) A doctor! (*Faints.*)

CHUBUKOV. Guttersnipe! Sissy! Windbag! I'm feeling faint. (*Drinks water.*) Faint!

NATALYA STEPANOVNA. What kind of hunter are you? You can't even sit on a horse! (*To her father.*) Papa! What's the matter with him! Look, Papa! (*Screams.*) Ivan Vassilievich! He's dead!

CHUBUKOV. I'm feeling faint! I'm suffocating! Air!

NATALYA STEPANOVNA. He's dead! (*Tugs at* LOMOV's *sleeve*.) Ivan Vassilich! Ivan Vassilich! What have we done! He's dead! (*Falls into an armchair.*) A doctor! A doctor! (*Hysterics.*)

CHUBUKOV. Oh! What now? What's wrong with you now?

NATALYA STEPANOVNA (*moans*). He's dead . . . dead!

CHUBUKOV. Who's dead? (*Glancing at* LOMOV.) He's dead! Lord in heaven! Water! A doctor! (*Holds a glass of water to* LOMOV's *mouth.*) Drink! No, he won't drink! It means he's dead, and things. I'm the most unfortunate of men! Why didn't I put a bullet through my head? Why didn't I cut my throat a long time ago? What am I waiting for? Give me a knife! Give me a gun! (LOMOV *stirs.*) He's coming to life. Drink some water! . . . That's it!

LOMOV. Sparks in front of my eyes . . . a mist . . . where am I?

CHUBUKOV. You'd better get married as soon as possible. . . . Go to the devil! She consents! (*Joins* LOMOV's *and* NATALYA STEPANOVNA's *hands.*) She has consented and all the rest and things. I give you my blessing and things. Only leave me in peace!

LOMOV. Eh? What? (*Getting up.*) Who?

CHUBUKOV. She has consented! Well, kiss each other . . . and . . . the devil take you!

NATALYA STEPANOVNA (*moans*). He's alive. . . . Yes, yes, I have consented. . . .

CHUBUKOV. Kiss each other!

LOMOV. Eh? Who? (*Kisses* NATALYA STEPANOVNA.) I'm so glad. . . . Excuse me, what's it about? Oh, yes, I understand, my heart, sparks. . . . I'm happy, Natalya Stepanovna. . . . (*Kisses her hand.*) My leg has gone to sleep. . . .

NATALYA STEPANOVNA. I . . . I also am happy. . . .

CHUBUKOV. What a load off my mind! . . . Oof!

NATALYA STEPANOVNA. But . . . you must admit it now: Humper is not as good as Pumper.

LOMOV. He's better! He's superior!

NATALYA STEPANOVNA. Inferior!

CHUBUKOV. Well, what a way to start connubial bliss! Let's have a little champagne!

LOMOV. He's better! He's superior!

NATALYA STEPANOVNA. He's inferior! Inferior! Inferior!

CHUBUKOV (*trying to shout them down*). Let's have some champagne! Champagne!

CURTAIN

THE RELUCTANT TRAGEDIAN:

Life in the Country

❧

A Joke in One Act

CHARACTERS

IVAN IVANOVICH TOLKACHOV, *paterfamilias*
ALEXEY ALEXEYEVICH MURASHKIN, *his friend*

The action takes place in Petersburg, in MURASHKIN's *apartment.* MURASHKIN's *study. Comfortable furniture.* MURASHKIN *is seated at his desk.*

(*Enter* TOLKACHOV, *carrying a glass lampshade, a toy bicycle, three hatboxes, a large bundle of clothes, a case of beer, and several smaller bundles. He looks around with a dazed expression on his face and slips down into the couch, exhausted.*)

MURASHKIN. My dear Ivan Ivanovich! I'm delighted to see you. What are you doing here?

TOLKACHOV (*breathing heavily*). Ah, my dear old friend! I've come to ask for a favor. . . . Please . . . lend me a revolver till tomorrow. Be a friend.

MURASHKIN. What do you want with a revolver?

TOLKACHOV. I need one. Dear Lord! Give me some water . . . right away, water! I have a lot of ground to cover before I rest tonight. In any case, do me a favor. Lend it to me!

MURASHKIN. Ivan Ivanich, what is this? What ground do you have to cover? I think you're up to something, aren't you? I can see by your face that you're up to something, and I don't like it. What's the matter with you? Are you upset about something?

TOLKACHOV. Wait. Let me catch my breath. Oh, dear Lord, I'm dog tired. I feel like a piece of shashlik roasting on a spit. I can't go on any longer. Be a friend. Don't ask me any questions. Don't insist on details. . . . Give me a revolver! I beg of you!

MURASHKIN. That's quite enough, Ivan Ivanich! You're such a coward! A family man like you, a civil servant! For shame!

TOLKACHOV. A family man? Me? I'm a martyr! A beast of burden, a nigger, a slave, a villain, serving my time until I start out for the next world. I'm a nonentity, a blockhead, an idiot! What am I living for? For what? (*He jumps up.*) Well, tell me: why am I living? Why all this endless mental and physical suffering? I can understand being a martyr to an idea. That, yes! But to be a martyr to God knows what, to a woman's skirt, to a lampshade, no! Allow me to decline! No, no, no! I've had enough! Enough!

MURASHKIN. Don't shout. The neighbors will hear.

TOLKACHOV. Let them. I don't care. If you don't give me a revolver, then somebody else will. And I'll put an end to this life! I've made up my mind!

MURASHKIN. Stop that. You've torn my button off! Please calm down. You know, I don't understand what's so bad about your life.

TOLKACHOV. What? You ask: what? Well, allow me to tell you. Please. Let me give you my opinion, and maybe I'll feel a little better. Let's sit down. Now listen. . . . Oh, my God! I can't catch my breath! For instance, just today. Imagine! As you well know, from ten in the morning until four in the afternoon, I'm busy blowing my trumpet around the office. It's hot, stuffy, the flies are not friendly; my dear friend, it's chaos! The secretary is on vacation. The boss, Hrapov, is on his honeymoon. The people in the office have their mind on the country, their love affairs, amateur theatricals! They're all sleepy and exhausted, good for nothing. . . . The secretary's work is being handled by somebody who is deaf in one ear: and she's also in love. And the clients act as if they'd lost their senses—rushing around, angry, threatening—everything is in such a commotion, you can't hear yourself talk. Confusion and commotion. You want to cry for help. And my work is deadly. I do the same things over and over again, check a reference, correct a reference, check, correct—it's as monotonous as the waves in the sea. You understand, it's simple: you feel as if your eyes are coming out of your head!

Give me some water! You leave the office exhausted, then you go home. You'd like to eat and get a good night's sleep, but no! You remember that you live in the country, and you're a slave there, a nothing, a piece of string, an icicle, a nonentity; call it whatever you like. Now you can run errands! There's a charming custom where we live in the country! When somebody goes into the city, every woman, not to mention your wife, has the authority to load you up with errands. My wife tells me to be sure to go to the dressmaker and scold her for making her blouse too wide in the bust and too narrow in the shoulders; Sonia's shoes have to be exchanged; my sister-in-law needs a sample of red silk, twenty kopecks' worth; two and one half yards of tape. Here. Let me read you the list.

(*He takes a slip of paper from his pocket and reads.*) A lampshade; a pound of pork sausage; cloves and cinnamon, five kopecks' worth; castor oil for Misha; ten pounds of granulated sugar; don't forget to bring a copper pot and a sugar bowl; carbolic acid, insect powder, face powder, ten kopecks' worth; twenty bottles of beer; some vinegar, and a corset for Mademoiselle Chanceau who lives at number eighty-two. Phew! And bring Misha's winter coat and galoshes home. This order is for my wife and family. But then there are errands to do for our dear friends and neighbors, may they go to the devil! Volodya Vlassin's birthday is tomorrow. Must buy a bicycle for him. Colonel Virin's wife is in a delicate condition, and so I'm obliged to call on the midwife daily to get her to come. And so on and so forth. There are five lists in my pocket and my handkerchief is all knotted up. So, my dear friend, between work and getting on the train, I run around town like a dog, with my tongue hanging out—running, running—and cursing my life. From the clothing store to the druggist, from the druggist to the dressmaker's, from the dressmaker's to the pork butcher, from there back to the druggist. You trip in one place and lose your money in another; in a third you forget to pay and they make a big thing out of it; in a fourth, you step on a lady's skirt, oof! You have so much exercise, you break down; every night your bones ache and you dream of crocodiles. . . . Well, now your errands are done, your purchases are made; how can you pack up and carry all that stuff? First, how can you put the heavy copper pot and the lampshade together, the tea with the carbolic acid? How can you carry the bottles and the bicycle? It's a labor of Hercules, a puzzle for the mind, a rebus! Well, you break your head thinking about it and the result is, no matter what you do, something breaks or spills. In the train you stand up, your arms spread out wide, bowlegged, supporting the bundles somehow with your chin. The boxes, the baskets, the bundles are all over you. The train starts; the people start pushing everything around. Your belongings are on somebody else's seat. They shout. They call the conductor. They threaten to throw you off the train. What can I do about it? I stand there with my eyes blinking like a beaten-down donkey.

But, listen! I arrive home. I'd like to have a nice drink and a decent meal for all my work. Don't I deserve it? No chance. My wife has been watching out for me for a long time. I've hardly slopped up my soup when she pounces. Wouldn't I just love to go to the theater or dancing? You can't say no! You are a husband, and the word "husband" translated into the language of people in the country means dumb animal—that can be driven and overloaded as much as they like, and you don't have to be afraid that the Society for the Prevention of Cruelty to Animals will interfere. You go. You stare at a play called *A Country Scandal* or something like that; you applaud when your wife does and you feel worse, worse, worse until you think you'll go out of your mind. At the dance, you go looking among the dancers for someone to dance with your wife, and if there is a shortage of eligible men, then you dance the quadrille by yourself, if you please. You can't believe it's after midnight when you get home from the theater or the dance. And now you're no longer a man but a wet rag. Finally you arrive at what you want: to undress and go to bed. It's wonderful to close your eyes and go to sleep . . . everything is so nice, warm, poetic, you understand; the children in the other room are not screeching any more; your wife is somewhere else; your conscience is clear. What more could a man want? You snuggle under the covers . . . and all of a sudden . . . suddenly . . . you hear . . . *bzzzzzz!* Mosquitoes!

(*He jumps up.*) Mosquitoes—may they be cursed! Ana-

thema! Damn them! Those mosquitoes! (*He shakes his fist.*)
Mosquitoes! A plague! An inquisition! *Bzzzzz* . . . The sound
they make is sad and mournful, as if they're begging your
pardon, but the little rascals sting, and then you scratch
yourself for a whole hour afterward. You smoke, you strike
out, you hide yourself from head to foot—it's no use! In the
end you give up, you sacrifice yourself to be torn to pieces,
damn it! And you haven't got the time to get used to the
mosquitoes when a new Egyptian plague begins: your wife
and her friend the tenor are singing a round of songs. They
sleep in the daytime and at night they rehearse for the amateur concerts. My God! A tenor—that's a torture no mos-
quito can compete with. (*He sings.*) "Don't say that my
youth is over . . ." "Once more you are my fascination . . ."
Oh, if I could get away! My mind is going! But I've worked
out a trick to stop hearing it all: I tap with my thumbs
around my ears. They go on chattering until four in the
morning, until they break up. Oh, my friend, give me a little
more water . . . I'm exhausted. . . . Then, without any sleep,
I get up at six and walk to the station. I run because I'm
afraid I'll be late. It's foggy, misty, cold, brrr! I go to town
and the merry-go-round starts all over again. That's the
truth, my friend. I tell you it's a life I wouldn't wish on my
worst enemy! You understand—I'm ill! I have asthma, heart-
burn; I'm always afraid. I have indigestion, my vision is
blurred. . . . Believe it or not, I'm becoming a psychopath. . . .

(*Looks over his shoulder.*) Don't tell anybody . . . I'm
going to visit a psychiatrist. They'll find the devil in me,
my friend. You see, when I'm upset and annoyed, when the
mosquitoes sting and the tenors sing, my vision becomes suddenly blurred; I run like a madman through the house and
I shout: "Give me blood! Blood!" At times like that I could
knife somebody or smash his head in with a chair. That's
what country life leads to! And nobody's sorry. Nobody
sympathizes! It serves me right. They even laugh at me.
But I'm alive and I want to live! This is not a farce, it's
a tragedy! Listen to me: if you don't give me a revolver,
you could at least sympathize!

MURASHKIN. But I do sympathize!

TOLKACHOV. I know you do. I can see that. Forgive me.

I've got to go get some anchovies and sausages. . . . I still need tooth powder before I can go to the station.

MURASHKIN. Where do you live in the country?

TOLKACHOV. In Dead River.

MURASHKIN (*joyfully*). Really? There's a coincidence. Listen: do you know a certain Olga Pavlova Finberg in that neck of the woods, by any chance?

TOLKACHOV. Yes, I know her quite well.

MURASHKIN. Can you imagine? What a piece of luck! If you would be so kind . . .

TOLKACHOV. What?

MURASHKIN. My dear friend, how would you like to do me a little favor? Be a friend. Promise me; will you do it?

TOLKACHOV. What?

MURASHKIN. As a favor! Please, dear friend, first be sure and give Olga Pavlova my best regards. Tell her I'm alive and well. Shake hands with her for me. Then take her a little something. She asked me to get her a sewing machine, but there was nobody to deliver it. . . . Take it to her, my friend! And while you're at it, take this canary in its cage . . . only watch out so the door doesn't break open. . . . Why are you looking at me like that?

TOLKACHOV. A sewing machine . . . a canary cage . . . a canary . . . songbirds . . . canary birds . . .

MURASHKIN. Ivan Ivanich, what's the matter with you? Why are you turning purple?

TOLKACHOV (*stamping his foot*). Give me that sewing machine! Where is the bird cage? Sit on me! Eat me alive! Torture me! Finish me off! (*Clenches his fists.*) I want blood! Blood! Blood!

MURASHKIN. You're out of your mind!

TOLKACHOV (*closing in on him*). I must have blood! Blood!

MURASHKIN (*horror-stricken*). He's gone out of his mind! (*He screams.*) Petrushka! Marya! Where are you? Help me, please!

TOLKACHOV (*chasing him around the room*). I will have blood! Blood!

CURTAIN

THE WEDDING

CHARACTERS

YEVDOKIM ZAHAROVICH ZHIGALOV, *a retired civil servant*

NASTASYA TIMOFEYEVNA, *his wife*

DASHENKA, *their daughter*

EPAMINOND MAXIMOVICH APLOMBOV, *Dashenka's bride-groom*

FYODOR YAKOVLEVICH REVUNOV-KARAULOV, *a captain of the second rank, in retirement*

ANDREY ANDREYEVICH NUNIN, *agent for an insurance company*

ANNA MARTINOVNA ZMEYUKINA, *midwife, thirty years of age, dressed in bright crimson*

IVAN MIHAILOVICH YAT, *a telegraph office worker*

HARLAMPI SPIRIDONOVICH DIMBA, *a Greek confectioner*

DMITRI STEPANOVICH MOZGOVOY, *a sailor in the imperial navy*

GROOMS, GENTLEMEN, WAITERS, *etc.*

*The scene takes place in one of the rooms in Andronov's
eatery. A brilliantly lit room. A large table, set for supper.
Waiters in frock coats are bustling about the table. Behind
the scenes, music is heard: the last part of a quadrille.*

(ZMEYUKINA, YAT, *and the* BEST MAN *cross the stage.*)

ZMEYUKINA. No, no, no!

YAT (*pursuing her.*) Have a little pity! Pity!

ZMEYUKINA. No, no, no!

THE BEST MAN (*pursuing them*). Messieurs—dames, you
mustn't behave this way! Where are you going? And what
about the *grande ronde? Grande ronde, s'il vous plaît!*

(*They go out. Enter* NASTASYA TIMOFEYEVNA *and*
APLOMBOV.)

NASTASYA TIMOFEYEVNA. Rather than upsetting me with
all your talk, you'd be much better off dancing.

APLOMBOV. I'm not any old Spinoza, twisting my legs into
a figure eight. I'm a man of decision and I have character,
and I see nothing entertaining in such silly pleasures. It's
not just a matter of dancing. I beg your pardon, Maman,
but there's quite a bit about your behavior that I do not
understand. For instance, in addition to the necessary household items, you also promised to give me, with your daughter, two lottery tickets. Where are they?

NASTASYA TIMOFEYEVNA. I have such a headache . . . it must be the weather . . . if only it would thaw!

APLOMBOV. Don't try to change the subject. Just today I found out those tickets were pawned. I beg your pardon, Maman, but only swindlers behave like that. You must understand I'm not behaving like an egoisticist—I don't need your tickets—but it's a matter of principle; and I do not allow myself to be swindled. I've made your daughter happy, and if you don't give me the tickets today, then I'll take it out on your daughter. I'm an honorable man!

NASTASYA TIMOFEYEVNA (looks at the table and counts the tablecloths). One, two, three, four, five . . .

A WAITER. The cook wants to know whether you'd like the ice cream served with rum, madeira, or just plain?

APLOMBOV. With rum. And tell the manager there isn't enough wine. Tell him to serve some more Haut-Sauternes. (To NASTASYA TIMOFEYEVNA.) You also promised and it was all agreed that there would be a general at supper this evening. So where is he, may I ask?

NASTASYA TIMOFEYEVNA. That, my dear, is no fault of mine.

APLOMBOV. Well then, whose is it?

NASTASYA TIMOFEYEVNA. It's Andrey Andreyevich's fault. . . . Yesterday he was here and he promised to bring a real, live general. (Sighs.) It must be he couldn't find one anywhere, or he would have brought him. . . . Don't you think it makes a difference to us? We begrudge nothing to our only daughter. Not even a general. . . .

APLOMBOV. And furthermore . . . everybody, including you, Maman, knows that Yat, that telegraph man, was after Dashenka before I proposed to her. Why did you invite him? Surely you knew that would be unpleasant for me?

NASTASYA TIMOFEYEVNA. How can you? Epaminond Maximovich, now you're a married man and you've already tortured Dashenka and myself long enough with your

endless complaining. What will it be like a year from now?
You're horrid; ugh, so horrid!

APLOMBOV. You don't like to hear the truth? Aha! So that's
it. Then behave decently. I only want you to do one thing:
behave decently!

(*Couples come dancing in, doing the* grande ronde,
from one door to the other. The first couple, the BEST
MAN *and* DASHENKA; *the last,* YAT *and* ZMEYUKINA.
They remain in the room. ZHIGALOV *and* DIMBA *enter
and go up to the table.*)

THE BEST MAN (*shouting*). Promenade! Messieurs, promenade! (*In the wings.*) Promenade!

(*The dancers exit.*)

YAT (*to* ZMEYUKINA). Have pity on me! Pity, adorable
Anna Martinovna.

ZMEYUKINA. Oh, you are the one. . . . I've already told
you I'm not in voice today.

YAT. Please, for me, sing! Just one single note! Be charita-
ble! Just one note!

ZMEYUKINA. I'm bored with you! (*Sits down and fans
herself.*)

YAT. No, you're just heartless! Such a cruel creature—if
I may express it thus, and yet you have such a beautiful,
beautiful voice! With such a voice, if you'll pardon the expression, you shouldn't be a midwife, but sing at recitals,
at public gatherings! For instance, that fioritura came out of
you . . . so divinely . . . (*Sings.*) "I loved you; loved then
in vain . . ." Beautiful!

ZMEYUKINA (*sings*). "I loved you, and may love again . . ."
Is that it?

YAT. That's it! Marvelous!

ZMEYUKINA. No, I'm not in voice today. There (*Giving

him the fan.), fan me a little, will you? . . . It's hot! (*To* APLOMBOV.) Epaminond Maximovich, why are you so melancholy? Really, is that how a bridegroom behaves? Aren't you ashamed of yourself, you bad boy! Well, what are you thinking about?

APLOMBOV. Marriage is a serious step! It must be considered thoroughly, from all angles.

ZMEYUKINA. What disgusting skeptics you all are! When I'm around you, I feel as if I shall suffocate! Give me some air! Do you hear? Give me some air! (*She sings.*)

YAT. Beautiful! Beautiful!

ZMEYUKINA. Fan me, fan me or I feel I shall have a stroke. Tell me, please; why am I suffocating so?

YAT. It's because you're sweating. . . .

ZMEYUKINA. Phew, how vulgar you are! Don't use such expressions! . . .

YAT. I'm sorry. Of course, you're accustomed to artistocratic society, if you'll pardon the expression . . . and . . .

ZMEYUKINA. Oh, leave me in peace! Give me poetry, rapture! Fan me, fan me. . . .

ZHIGALOV (*to* DIMBA). Let's have some more, huh? (*Pours.*) One can always drink. Just as long as one doesn't forget one's business, eh, Harlampi Spiridonich? Drink, but be businesslike. . . . And as for drinking, well, why not drink? It's allowed. . . . To your health! (*They drink.*) And do you have tigers in Greece?

DIMBA. That we have.

ZHIGALOV. And lions?

DIMBA (*speaks with a Greek accent*). Lions, too. There's nothing in Russia; in Greece there's everything . . . my father, my uncles, my brothers . . . and here there's nothing.

APLOMBOV. I'm right with you, Papa, all the way. Why should we start a learned discussion? I myself having nothing to say against scientific discoveries, but this is neither the time nor the place. (*To* DASHENKA.) What's your opinion, *ma chère?*

DASHENKA. They want to show off how educated they are, always talking about things you can't understand.

NASTASYA TIMOFEYEVNA. Thank God, we've lived our time without education, and now we're marrying off our third daughter to a good man. In your opinion, if you think we're not educated, then why did you want to come here? Go to your educated friends!

YAT. Nastasya Timofeyevna, I have always respected your family, and if I started talking about electric light, then it doesn't mean that I did it out of pride. I'd like to drink to that. I've always sincerely wished that Daria Yevdokimovna should have a good husband. Nowadays, Nastasya Timofeyevna, it's hard to find a good husband. Nowadays everybody is looking to find somebody who can give them something, money. . . .

APLOMBOV. That's a dig!

YAT (*shaking*). That was in no way a dig. . . . Present company excepted. . . . It was just meant . . . in general—Pardon me! We all know you're marrying for love . . . the dowry you're getting is nothing!

NASTASYA TIMOFEYEVNA. It is not nothing! Be careful what you say, sir! Besides the thousand rubles in cash, we're giving three dresses, the bed, and all the furniture. Try and find another dowry like that!

YAT. I didn't say that. . . . The furniture is really wonderful and . . . the dresses, of course, but I never meant what they said they were offended that I hinted at.

NASTASYA TIMOFEYEVNA. Don't start hinting. We have respect for you on account of your parents, and we've invited you to the wedding and now you won't stop talking. If you knew that Epaminond Maximich was marrying for money, why didn't you mention it before? (*Tearfully.*) I brought her up, nursed her, cherished her, cared for her more than if she were a diamond or an emerald, my little daughter . . .

APLOMBOV. And you believe him? I ask you! Thank you very much! (*To* YAT.) And as for you, Mr. Yat, although you are an acquaintance, I will not allow you to behave this way in somebody else's house! Please get out!

YAT. What are you saying?

APLOMBOV. I wish you were as honest a person as I am! In a word, get out!

(*Sound of music: a flourish.*)

VOICES OF GENTLEMEN PRESENT. Leave him alone! Stay seated! Now, will you? Stay seated! Sit down! Stop it!

YAT. I never did. . . . You see, I . . . don't even understand. . . . Please, I'll go . . . only give me the five rubles you borrowed from me last year with a piqué waistcoat as collateral, if you'll pardon the expression. I'll have another drink and . . . I'll be on my way; only give me what you owe me first.

GENTLEMEN. Well, stay, stay there! That's enough! Is it worth fighting over such trifles?

THE BEST MAN (*shouts*). To the health of the bride's parents, Yevdokim Zaharich and Nastasya Timofeyevna!

(*Music; flourish. Cheers.*)

ZHIGALOV (*touched, bows in all directions*). I thank you! Dear guests! I am very grateful to you for not having forgotten and for having come here without complaining or second thoughts. . . . And don't think that I'm a cunning fellow out to swindle people for my own profit. I say all this out of deep feeling, straight from my heart. For good people, I begrudge nothing. We thank you from the bottom of our heart. (*Throws kisses.*)

had, so to speak, its special meaning! For example: topsail along shrouds to foresail and mainsail! Hoist away! Now what does that mean? A sailor must understand! Ho-ho. To the minutest mathematical detail.

NUNIN. To the health of His Excellency Fyodor Yakovlevich Revunov-Karaulov!

(*The musicians play a march. Cheers.*)

YAT. But, Your Excellency, you have just expressed yourself concerning the hard work done in the navy. Now really, is telegraphy any easier? Nowadays, Your Excellency, nobody can go into telegraph work if he doesn't know how to read and write French and German. And our hardest work is the transmission of telegrams. It's frightfully difficult! Please, just listen. (*Taps with his fork on the table, imitating a telegraph transmitter.*)

REVUNOV-KARAULOV. What does that mean?

YAT. It means: "I respect you, Your Excellency, for your virtues." You think that's easy? Just listen. (*Taps.*)

REVUNOV-KARAULOV. Do it louder . . . I can't hear . . .

YAT. And this means: "Madame, how happy I am to hold you in my embrace!"

REVUNOV-KARAULOV. Which Madame are you talking about? Yes . . . (*To* MOZGOVOY.) And then, if there is a headwind, you must . . . you must hoist the topgallant sail and the royal. And this is the order: "On the crosstrees along shrouds to the topgallant and the royal. . . ." And at the same time, as the sails began to luff and take hold from below the topgallant and the royal sheets, the flags and the braces . . .

THE BEST MAN (*rising*). Honored guests . . .

REVUNOV-KARAULOV. Yes. There are enough different commands to give. . . . Yes. . . . Furl the topgallant sail and hoist the royal halyards! All right? Now, what does that mean and what is it for? But it's very simple! You know that

if the topgallant sails and the royal sheets are taken hold of
while raising the halyards . . . all together, at one time . . .
thereby leveling the royal sheets and hoisting the royal
halyards, and at the same time recognizing the necessity to
slacken the braces from their sails, and when the sheets are
already luffing, halyards are hoisted, then the topgallants
and the royal are set and the yards are hauled close to the
direction of the driving wind. . . .

NUNIN (*to* REVUNOV-KARAULOV). Fyodor Yakovlevich, the
mistress of the house asks you to speak about something
else. The guests don't understand it and it's boring. . . .

REVUNOV-KARAULOV. What? What's boring? (*To* Mos-
COVOY.) Young man! Now suppose the ship is lying with
the wind, on the starboard tack, under full sail, and you
must bring her before the wind. What should the order be?
Well, this is it: all hands on deck, come before the wind!
He-he. . . .

NUNIN. Fyodor Yakovlevich, that's enough. . . . Eat . . .
come on. . . .

REVUNOV-KARAULOV. As soon as the men are on deck, the
order is given: "To your stations, round before the wind!"
Ach, what a life! You give the order, and at the same time
you keep your eye on how the sailors run like lightning,
scattering to their stations, carrying sails and braces. And
you can't stand it any longer, so you shout: "Brave lads!"
(*Chokes and coughs.*)

THE BEST MAN (*rushing to take advantage of the ensuing
pause*). And on this day, we have, so to speak, come together for a celebration in honor of our beloved . . .

REVUNOV-KARAULOV (*getting nervous*). Yes! You have to
remember all that! For instance, foresail sheet! Mainsail
sheet!

THE BEST MAN (*becoming offended*). Why does he keep
on interrupting? He doesn't let us make a single speech!

NASTASYA TIMOFEYEVNA. We are ignorant people, Your

Excellency, we don't understand any of this, and it would be nicer if you would tell us something less abstruse. . . .

REVUNOV-KARAULOV (*not catching what she said*). I've already had supper, thank you. Did you say goose? Thank you. . . . Yes, I remember the old days . . . it certainly was pleasant, young man! You sail on the sea, you have no worries, and . . . (*In a trembling voice.*) Do you remember the joy of being in control? What sailor doesn't glow at the memory of that maneuver? As soon as the order is given, "Pipe all hands on deck," everybody's in control, as if an electric spark had run through them all. From the captain to the lowliest sailor—everybody feels the spark . . .

ZMEYUKINA. Such a bore! A bore!

(*A general murmur among the guests begins.*)

REVUNOV-KARAULOV (*hasn't understood*). Thank you, I've had supper. (*Exalted tone.*) Everybody is ready and looks to the boatswain. . . . "Foretop sails and mainsail braces to the starboard side, mizzenbraces to port, counterbraces to port," the senior officer orders. Everything happens in a twinkling. Top sheets, jib sheets laxed . . . taken to starboard! (*Leaps up.*) The ship takes the wind, and finally the sails begin to fill. The senior officer says: "To the braces, to the braces, look sharp!" and keeps his eyes on the mainsail, and when finally the sail begins to fill, at the moment the ship begins to turn, he yells out the thunderous command: "Let go the braces! Loose the stays! Let go the braces!" Then everything flies and creaks—the tower of Babel! And everything is accomplished without error. The ship has come about!

NASTASYA TIMOFEYEVNA (*bursting*). General, you're behaving disgracefully . . . it's shameful for someone your age!

REVUNOV-KARAULOV. Did you say cabbage? No, I've eaten. . . . Thank you very much.

NASTASYA TIMOFEYEVNA (*loudly*). I said you should be ashamed of yourself, at your age! A general, behaving so disgracefully!

Nunin (*embarrassed*). Ladies and gentlemen, well well . . . what's the use? Really . . .

Revunov-Karaulov. In the first place, I'm not a general, but a captain second class, which, according to the military order of rank, is equivalent to a lieutenant-colonel.

Nastasya Timofeyevna. If you're not a general, then why did you take our money? We didn't pay you money to behave like this!

Revunov-Karaulov (*puzzled*). What money?

Nastasya Timofeyevna. You know what money. What you got from Andrey Andreyevich . . . the twenty-five rubles. . . . (*To* Nunin.) As for you, Andreyushka, you've committed a sin! I didn't ask you to hire one like this!

Nunin. Well, well . . . forget it! What's the use?

Revunov-Karaulov. Hired . . . paid . . . what is all this?

Aplombov. Pardon me, but I must ask you . . . did you by any chance receive twenty-five rubles from Andrey Andreyevich?

Revunov-Karaulov. What twenty-five rubles? (*Grasping the situation.*) So that's it! Now I understand everything. . . . What a dirty trick! What a dirty trick!

Aplombov. Well, did you receive money?

Revunov-Karaulov. I never received any money! Get away from me! (*Leaves the table.*) What a dirty trick! What meanness! To insult an old man, a sailor, an officer who has served, in this way. . . . If I were in decent company, I would challenge you to a duel, but what can I do now? (*In a dither.*) Where's the door? Which way out? Waiter, show me the way out! Waiter! (*He goes out.*) What meanness! What a dirty trick! (*Exits.*)

Nastasya Timofeyevna. Andreyushka, where are those twenty-five rubles?

NUNIN. What's the use of talking about such trifles? Is it so important! Everybody's having a good time, what the hell are you trying to do . . . (*He shouts.*) To the health of the youngsters! Music! A march! Music!

(*The band plays a march.*)

To the health of the youngsters!

ZMEYUKINA. It's stuffy in here! Give me some air! With you around me, I'll choke.

YAT (*delighted*). You beauty! You beautiful creature!

(*General uproar.*)

THE BEST MAN (*trying to shout everybody down*). Honored guests! On this occasion, if I may be allowed to speak . . .

CURTAIN

THE ANNIVERSARY

A Joke in One Act

CHARACTERS

ANDREY ANDREYEVICH SHIPUCHIN, *chairman of the N—— Mutual Credit Company, a middle-aged man with a monocle*

TATYANA ALEXEYEVNA, *his wife, twenty-five years old*

KUSMA NICOLAEVICH HIRIN, *the bank's bookkeeper, an old man*

NASTASYA FEDOROVNA MERCHUTKINA, *an old woman wearing an old-fashioned cloak*

SHAREHOLDERS OF THE BANK

EMPLOYEES OF THE BANK

The action takes place in the N—— mutual credit bank. Office of the chairman of the board of directors. At left, a door, leading to the bank's main office. There are two desks. The furniture makes a pretence at refined luxury: velvet-covered armchairs, flowers, statuary, carpets, telephone. It is midday.

HIRIN (*alone; wearing felt boots. Shouting through the door.*) Send out to the drugstore for fifteen kopecks' worth of valerian drops, and tell them to bring fresh water to the chairman's office! Do I have to tell you a hundred times! (*Goes over to a desk.*) I'm exhausted. I've been working four days here without any sleep, writing here from morning till night and at home from night to morning. (*Coughs.*) On top of all that, I'm feeling feverish all over. I have the shivers, a temperature, and a cough; my feet hurt me and I keep seeing exclamation points before my eyes. (*Sits down.*) That clown, that scoundrel of a chairman, is to read a report at the company meeting today: "Our Bank, Its Present and Future." He thinks he's some sort of Gambetta. . . . (*Writes.*) Two . . . one . . . one . . . six . . . zero . . . nought . . . seven . . . then six . . . nought . . . one . . . six. . . . He wants to pull the wool over their eyes, and I sit here and work for him like a galley slave! That report is full of rubbish, nothing else, and I have to sit here day in, day out, clicking and counting, damn his soul! (*Clicks and counts on the abacus.*) I can't bear it! (*Writes.*) Well, it comes to . . . one . . . three . . . seven . . . two . . . one . . . nought. . . . He promised to reward me for my work. If all goes well today and he pulls the wool over their eyes, he promised me a gold medal and three hundred for a bonus. . . . We'll see. (*Writes.*) But if my work is wasted, then, my friend, we shall see what we shall see. . . . I'm a hot-tempered man . . . my friend, when I'm roused, I'm capable of committing a crime. . . . I am!

(*Behind the scenes, noise and applause. The voice of* SHIPUCHIN: *"Thank you! Thank you! I'm touched!" Enter* SHIPUCHIN. *He wears evening dress and a white tie; in his hands he holds an album which has just been presented to him.*)

SHIPUCHIN (*standing in the doorway and turning toward the outer office*). This present of yours, my dear employees, will be kept till my dying day, as a remembrance of the happiest days of my life! Yes, yes, dear people! Once again, I thank you! (*Throws a kiss into the air and goes to* HIRIN.) My dear, my most esteemed Kusma Nicolaevich!

(*While* SHIPUCHIN *is on the scene, employees come and go with papers which require his signature.*)

HIRIN (*getting up*). May I have the honor of congratulating you, Andrey Andreyich, on the fifteenth anniversary of our bank, and of wishing you . . .

SHIPUCHIN (*vigorously shaking his hands*). Thank you, my dear! Thank you! On this important day, this joyful jubilee, I dare say we might even kiss. . . . (*They kiss.*) I'm so happy, so very happy! Thank you for your services . . . for everything, for everything I thank you! If, while I have had the honor of being the chairman of the board of directors of this bank, if I have accomplished anything useful, I am primarily obliged to all of my colleagues. (*Sighs.*) Yes, my boy, fifteen years! or don't call me Shipuchin! (*Quickly.*) Well, how is my report coming? Is it on the way?

HIRIN. Yes. Only five pages more.

SHIPUCHIN. Excellent. Then it will be ready by three o'clock?

HIRIN. If nothing hinders me, then it will. What's left is only a trifle.

SHIPUCHIN. Splendid, splendid, or don't call me Shipuchin!

The general meeting is at four o'clock. Please, my dear, give me the first part to study. . . . Give it here. (*Takes the report.*) I pin my highest hopes on this report. . . . This is my *profession de foi*, or, to express it better, my fireworks. . . . My fireworks, or don't call me Shipuchin! (*He sits down and reads the report to himself.*) But I'm hellishly tired. . . . Last night I had an attack of gout; all morning I've been fussing and running around all over; and all this nervousness, the ovations, the excitement . . . I'm tired!

HIRIN (*writes*). Two . . . nought . . . nought . . . three . . . nine . . . two . . . nought . . . the figures are turning green in front of my eyes . . . three . . . one . . . six . . . four . . . one . . . five . . . (*Clicks and counts beads.*)

SHIPUCHIN. Also, there was a little unpleasantness. . . . This morning your wife came to see me and complained about you again. She said that you chased her and her sister-in-law with a knife. Kusma Nicolaevich, now what is this all about? Ai, ai!

HIRIN (*sternly*). Since it's the anniversary, Andrey Andreyevich, I'll be bold enough to request a favor of you. I beg of you, out of respect for my backbreaking labor, don't interfere in my family life. I ask you!

SHIPUCHIN (*heaving a sigh*). You have an impossible character, Kusma Nicolaevich! You're an excellent man, a respectable fellow, but with women you behave like some Jack the Ripper. Really, I don't understand why you hate them so much.

HIRIN. And you know what I don't understand: why you love them so much! (*Pause.*)

SHIPUCHIN. The employees have just presented me with an album, and the shareholders are, I understand, waiting to give me a speech and a silver urn. (*Playing with his monocle.*) Very nice, or don't call me Shipuchin. It's only what I deserve. To maintain the reputation of a bank, a certain pomp is necessary, damn it! You're one of us, so of course you know all that. . . . I wrote the speech myself and I also bought the silver urn myself . . . and the binding for the speech cost forty-five rubles, but you can't do with-

out it! They wouldn't have thought of it by themselves.
(*Looks around.*) Look at that furniture! What furniture!
They say I'm stingy, that all I require is the polishing of
the door handles, that the employees wear fashionable neck-
ties, and that a fat porter should stand out in front. No, my
dear friend. Door handles and fat porters are not trifles. At
home I can behave like a petty bourgeois as much as I
like; I can eat and sleep like a pig, I can drink myself
under the table. . . .

HIRIN. Please, I beg of you, no hints . . .

SHIPUCHIN. Who's hinting! What an impossible character
you have. . . . What I was saying was at home I can be a
petty bourgeois, a parvenu; I can indulge myself, but
here everything must be *en grand.* This is a bank! Here
every detail must be respected; everything must have a
solemn appearance. (*Picks up a scrap of paper from the
floor and throws it in the fireplace.*) This has been my
great merit: I have raised the reputation of the bank up to a
high level. Tone is a big thing. Big—or don't call me
Shipuchin. (*Looks* HIRIN *up and down.*) My dear, any
minute now a deputation of the bank's shareholders may arrive and you're wearing those felt boots and that scarf and
that coat with that wild color. . . . You might have put on
a frock coat. After all, a black frock coat . . .

HIRIN. I care more about my health than about the shareholders of your bank. I'm feverish all over.

SHIPUCHIN (*perturbed*). But you must admit you're un-
tidy. You're spoiling the ensemble!

HIRIN. If the deputation comes, I'll hide. It doesn't make
any difference. (*Writes.*) Seven . . . one . . . eight . . .
two . . . one . . . five . . . nought . . . I don't like untidiness myself . . . seven . . . two . . . nine. . . . (*Clicks
his beads.*) I can't bear untidiness. You would have done
better not to invite ladies to the jubilee dinner today. . . .

SHIPUCHIN. Such nonsense!

HIRIN. I know you're going to fill the hall with them today just for the sake of a stylish show, but, watch out,

they'll spoil the whole thing for you. They'll make mischief and confusion.

SHIPUCHIN. On the contrary, the society of ladies is elevating!

HIRIN. Yes . . . your wife is educated, it seems, but on Monday of last week she blurted something out that took me two days to get over. All of a sudden, in front of strangers, she asked: "Is it true," she asked, "that my husband bought shares of the Driazhko-Priashko Bank for our bank, and then the price fell on the exchange? Oh, my husband is so worried about it!" This she said in front of strangers! Why you take them into your confidence, I do not understand! Do you want them to get you into criminal court?

SHIPUCHIN. That's enough! Enough! I don't like that kind of talk on an anniversary! By the way, that reminds me. (*Looks at his watch.*) My wife should be here soon. As a matter of fact, I should have gone to the station to meet her, poor thing, but there was no time . . . and I'm tired. To tell the truth, I'm not glad she's coming! I mean I'm glad, but I'd be much happier if she had stayed a few more days with her mother. She'll want me to spend the whole evening with her, and we had made plans for a little excursion after the dinner. . . . (*Jumps up.*) My nerves have started to get the better of me. My nerves are so strained that a mere trifle is enough to make me burst into crying. No, no, I must be strong, or don't call me Shipuchin!

(*Enter* TATYANA ALEXEYEVNA *in a raincoat with a little traveling bag across her shoulder.*)

Ach! Speak of the devil!

TATYANA ALEXEYEVNA. Darling! (*Runs to her husband, prolonged kiss.*)

SHIPUCHIN. We were just talking about you! (*Looks at his watch.*)

TATYANA ALEXEYEVNA (*panting*). Did you miss me? Are

you all right? I haven't been home yet. I came here straight from the station. I have so much to tell you about, so much . . . I can hardly restrain myself . . . I won't take my coat off. I'll only stay a minute. (*To* HIRIN.) How are you, Kusma Nicolaevich! (*To her husband.*) Is everything all right at home?

SHIPUCHIN. Yes, everything is fine. You've gotten a little plumper and prettier this week. . . . So, how was the trip?

TATYANA ALEXEYEVNA. Marvelous. Mama and Katya send you their regards. Vassili Andreyevich embraces you. (*She kisses him.*) Auntie sent you a pot of jam and everybody's very annoyed because you never write. Zina told me to give you a kiss. (*Kisses him.*) Oh, if you knew what was going on! What's happening! It frightens me to talk about it! Such goings on! I can see from your expression that you're not glad to see me!

SHIPUCHIN. On the contrary . . . darling . . . (*Kisses her.*)

(HIRIN *coughs angrily.*)

TATYANA ALEXEYEVNA (*sighs*). Oh, poor Katya! Poor, dear Katya! I'm so sorry for her, so very sorry!

SHIPUCHIN. Darling, we're celebrating our anniversary today; any minute now a deputation of the bank's shareholders may be arriving; and you aren't properly dressed.

TATYANA ALEXEYEVNA. That's true, it's the jubilee! Congratulations, everybody! . . . I wish you— So, there's going to be a gathering and a dinner. . . . That's what I like. And remember that beautiful speech you've been making up all this time for the bank's shareholders? Are you going to read it today?

(HIRIN *coughs angrily.*)

SHIPUCHIN (*embarrassed*). My darling, we don't talk about that. . . . Really, you'd better go home.

TATYANA ALEXEYEVNA. Right away, right away. I'll tell

you everything in a minute and then I'll go. I'll tell you everything from the beginning. Well . . . when you saw me off, I remember, I sat down next to that stout lady, and I began to read. I don't like talking on trains. I kept on reading for three stations and I didn't say a word to a living soul. . . . So, the evening set in and you know, I got such gloomy thoughts! A young man was sitting opposite me, not too bad looking; and we started talking . . . a sailor came along, then a sort of student. . . . (*Laughs.*) I told them I wasn't married . . . they made such a fuss over me! We chattered until midnight, the dark-haired one kept telling screamingly funny anecdotes, and the sailor was singing all the time. My chest began to ache from the laughing. And when the sailor—oh, those sailors!—when the sailor accidentally found out my name is Tatyana, then you know what he sang? (*Sings in a bass voice.*)

> Onegin, I conceal it badly,
> I love Tatyana madly . . .

(*Laughs.*)

(HIRIN *coughs angrily.*)

SHIPUCHIN. Tanya darling, we're disturbing Kusma Nicolaevich. Go home, darling . . . tell me later. . . .

TATYANA ALEXEYEVNA. Never mind, never mind. Let him hear it, too. It's very interesting. I'm almost finished. Seryozha came to meet me at the station. Some young man turned up, a tax inspector, it seems . . . rather handsome, especially his eyes. . . . Seryozha introduced me and we three went off together . . . it was wonderful weather. . . .

(*Offstage voices: "It's not possible! Not possible! What do you want?" Enter* MERCHUTKINA.)

MERCHUTKINA (*at the door, waving her arms*). What are you grabbing me for? What next? I want to speak to him myself. . . . (*Enters; to* SHIPUCHIN.) My pleasure, Your Excellency. . . . Allow me to introduce myself. I am the wife of a provincial secretary, Nastasya Federovna Merchutkina.

SHIPUCHIN. What can I do for you?

MERCHUTKINA. If you'll pardon my saying so, Your Excellency, my husband, provincial secretary Merchutkin, has been sick for the last five months, and while he was at home, recuperating, they laid him off from his job, Your Excellency, and when I went to collect his salary, they, if you'll pardon my saying so, they'd gone and deducted twenty-four rubles and thirty-six kopecks from his salary. What for? I ask you. "Well," they said, "he had taken it from the employees' mutual aid fund and others had to guarantee the loan." How could that be? He can't take anything without my permission! It couldn't be, Your Excellency! I'm a poor woman. . . . I can only make ends meet by taking in lodgers. . . . I'm weak and defenseless. . . . I have to put up with insults from everybody and I never hear a kind word from anybody.

SHIPUCHIN. Excuse me. . . . (*Takes her petition from her and reads it standing up.*)

TATYANA ALEXEYEVNA (*to* HIRIN). I'll have to begin from the beginning. . . . Last week, I got a letter suddenly from Mama. She wrote that sister Katya had received a proposal from a certain Grendilevski. A nice, modest young man, but without any means or any definite position. And unfortunately, you can imagine, Katya was crazy about him. What could we do about it? Mama wrote to me to come right away and influence Katya. . . .

HIRIN (*sternly*). Excuse me, but you've made me lose my place! You, your mama, and your Katya, and now I've lost my place and I don't understand any of it!

TATYANA ALEXEYEVNA. What does it matter? Listen when a lady is talking to you! Why are you so angry today? Are you in love? (*She laughs.*)

SHIPUCHIN (*to* MERCHUTKINA). Excuse me, but what is all this about? I don't understand any of it. . . .

TATYANA ALEXEYEVNA. Are you in love? Aha! You're blushing!

SHIPUCHIN (*to his wife*). Tanyusha, darling, leave the office for a moment. I won't be long.

TATYANA ALEXEYEVNA. All right. (*Goes out.*)

SHIPUCHIN. I don't understand any of it. Obviously, my dear lady, you've come to the wrong place. Your petition has nothing to do with us here. Be so kind as to address yourself to the department where your husband was employed.

MERCHUTKINA. My God, I've been in five different places already. They wouldn't even read my petition. I almost lost my mind, but thanks to my son-in-law, Boris Matveyitch, I thought of coming to you. "Mamushka," he said, "go to Mr. Shipuchin; he's an influential man, he can do anything...." Help me, Your Excellency!

SHIPUCHIN. Mrs. Merchutkin, we can't do anything for you. Please understand: your husband, as far as I can make out, was employed in the army medical department of the war office, while ours is an absolutely private institution, a commercial bank. How can you not understand that!

MERCHUTKINA. Your Excellency, as for my husband's being sick, I have a doctor's certificate. Here it is, if you'd be so kind as to look....

SHIPUCHIN (*irritated*). That's excellent. I believe you, but I repeat, that is no concern of ours.

(*Offstage* TATYANA ALEXEYEVNA *laughs; then a man's laughter is heard.*)

(*Glancing at the door.*) She's interfering with the employees. (*To* MERCHUTKINA.) It's unusual and even a little ridiculous. Really, doesn't your husband know where you should apply?

MERCHUTKINA. In my book, Your Excellency, my husband knows from nothing. He only says one thing: "It's none of your business! Get out!" Yes, that's all he says....

SHIPUCHIN. I repeat, my dear lady: your husband was employed by the army medical department, and this is a bank, a private, commercial institution....

MERCHUTKINA. All right, all right . . . I understand, sir. In that case, Your Excellency, order them to pay me at least fifteen rubles! I don't mind not getting it all at once.

SHIPUCHIN (sighs). Oof!

HIRIN. Andrey Andreyevich, I'll never finish the report at this rate!

SHIPUCHIN. In a moment. (To MERCHUTKINA.) You don't seem to understand. But please try: to make such a request from us is just as strange as trying to get a divorce at the drugstore, or a pawnshop.

(Knock at the door. Voice of TATYANA ALEXEYEVNA: "Andrey? Can I come in?")

(Shouts.) Wait a minute, dear! (To MERCHUTKINA.) If they don't pay you, what have we got to do with it? And besides, my dear madam, we're having an anniversary today . . . we're busy . . . somebody might come in here at any moment . . . excuse me . . .

MERCHUTKINA. Your Excellency, have pity on me, an orphan! I'm a weak, defenseless woman . . . tortured to death. . . . I have to take my boarders to court, run around for my husband, run the household, and besides, my son-in-law's out of work.

SHIPUCHIN. Mrs. Merchutkin, I— No, excuse me, I can't talk to you! My head is in a whirl . . . you're disturbing us and wasting our time. . . . (Sighs, aside.) What a blockhead, or don't call me Shipuchin! (To HIRIN.) Kusma Nicolaich, will you please explain to Madame Merchutkin? (Waves his hand and goes out to the board of directors' office.)

HIRIN (approaching MERCHUTKINA, angrily). What do you want?

MERCHUTKINA. I'm a weak, defenseless woman. . . . I may look strong, but if you took me to pieces, you'd see there wasn't a single healthy bone in my body! I can hardly stand on my legs and my appetite is gone. I drank coffee today and I didn't get any pleasure out of it.

HIRIN. I ask you: what do you want?

MERCHUTKINA. Tell them, kind sir, to pay me fifteen rubles and the rest within a month.

HIRIN. But you were told in plain language: this is a bank!

MERCHUTKINA. All right, all right. . . . And if you want, I can show you the medical certificate.

HIRIN. Have you got a head on your shoulders, or haven't you?

MERCHUTKINA. My dear sir, really, I'm asking for what's mine by law. I don't want what's not mine.

HIRIN. I ask you, madam: do you have a head on your shoulders, or not? Well, the hell with you, I haven't got time to talk to you! I'm busy. . . . (*Indicates the door*). Please!

MERCHUTKINA (*surprised*). But what about the money? . . .

HIRIN. I see, you don't have a head on your shoulders, only this. . . . (*Taps with his finger on the table, then on his head.*)

MERCHUTKINA (*offended*). What? All right, all right . . . you can behave that way with your own wife . . . but I'm the wife of a provincial secretary. . . . With me, you'd better watch out.

HIRIN (*flaring, in a low voice*). Get out!

MERCHUTKINA. Ah, ah, ah . . . watch out!

HIRIN (*in a low voice*). If you don't get out this second, I'll send for the porter! Out! (*Stamps his feet.*)

MERCHUTKINA. All right, all right! I'm not scared of you. I've seen the likes of you. You penpusher, you!

HIRIN. I've never seen a more repulsive creature in my entire life! Oof! You're drilling a hole in my head! . . .

(*Breathes heavily.*) I'll tell you once more . . . are you listening? If you don't get out of here, you old nightmare, I'll grind you up into a powder. I've got such a temper that I'm capable of crippling you for life! I'm capable of committing a crime!

MERCHUTKINA. Your bark is worse than your bite! I'm not afraid. I've seen your kind before.

HIRIN (*in despair*). I can't bear to look at her! It makes me sick! I cannot! (*He goes to the desk and sits down.*) They're filling the bank with women and I can't write the report! I cannot!

MERCHUTKINA. I don't want anybody else's money, but my own, according to law. You shameless fellow! Sitting in an office with felt boots on! You peasant!

(*Enter* SHIPUCHIN *and* TATYANA ALEXEYEVNA.)

TATYANA ALEXEYEVNA (*following her husband*). We spent the evening at the Berezhnitskys'. Katya was wearing a blue neckerchief, a taffeta dress trimmed with lace, open at the neck . . . it suits her to wear her hair high on top of her head, and I myself arranged it for her . . . when she was all ready to be presented, she was simply fascinating!

SHIPUCHIN (*already has a migraine*). Yes, yes . . . fascinating! They may be coming any minute.

MERCHUTKINA. Your Excellency!

SHIPUCHIN (*despondent*). What now? What do you want?

MERCHUTKINA. Your Excellency! (*Points to* HIRIN.) That . . . that man . . . tapped on the desk and then on his forehead . . . you told him to look into my case and he jeered at me and said all kinds of things. . . . I'm a weak, defenseless woman.

SHIPUCHIN. Very well, madam. I'll look into it . . . and take the necessary measures. Now go away . . . later! (*Aside.*) My gout is starting up! . . .

HIRIN (*approaches* SHIPUCHIN *quietly*). Andrey Andreyevich, tell them to send for the porter and have him throw her out! What is all this?

SHIPUCHIN (*frightened*). No! No! She'll raise an uproar. There are many offices in the building.

MERCHUTKINA. Your Excellency!

HIRIN (*in a tearful voice*). But I've got to finish writing my report! I don't have time! (*Returns to his desk.*) I cannot!

MERCHUTKINA. Your Excellency, when will I be paid? I need the money right away.

SHIPUCHIN (*aside, indignantly*). A re-mar-ka-bly mean woman! (*To her, softly.*) Madam, I've already told you. This is a bank, a private commercial institution. . . .

MERCHUTKINA. Be kind, Your Excellency. Be a father to me. . . . If the medical certificate isn't enough, then I can get you a notarized certificate. Tell them to give me the money!

SHIPUCHIN (*sighs heavily*). Oof!

TATYANA ALEXEYEVNA (*to* MERCHUTKINA). Old lady, haven't they told you you're disturbing them? Really, you're the one.

MERCHUTKINA. Listen, beauty, nobody wants to take my side. I have only one pleasure, drinking and eating, and today I drank coffee without any pleasure at all.

SHIPUCHIN (*exhausted, to* MERCHUTKINA). How much do you want?

MERCHUTKINA. Twenty-four rubles, thirty-six kopecks.

SHIPUCHIN. Very well! (*Takes a twenty-five-ruble note from his wallet and gives it to her.*) Here are twenty-five rubles. Take them . . . and go!

(HIRIN *coughs angrily.*)

MERCHUTKINA. I thank you most humbly, Your Excellency. . . . (*Conceals the money.*)

TATYANA ALEXEYEVNA (*sits by her husband*). I should be going home. (*Looks at her watch.*) But I'm still not finished. . . . I'll finish in a moment, and then I'll go. . . . What goings on! . . . Oh, what goings on! So, we went to spend the evening at the Berezhnitskys' . . . it wasn't much, it was enjoyable, but not especially. . . . Katya was there, and of course, Grendilevski, who's sweet on her. Well, I had a talk with Katya. I shed a few tears, influenced her on the spot that evening to have a talk with Grendilevski and tell him no. So everything was settled, I thought, as well as it could be. Mama was calmed down, Katya was saved and now I could be calm, too. . . . Well, what do you think? Just before supper Katya and I were taking a walk down the path, when suddenly . . . (*Excited.*) when suddenly we heard a shot. . . . No, I can't tell about it in cold blood. . . . (*Fans herself with her handkerchief.*) No, I can't!

SHIPUCHIN (*sighs*). Oof!

TATYANA ALEXEYEVNA (*cries*). We ran to the summer-house and there . . . there lay poor Grendilevski . . . with a pistol in his hand. . . .

SHIPUCHIN. No, I can't stand it! I can't stand it! (*To* MERCHUTKINA.) Now what do you want?

MERCHUTKINA. Your Excellency, is it impossible for my husband to get his job back in this place again?

TATYANA ALEXEYEVNA (*weeping*). He'd shot himself right in the heart . . . right there. . . . Katya fainted, the poor thing . . . and he was terribly frightened, lying there . . . and asked us to send for a doctor. The doctor came quite soon and . . . and saved the unhappy man. . . .

MERCHUTKINA. Your Excellency, is it impossible for my husband to go to work here again?

SHIPUCHIN. No, I can't bear it! (*Cries.*) I can't bear it!

(*Stretches out both his hands to* HIRIN, *in desperation.*)
Get rid of her! Get rid of her, I implore you!

HIRIN (*goes up to* TATYANA ALEXEYEVNA). Get out!

SHIPUCHIN. Not her, this one . . . the terrible woman. . . .
(*Pointing at* MERCHUTKINA.) This one!

HIRIN (*not understanding him, to* TATYANA ALEXEYEVNA).
Get out of here! (*Stamps his feet.*) Get out!

TATYANA ALEXEYEVNA. What? What are you saying? Are
you mad?

SHIPUCHIN. This is terrible! I'm an unfortunate man!
Throw her out! Out with her!

HIRIN (*to* TATYANA ALEXEYEVNA). Get out! I'll cripple
you! I'll mangle you! I'll commit a crime!

TATYANA ALEXEYEVNA (*running from him; he goes after
her*). How dare you! You lout! (*Shouts.*) Andrey! Help
me! Andrey! (*She screams.*)

SHIPUCHIN (*chasing them*). Stop! I beg of you! Quiet!
Have mercy on me!

HIRIN (*chasing after* MERCHUTKINA). Get out! Catch her!
Smash her! Cut her up! Make mincemeat out of her!

SHIPUCHIN (*shouts*). Stop! I beg of you! I implore you!

MERCHUTKINA. Lord in heaven! Saints above! (*Screams.*)
Lord in heaven! . . .

TATYANA ALEXEYEVNA (*shouts*). Help! Help! . . . Oh . . .
oh . . . I'm going to faint! I'm fainting! (*Jumps up on a
chair, then falls on to the sofa and moans, as if she had
fainted.*)

HIRIN (*chasing* MERCHUTKINA). Beat her! Thrash her!
Cut her to pieces!

MERCHUTKINA. Oh, oh . . . Lord, everything is black

in front of my eyes! Oh! (*Falls unconscious into* SHIPUCHIN's *arms.*)

(*Knock at the door, and a voice from backstage:* "The deputation!")

SHIPUCHIN. The deputation . . . reputation . . . occupation . . .

HIRIN (*stamps his feet*). Get out, damn it! (*Turns up his sleeves.*) Give her to me! I may commit a crime!

(*Enter the deputation of five men, all in frock coats. One carries the speech in a velvet binding, and another, the silver urn. From the office door, the employees look in.* TATYANA ALEXEYEVNA *is on the sofa,* MERCHUTKINA *is in* SHIPUCHIN's *arms; both are moaning quietly.*)

A SHAREHOLDER (*reading in a loud voice*). "Most respected and esteemed Andrey Andreyevich! Casting a retrospective glance at the past of our financial establishment, and taking a survey in our minds of the history of its gradual development, we receive to the highest degree a gratifying impression. It is true that in the early stages of its existence the small dimensions of its capital and the absence of any financial operations, as well as the uncertainty of its aims, put the Hamlet question squarely before us: 'To be or not to be?' And at one time voices had even been raised in favor of the closing of the bank. But then you set yourself up as head of our establishment. Your knowledge, energy, your inherent tact were the cause of our extraordinary success and rare prosperity. The reputation of the bank . . ." (*Coughs.*) "The reputation of the bank . . ."

MERCHUTKINA (*moaning*). Oh! Oh!

TATYANA ALEXEYEVNA (*moaning*). Water! Water!

SHAREHOLDER (*continuing*). "The reputation . . ." (*Coughs.*) "reputation of the bank has been raised by you to such a height that our establishment can now compete with the best foreign concerns . . ."

SHIPUCHIN. Deputation . . . reputation . . . occupation . . .

> Two friends went out for an evening walk
> And they had a sensible talk;
> Don't say your youth was wasted
> That by jealousy I was devastated . . .

SHAREHOLDER (*continues, embarrassed*). "For that very reason, as we cast an objective glance at the present, we, much esteemed and dear Andrey Andreyevich . . ." (*Lowering his voice.*) In that case, later we'll . . . better do it later. . . .

(*The deputation goes out, embarrassed.*)

CURTAIN

CHRONOLOGY OF
CHEKHOV'S LIFE AND PRINCIPAL WORKS

The Plays

1881	*Platonov*
1885	*On the Highroad*
1886–1903	*On the Harmfulness of Tobacco*
1887	*Swan Song*
1887–1889	*Ivanov*
1888	*The Bear*
1888–1889	*The Proposal*
1889	*Tatyana Repina*
1889	*The Reluctant Tragedian*
1889–1890	*The Wood Demon*
1889–1890	*The Wedding*
1891	*The Anniversary* (revised 1902)
1895	*The Night Before the Trial*
1896	*The Sea Gull*
1897	*Uncle Vanya*
1900–1901	*The Three Sisters*
1903–1904	*The Cherry Orchard*

1860	Anton Chekhov born January 17, 1860, in Taganrog, Russia.
1876	His father's business fails. The family moves to Moscow.
1879	Begins study of medicine, Moscow University.
1879	Begins writing humorous sketches for periodicals.
1880	First story: "A Letter from a Don Squire Stepan Vladimirovich N. to His Learned Neighbor Doctor Friedrich," published in periodical known as *Dragonfly*. Wrote over four hundred stories, short sketches,

1880s	pastiches to a number of papers and periodicals, published under several amusing pseudonyms: Antosha Chekhonté, My Brother's Brother, A Doctor Without Patients, A Quick-tempered Man, A Man Without a Spleen, Rover, Ulysses.
1881–1882	Earliest extant play, *Platonov* (known as *A Country Scandal* and *Don Juan in the Russian Manner*, in adaptations), rejected by actress Yermolova and discarded during his lifetime.
1884	Receives his medical degree. Practices medicine throughout life, medicine his "wife" and writing his "mistress."
1884	*Tales of Melpomene*, collection of humorous pieces by Antosha Chekhonté.
1884	First attacks of tuberculosis, which eventually claims his life.
1885	*Motley Stories*, by Antosha Chekhonté, Moscow.
1885	Meets Suvorin, editor of the Petersburg newspaper *New Times*, who becomes his friend, correspondent, publisher, and mentor. Paves the way for the publication of his more serious work.
1886	Letter from renowned writer Grigorovich, urging Chekhov to write seriously.
1887	*At Twilight*, stories, published by Suvorin, Petersburg.
1887–1889	*Ivanov*, produced at Korsh Theater, Moscow (1887), and at Alexandrinsky Theater, Petersburg (1889).
1888	*The Steppe*, journal of travel impressions.
1888	Awarded Pushkin prize by the Imperial Academy of Sciences, Petersburg.
1888	*Stories*, collected, published by Suvorin, Petersburg.
1889	Elected member of the Society of Lovers of Russian Literature.
1889–1890	*The Wood Demon*, produced by the Abramova Theater, Moscow (1889).
1890	Much-discussed voyage to Island of Sakhalin—takes census of prisons and the conditions of the prisoners.
1891	Trip abroad to Austria, Italy, France.
1891	Impressions of Sakhalin Island, "The Duel," "Women" (stories).
1892	"Ward No. 6," "The Grasshopper," "The Wife," "In Exile," "Neighbors" (stories).
1892	Buys a farm at Melikhovo and moves entire family to country.

1893–1894	Notes on Sakhalin Island journey appear in review *Russian Thought.*
1894	Illness more severe; advised by doctors to go to Crimea for health.
1895	"Three Years," "Murder," "Ariadne," (stories).
1896	*The Sea Gull,* produced by Alexandrinsky Theater, Petersburg. Published in December issue, *Russian Thought.*
1897	"My Life," "Peasants" (stories). Works on census, builds several schools in region of Melikhovo. Illness more severe. Doctors order trip to south of France.
1898	Breaks with Suvorin over the Dreyfus affair. Chekhov pro-Dreyfus.
1898	*The Sea Gull* produced by Moscow Art Theater— great success.
1898	*Uncle Vanya* played in the provinces.
1898	"The Lodger," "The Husband," "The Darling" (stories).
1898	Chekhov's father dies; Chekhov decides to settle in Crimea with family. Builds house near Yalta.
1899	Sells Melikhovo farm, moves to Crimea. "The Lady with the Toy Dog" (story).
1899	*Uncle Vanya* produced by Moscow Art Theater. "In the Ravine" (story).
1899	Complete works to be published by Petersburg publisher Marx.
1900	Elected member of Academy of Sciences, Petersburg.
1901	Marries Olga Knipper, one of Moscow Art Theater's major actresses.
1902	Chekhov resigns in protest from Academy of Sciences, protesting expulsion of Maxim Gorky.
1902	"The Bishop" (story).
1903	"The Bride" (story).
1904	*The Cherry Orchard* produced by Moscow Art Theater.
1904	Goes to Badenweiler, German health resort; dies at Badenweiler, July 2, 1904.